# AppleScript:
## A Beginner's Guide

## About the Author

**Guy Hart-Davis** is the author of *Mac OS X Leopard QuickSteps, How to Do Everything: iPod, iPhone, & iTunes, HTML, XHTML & CSS QuickSteps*, and several other equally fine computer books.

## About the Technical Editor

**Greg Kettell** is a Windows programmer by day, but by night loves his Mac. Greg has served as an author, contributing author, and/or technical editor for an ever-increasing number of technical books.

# AppleScript:
## A Beginner's Guide

*Guy Hart-Davis*

New York   Chicago   San Francisco
Lisbon   London   Madrid   Mexico City
Milan   New Delhi   San Juan
Seoul   Singapore   Sydney   Toronto

The McGraw·Hill Companies

**Library of Congress Cataloging-in-Publication Data**

Hart-Davis, Guy.
  AppleScript : a beginner's guide / Guy Hart-Davis.
      p.    cm.
  Includes bibliographical references and index.
  ISBN 978-0-07-163954-5 (alk. paper)
    1. AppleScript (Computer program language)   2. Macintosh (Computer)—
Programming.   I. Title.
  QA76.73.A67H37      2010
  005.4'3—dc22                                       2009048211

McGraw-Hill books are available at special quantity discounts to use as premiums and sales promotions, or for use in corporate training programs. To contact a representative, please e-mail us at bulksales@mcgraw-hill.com.

**AppleScript: A Beginner's Guide**

1234567890  WFR WFR  019

ISBN  978-0-07-163954-5
MHID    0-07-163954-3

**Sponsoring Editor**   Roger Stewart
**Editorial Supervisor**   Patty Mon
**Project Manager**   Vipra Fauzdar, Glyph International
**Acquisitions Coordinator**   Joya Anthony
**Technical Editor**   Greg Kettell
**Copy Editor**   Lisa McCoy
**Proofreader**   Christine Andreasen
**Indexer**   Jack Lewis
**Production Supervisor**   Jean Bodeaux
**Composition**   Glyph International
**Illustration**   Glyph International
**Art Director, Cover**   Jeff Weeks
**Cover Designer**   Jeff Weeks

*This book is dedicated to Teddy,*
*who helped develop some of the sample scripts.*

# Contents at a Glance

# Contents

**PART II  Learning Essential AppleScript Programming Techniques**

# Acknowledgments

My thanks go to the following people for their help with this book:

- **Roger Stewart** for getting the book approved and pulling strings.
- **Joya Anthony** for managing the acquisitions end of the process.
- **Greg Kettell** for reviewing the book for technical accuracy and contributing many helpful suggestions.
- Lisa McCoy for editing the book with a light touch and a good sense of proportion.
- Vipra Fauzdar for coordinating the production of the book.
- Glyph International's skillful typesetters for laying out the book.
- Jack Lewis for creating the index.

# Introduction

This book shows you how to harness the power of AppleScript to make your Mac do your work for you.

AppleScript not only comes for free, built into every copy of Mac OS X, but it works across all Mac OS X applications, so you can automate almost any operation you can think of.

## Is This Book for You?

Yes.

If you want to get more done on your Mac—at work, at home, on the road, or all three—then this book is for you.

This book takes you from knowing nothing about AppleScript to using it confidently to manipulate all the applications you use.

The book is clear and easy to read, and it moves along at a rapid pace. As you progress, the Try This sections give you step-by-step practice in the essential skills for using AppleScript effectively.

# What Does This Book Cover?

This book shows you how to get started with AppleScript and how to achieve impressive results in minimal time.

Here is a chapter-by-chapter breakdown of what you will learn:

- Chapter 1, "Grasping the Essentials of AppleScript," makes sure you know what AppleScript is and what you can do with it. You learn about the key terms for working with AppleScript: objects, keywords, commands, and properties.

- Chapter 2, "Up to Speed with AppleScript Editor," teaches you to use AppleScript Editor, the tool that Mac OS X includes for creating and editing scripts. You learn how to launch AppleScript Editor, understand its user interface, and customize AppleScript Editor to suit your needs. You also learn how to put the Mac OS X Script menu on your Mac's menu bar and run scripts instantly from it.

- Chapter 3, "Creating Your First Script," walks you through creating a script in AppleScript Editor. You create and save a script, build **tell** statements and **tell** blocks, and compile and run the script. Along the way, you learn how to open and arrange Finder windows, and how to launch, manipulate, and close other applications.

- Chapter 4, "Working with Variables, Classes, Operators, and Coercions," explains how to store data temporarily in your scripts for later use. You learn how to create variables, assign data to them, and retrieve the data; how to use AppleScript's operators to perform operations (such as addition or division) or to make comparisons; and how to use different classes of objects and change data from one type to another.

- Chapter 5, "Working with Text, Numbers, and Dates," teaches you how to work with three essential types of content: text (such as words and paragraphs), AppleScript's two different types of numbers, and dates.

- Chapter 6, "Working with the Finder, Files, and Folders," shows you how to use AppleScript to control the Finder and to manipulate files and folders. For example, you learn how to create folders, rename them, move them, and delete them.

- Chapter 7, "Making Decisions in Your Scripts," explains how to make decisions by using the three If structures that AppleScript provides. Making decisions is vital to creating powerful and flexible scripts—and AppleScript makes the language of decisions as easy and natural as it can be.

- Chapter 8, "Using Dialog Boxes to Get User Input," covers using dialog boxes to let the user control your scripts and provide input to them. You learn about AppleScript's dialog box, its alerts, and the special commands it provides for displaying dialog boxes that enable the user to choose files, folders, or other items.

- Chapter 9, "Repeating Actions in Your Scripts," teaches you how to repeat actions in your code—either once, or a fixed number of times, or exactly however many times turns out to be necessary. AppleScript provides a handful of different kinds of loops for repeating actions, but you will find it easy to get the hang of them.

- Chapter 10, "Debugging Scripts and Handling Errors," shows you how to write code that either suppresses errors or handles them neatly. Even if you keep your scripts simple, errors can easily occur, so handling them is a vital skill.

- Chapter 11, "Running Scripts Automatically," explains the different options that AppleScript offers for running scripts automatically rather than running them manually. For example, you can create a "droplet" application that runs when you drop a file on it, attach a script to a folder as a Folder Action, or set it to run automatically when you log in. Then there are other possibilities… .

- Chapter 12, "Automating iTunes and iPhoto," shows you how to let AppleScript loose on the Mac's multimedia marvels. You learn how to work with tracks and playlists in iTunes, and how to work with albums, photos, and keywords in iPhoto.

- Chapter 13, "Automating Apple Mail," teaches you how to script Apple's Mail application. Coverage includes creating and configuring mail accounts, creating and sending messages, dealing with incoming messages, and working with tasks.

- Chapter 14, "Automating Microsoft Word," explains how to manipulate Microsoft Word 2008 via AppleScript. Word is a big application, and this is a big chapter, teaching you how to work with documents, windows, and views; insert and manipulate text; and set up your documents using sections and headers and footers. You even learn how to corral Word's built-in dialog boxes and use them in your scripts.

- Chapter 15, "Automating Microsoft Excel," digs into using AppleScript with Microsoft Excel 2008. You learn to launch and quit Excel; create, save, open, and close workbooks; work with worksheets, ranges, and charts; and much more.

- Chapter 16, "Automating Microsoft Entourage," teaches you to use AppleScript to automate essential tasks in Microsoft Entourage. Among other things, this chapter shows you how to create and send e-mail messages and attachments, deal with incoming e-mail messages (with or without attachments), and work with contacts.

# What Are Those Lines, and What Are the Funny Fonts For?

To make its meaning clear but concise, this book uses a number of conventions, four of which are worth mentioning here:

- The pipe character, or vertical bar, indicates choosing an item from the menus. For example, "choose File | Open Dictionary" means that you should click the File menu on the Mac OS X menu bar to open the menu, and then click the Open Dictionary command on it.

- Terms in **boldface** in regular text are AppleScript terms. The boldface is just there to make the terms stand out and help the sentences make sense.

- The code lines show examples of AppleScript code. Here is how such a code snippet looks:

```
display dialog "Keep playing this version, or play the next?" ¬
    buttons {"Keep Playing This Version", "Play the Next Version", ¬
    "Cancel"} with title "Gimme Shelter"
if the button returned of the result is "Play the Next Version" then
    next track
else
    return
end if
```

- The ¬ characters at the end of the code lines are *continuation characters* that indicate the same line of code continues on the same line of text.


Turn the page, and we will get started.

# Part I

# Getting Started
# with AppleScript

# Chapter 1

## Grasping the Essentials of AppleScript

## Key Skills & Concepts

- Knowing what AppleScript is and what you can do with it

- Understanding what scripts are

- Understanding objects, keywords, commands, and properties

Welcome to automating your Mac with AppleScript! This short chapter brings you up to speed on what AppleScript is and what you can do with it. The chapter then covers the essentials you need to know about scripts before you start working with them, and then explains key terms—objects, keywords, commands, and properties—for working in AppleScript.

# Knowing What AppleScript Is and What You Can Do with It

AppleScript is a power-packed programming language that comes with Mac OS X. You can use AppleScript to automate almost any repetitive task on your Mac, saving you time and effort.

AppleScript works both with Mac OS X and its built-in components (such as the Finder and Spotlight) and with most applications that run on Mac OS X. For example, you can automate tasks in Apple applications such as TextEdit, Apple Mail, iPhoto, iTunes, and the iWork applications—not to mention essential third-party applications such as the Microsoft Office applications (Word, Excel, PowerPoint, and Entourage), Adobe Photoshop, and FileMaker Pro.

## What You Can Do with Scripts

A script can do anything from a single action (such as automatically emptying the Trash securely) to running as a complete application—for example, opening Microsoft Excel, using it to create a spreadsheet file, drawing in data from existing files and inserting it in the worksheets, saving the file, and generating a Portable Document Format (PDF) file from it for distribution.

## Why AppleScript Is Easy to Learn

Many programming languages are hard to learn because they use not only complicated concepts, but also abstruse syntax that looks like an explosion in a punctuation factory.

By contrast, AppleScript is easy to read and understand, so you can get moving with it immediately. For example, if you read the following AppleScript command, you can immediately understand what it does:

```
tell the application "Microsoft Excel" to make new document
```

When you run that command, Microsoft Excel creates a new workbook. (If Excel isn't running, Mac OS X launches it automatically.)

Yes, AppleScript is that English-like and straightforward. That doesn't mean AppleScript isn't powerful, just that its power is delivered in a friendly and easy-to-use way.

# Understanding What Scripts Are

This section runs you quickly through essential concepts you need to grasp before you get started with AppleScript.

## What a Script Is

A script is a document that contains a sequence of commands. For example, a script can contain commands to do the following:

1. Open the TextEdit application and create a new document.

2. Type some text in the document.

3. Save the document.

4. Quit TextEdit.

Normally, Mac OS X executes the script's commands in order from first to last, but you can build control structures to repeat or skip sections of code. For example, you can create a loop that runs for a certain number of repetitions or until a condition is met.

## Where Scripts Are Stored

Mac OS X comes with various scripts that are installed in the /Library/Scripts/ folder and its subfolders. These scripts are available to all the users of your Mac.

Your own scripts are stored in the ~/Library/Scripts/ folder (where ~ represents your home folder) and are available only to you. You can move them to other folders as needed.

## Ask the Expert

**Q:** Can I record scripts the way I can record macros in Microsoft Office?

**A:** AppleScript Editor lets you record actions in some applications, such as the Finder and iChat—but very few applications have this capability.

You open the script to which you want to add the actions, turn on recording, and then perform the actions in the application (for example, the Finder). AppleScript Editor records what you do and writes down the commands for the actions. When you've finished, you turn off recording and polish up the recorded code in AppleScript Editor.

## How You Create Scripts

To create scripts, you open the AppleScript Editor application (as described in Chapter 2) and type commands into it. You save a script as you would most any other document, giving it a name of your choice and using one of the Scripts folders explained in the previous section. You can also save a script to a different folder if you prefer.

## How You Run Scripts

You can run a script in any of these ways:

- **From AppleScript Editor** When you're creating a script, you can run it by clicking the Run button on the toolbar in AppleScript Editor, by pressing ⌘-R, or by choosing Script | Run. If the script works, great; if not, you're in the right place to change it.

### NOTE
You can run any script at any time by opening it in AppleScript Editor and using one of the Run commands described in the main text, but usually, other ways of running a finished script are more convenient unless you need to open a script for another reason—for example, to change it.

- **From the Script menu** If you add the Script menu to the Mac OS X menu bar, you can instantly run any script stored in your Mac's /Library/Scripts/ folder or in your ~/Library/Scripts/ folder. See Chapter 2 for details.

- **From the Finder** If you save a script to a different folder than your Mac's /Library/Scripts/ folder or in your ~/Library/Scripts/ folder, you can run the script by opening the folder and double-clicking the script file.

- **From the Dock** If you save a script as an application, you can add it to the left side of the Dock and run it as you would any other application.

# Understanding Objects, Keywords, Commands, and Properties

This section introduces four essential terms for working with AppleScript: objects, keywords, commands, and properties.

## What Objects Are

To take actions in AppleScript, you work with objects. An *object* is simply an identifiable item on your Mac—for example:

- Your Mac itself is an object.
- Each disk on the Mac is an object.
- Each folder on the Mac's disks is an object.
- Each file in each folder is an object.
- The items in each file are objects—for instance, an image object on a slide in a presentation or a paragraph object in a word-processing document.
- Each application is an object.

The objects are arranged in an organizational structure called an *object hierarchy*. That term sounds complex, but the object hierarchy is simply a map that shows you how to reach the objects you need.

At the top of the hierarchy are objects that are directly accessible to AppleScript— objects you can get at directly, such as the computer and your home folder. Those objects contain other objects that you can reach by going through the directly accessible objects. For example, you can get to your Documents folder by going through your home folder (because the home folder contains the Documents folder).

## What Keywords Are

In AppleScript, a *keyword* is a predefined term with a special meaning. For example:

- **before** and **after** are keywords used to describe the position of an item in a range of items—for instance, in a range of open Finder windows, you may need to work with the window after the front window or the window before the last window.
- **first**, **second**, **third**, and so on through **tenth** are keywords used to describe the position of an object in a container object—for instance, the second item in the Documents folder.
- **me** is a keyword that refers to the current script.

## Ask the Expert

**Q:** **Can you give an example to help me understand the object hierarchy?**

**A:** The object hierarchy can be difficult to picture, but it works in much the same way as when you're working interactively with your Mac.

For example, the Desktop is right there, so you can access it directly with your mouse. By contrast, if you want to apply boldface to a character in a paragraph in a Word document, you normally proceed like this:

1. Open Word.

2. Open the document in Word.

3. Go to the paragraph in the document.

4. Find the character.

5. Apply the boldface.

In the same way, AppleScript can access your Desktop directly. But if you want to make a change to that character using AppleScript, you need to work like this:

1. Tell AppleScript to open Word.

2. Tell Word to open the document.

3. Tell Word which paragraph contains the character and which character it is (for example, the fifth character in the third paragraph).

4. Tell Word to apply the boldface.

When you use a keyword in a script, it's important to use it only in its AppleScript sense. Avoid creating variable names that conflict with AppleScript's keywords, because this is a recipe for errors and confusion.

## What Commands Are

A *command* is an action that you can take with an object. Here are three examples:

● **activate** This command brings the specified application to the front. If the application isn't running, Mac OS X launches it and then brings it to the front.

- **mount volume**   This command mounts an AppleShare volume in the Mac's file system.
- **choose file**   This command displays the Choose A File dialog box so that the user can choose a file.

## What Properties and Values Are

Each object has *properties*—attributes—that describe what the object is and control how it behaves. Each property is set to a value; the type of value depends on the type of property.

Some properties are *read-only*, which means that you can *get* (return) the value but not change it. But most properties are read-write, which means that you can *set* their values as well as get them.

For example, you're probably familiar with the View Options window for Finder windows in List view (see Figure 1-1). The Text Size pop-up menu is the interactive means of setting the text size to use in List view; the AppleScript way is to change the value of the **text size** property. Similarly, you can set the **icon size** property to **large icon** or **small icon**—this is the AppleScript equivalent of choosing the small option button or the large option button in the Icon Size area of the window.

**Figure 1-1**   AppleScript provides properties for the List view options settings you can choose in this window.

# Chapter 2
## Up to Speed with
## AppleScript Editor

## Key Skills & Concepts

- Launching AppleScript Editor
- Meeting the AppleScript Editor window
- Setting up AppleScript Editor for working comfortably
- Putting the Script menu on the menu bar in Leopard
- Running a script from the Script menu

Your tool for creating AppleScript is AppleScript Editor, which is included with Mac OS X. This chapter shows you how to launch AppleScript Editor, understand its user interface, and customize AppleScript Editor to suit your needs. You'll also learn how to put the Mac OS X Script menu on your Mac's menu bar and run scripts instantly from it.

# Launching AppleScript Editor

AppleScript Editor lives in the Utilities folder in your Applications folder, so you can launch it like this:

1. Activate the Finder by clicking the Finder icon on the Dock or clicking open space on your Desktop.

2. Choose Go | Utilities to open a Finder window showing the Utilities folder. Alternatively, press ⌘-SHIFT-U.

3. Double-click the AppleScript Editor icon.

### NOTE

In Mac OS X version 10.5 (Leopard) and earlier versions, Script Editor is in the Applications/AppleScript/ folder rather than in the Utilities folder. Activate the Finder, choose Go | Applications to open a Finder window showing the Applications folder, double-click the AppleScript folder, and then double-click the Script Editor icon.

Once you've launched AppleScript Editor, make its icon stay in the Dock so that you can launch it instantly. CTRL-click or right-click the AppleScript Editor icon in the Dock, click or highlight Options, and then choose Keep In Dock from the shortcut menu.

## Ask the Expert

**Q:** Why is my editor named Script Editor rather than AppleScript Editor?

**A:** In Snow Leopard, Apple changed the editor's name from Script Editor to AppleScript Editor. So if you're using Leopard or an earlier version of Mac OS X, your editor is named Script Editor.

You'll find that Script Editor behaves in almost exactly the same way as AppleScript Editor described in this book but that the interface is different—in particular, that the lower pane is laid out differently, and that AppleScript Editor's preferences contain settings that used to be in AppleScript Utility in earlier versions of Mac OS X. You'll see the main differences later in this chapter.

## Meeting the AppleScript Editor Window

Figure 2-1 shows AppleScript Editor window with its key components labeled. As you can see, AppleScript Editor has a straightforward interface.

- **Toolbar**  The toolbar contains buttons for recording, running, and compiling scripts, and for bundling their contents into an application bundle or script bundle (a package that contains not only the script, but also any other items it needs, such as documents and images).

**TIP**

You can toggle the display of the toolbar by clicking the jellybean button at the right end of the AppleScript Editor title bar or by choosing View | Hide Toolbar or View | Show Toolbar. If you want to change the selection of buttons on the toolbar, choose View | Customize Toolbar and then work in the dialog box that appears.

- **Navigation bar**  The navigation bar is the thin horizontal strip under the toolbar. At its left end, the language pop-up menu lets you switch between AppleScript and other scripting languages that AppleScript Editor supports; normally, you'll want to leave this menu set to AppleScript. To the right of the language pop-up menu is the elements pop-up menu, which you can use to select elements (such as variables or properties) that you've defined in the script. Until you select an element, the elements pop-up menu shows "<No selected element>," as shown in the figure.

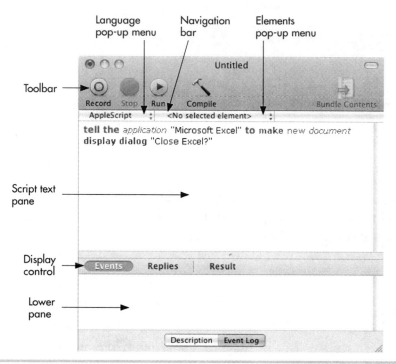

**Figure 2-1** AppleScript Editor has a streamlined interface that enables you to create code quickly and easily.

- **Script text pane**  This pane is where you create and edit each script.

- **Lower pane**  This pane displays two main different types of information, depending on which of the tabs at the bottom of the window is selected. When the Description tab is selected, the pane displays the description of the script—text you write to explain what the script is and what it does. When the Event Log tab is selected, the pane displays the event log. The event log contains three different categories of information, which you can switch among by clicking the three visibility buttons.

  - **Events**  Click this visibility button to see the events the script has sent. This helps you keep track of exactly what's happening in the script.

  - **Replies**  Click this visibility button to see the values the script has returned for the events. This information helps you see the information the script is getting.

  - **Result**  Click this visibility button to see the result of running the script—for example, which button in a dialog box the user clicked.

If you're using Mac OS X Leopard (10.5) or an earlier version, your AppleScript tool is named Script Editor rather than AppleScript Editor. As you can see in Figure 2-2, the Script Editor window has three tabs at the bottom—Description, Result, and Event Log—instead of the two that AppleScript Editor has, and it does not have the three visibility buttons.

**Figure 2-2**   In Leopard or earlier versions of Mac OS X, you use Script Editor rather than AppleScript Editor to create your code. The differences are minor.

# Setting Up AppleScript Editor for Working Comfortably

To make sure you can work swiftly and comfortably in AppleScript Editor, spend a few minutes setting its preferences.

With AppleScript Editor open, press ⌘-, (⌘ and the COMMA key) or choose AppleScript Editor | Preferences to open the Preferences window. This window's title bar shows the category of preferences you're setting—General, Editing, Formatting, History, or Plug-ins—rather than the word "Preferences." If the title bar doesn't show General at first, click the General button to open the General preferences pane.

## Choosing General Preferences

The General preferences pane (see Figure 2-3) enables you to choose your default script editor and default language for scripting, decide whether to show inherited items in the dictionary viewer, and choose whether (and if so, how) to display the Script menu in the menu bar.

### NOTE

In Script Editor in Leopard and earlier versions of Mac OS X, the General preferences pane contains only the Default Language pop-up menu and the Show inherited items in dictionary viewer check box. The other controls appear in AppleScript Utility, discussed in the section "Putting the Script Menu on the Menu Bar in Leopard," later in this chapter.

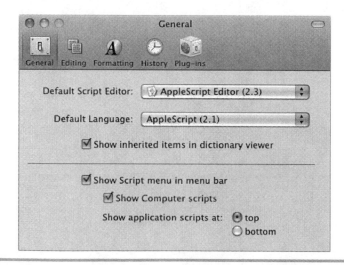

**Figure 2-3** In the General preferences pane, make sure AppleScript Editor is set to use AppleScript.

Here's what you need to know:

- **Default Script Editor**   In this pop-up menu, pick the script editor you want to use for AppleScript. Make sure AppleScript Editor is selected, unless you've installed another AppleScript-capable script editor, such as Smile, Script Debugger, or Xcode.

- **Default Language**   In this pop-up menu, choose the language you'll use in AppleScript Editor. For this book, you'll want AppleScript. Depending on how your Mac is set up, this may be your only choice.

**NOTE**

AppleScript Editor supports the Open Scripting Architecture (OSA for short), which enables AppleScript Editor to handle other scripting languages, such as UserTalk, JavaScript, or QuicKeys (http://startly.com).

- **Show Inherited Items In Dictionary Viewer**   This check box lets you decide, when viewing a dictionary file, whether to view only the items that belong to the object itself or to also view the objects it inherits from the class above it in the object hierarchy. Turn this setting on for now, because it's usually helpful. You'll work with inherited items extensively throughout the course of this book.

**NOTE**

In the AppleScript sense, a *dictionary* is a file that contains all the AppleScript terms associated with an application. For example, to browse the list of objects, commands, and properties available for scripting Safari, you open the Safari dictionary.

- **Show Script Menu In Menu Bar**   Select this check box to make the Script menu appear on the menu bar. It appears as a stylized *S* that looks like a scroll, as shown on the left here.

- **Show Computer Scripts**   Select this check box if you want the scripts stored in your Mac's /Library/Scripts/ folder to appear in the Script menu. Having these scripts appear is usually helpful at first, especially when you're learning to use AppleScript, so select this check box. Later, when you've stuffed the Script menu with essential scripts you've created, you may want to suppress the display of the computer scripts so that the Script menu is easy to use.

**NOTE**

The /Library/Scripts/ folder is referred to either as the "computer scripts folder" or the "local scripts folder." Your own scripts folder is the "user scripts folder."

- **Show Application Scripts At**   In this area, select the Top option button or the Bottom option button to choose where to display application scripts on the Script menu. These are scripts that you place in a folder named Applications in your ~/Library/Scripts/ folder. Usually, you'll want to select the Top option button, as it makes the scripts easier to access.

# Choosing Editing Preferences

The Editing preferences (see Figure 2-4) can help you work more quickly and accurately in AppleScript Editor, so it's important to set them to suit your needs. This section explains the preferences and offers suggestions on how to set them.

## Choosing Wrapping and Tabs Preferences

Lines of code can become much longer than the width of AppleScript Editor, so normally it's a good idea to select the Wrap Lines check box. When this setting is on, AppleScript Editor automatically wraps lines of code to fit in the window so you can see each entire line.

The alternative is to clear the Wrap Lines check box and then scroll to the right as needed to see the hidden part of the line and then scroll back to see the beginning of the next line. Some people prefer working this way.

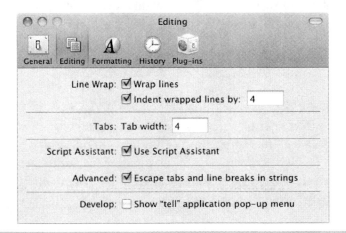

**Figure 2-4**   Editing preferences let you control line wrap, tabs, and whether the Script Assistant offers you its help.

When you wrap a line of code, normal practice is to indent each line after the first so that you can easily see what's a starting line and what's a wrapped line. Usually, it's helpful to have AppleScript Editor indent the lines for you, so you'll probably want to select the Indent Wrapped Lines By check box. The normal indentation is 4 spaces, but you can change this number if you want more indentation or less.

### NOTE
You can also break your lines of code manually so that they don't become too long. See Chapter 3 for details.

You can indent code manually by typing spaces, but it's quicker to press TAB and have AppleScript Editor automatically enter a group of spaces for you. Use the Tab Width box to set the number of spaces AppleScript Editor enters for a tab. Normally, you'll want the tab width to match your Indent Wrapped Lines By setting so that you can press TAB to indent lines to the same level; the default setting is again 4 spaces.

## Choosing Whether to Use the Script Assistant
The Script Assistant feature watches as you type in AppleScript Editor and tries to save you time by either completing code items for you or displaying suggestions for completing your code. Here are the details:

- When Script Assistant identifies enough of a word to be able to suggest ways to complete the word, it displays an ellipsis (...) to let you know, as shown here.

- To see the suggestions, press F5. In the pop-up list that appears (as shown here), you can enter it in your code. Either double-click the item you want, or press DOWN ARROW or UP ARROW to reach the term, and then press RETURN.

- When Script Assistant has uniquely identified the term you're typing, or has identified the most likely term, it enters the term in your code without asking you. The part that Script Assistant has entered appears in gray, and the insertion point remains after the last character you typed. You can accept the suggestion by pressing ESC or F5, or reject the suggestion by typing through it.

## Choosing Whether to Escape Tabs and Line Breaks

Near the bottom of the Editing preferences, the Escape Tabs And Line Breaks Strings check box sounds bewildering, but it's straightforward enough.

A *string* is a sequence of text characters, such as your name. Normally, when you enter a string, AppleScript Editor shows it as text, and any tabs, line breaks, or carriage returns appear in the normal way they do on screen—for example, a tab appears as a chunk of white space in AppleScript Editor, and a carriage return makes the text wrap down to a new line.

To make your code more compact, AppleScript Editor can automatically replace tabs with the **\t** code and line breaks and carriage returns with the **\n** code. AppleScript Editor replaces these items when you compile or run your code rather than when you type it in. Your code appears more compact as a result, but it's harder to read because of the escaped characters—for example, **documents.\nChoose** indicates the word "documents." followed by a carriage return and the word "Choose."

### NOTE
A line-feed is the character created when you press SHIFT-RETURN. A carriage return is the character created when you press RETURN.

## Choosing Whether to Show the Tell Application Pop-up Menu

Right at the bottom of the Editing preferences is the Show "Tell" Application Pop-up Menu check box. This appears only in AppleScript Editor (in Snow Leopard), not in Script Editor in Leopard or earlier versions of Mac OS X.

Select this check box to add to the navigation bar a pop-up menu that lets you direct a **tell** block to the current application or a particular application. Briefly, a **tell** block is what you use to direct a command to an application rather than to AppleScript itself; you'll start using **tell** blocks in the next chapter, after which you'll never stop.

# Choosing Formatting Preferences

The Formatting preferences (see Figure 2-5) let you control how code looks in AppleScript Editor. AppleScript Editor by default uses the typewriter-like Courier font for uncompiled new text, so you can easily distinguish what's new from the compiled items,

**Figure 2-5**   In the Formatting preferences, choose fonts and colors for different types of text in AppleScript Editor.

which appear in the Verdana font in different colors according to their type. For example, operators (such as + and ,) appear in black and regular weight, while language keywords appear in bold blue, making them stand out.

To change a category's font, size, or color, double-click the category, and then work in the Font panel that AppleScript Editor opens. Click the Apply button in the Formatting preferences when you want to apply the font formatting; click the Revert button if you find yourself regretting the change. And if you want to restore AppleScript Editor's standard fonts and colors, click the Use Defaults button.

### *TIP*

If you want to change several categories at once, select them by clicking the first category and then ⌘-clicking each of the others. You can also select a range of categories by clicking the first and then **SHIFT**-clicking the last. Then double-click anywhere in the selection to open the Fonts panel. This trick is useful when you want to change the font family or size of several different categories at once—for example, when you grow tired of the Verdana font.

# Choosing History Preferences

The History preferences (see Figure 2-6) let you choose how many items of the results and the Event Log to keep to hand.

To keep Event Log items, select the Enable Event Log History check box, and then choose between the Unlimited Entries option button and the Maximum Entries option button; again, if you choose Maximum Entries, type the number you want in the text box (the default number is 10).

### NOTE

In Script Editor in Leopard and earlier versions of Mac OS X, the History preferences pane also includes an Enable Result History check box. If you select this check box, you can choose between the Unlimited Entries option button and the Maximum Entries option button; if you choose the latter, type the number you want in the text box (the default number is again 10).

For Event Log items, you can also select or clear the Log Only When Visible check box. When selected, this check box makes AppleScript Editor log only the Event Log items that occur when the Event Log pane is displayed. When this check box is cleared, AppleScript Editor logs the items whether or not the Event Log pane is displayed.

### NOTE

Usually, you'll do best to select the Enable Event Log History check box, because you can save time and effort by having this information available. Whether to log all entries or just the last few depends on the types of scripts you create and how you create them, so experiment with the different settings and find out what suits you best.

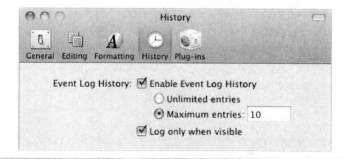

**Figure 2-6** In the History preferences, choose how many Result History items and Event Log items to keep.

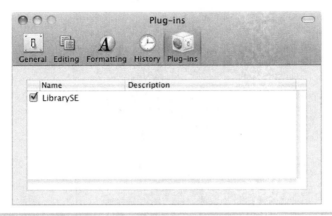

**Figure 2-7**    The Plug-ins preferences pane lets you turn off plug-ins when you don't want to use them.

## Choosing Plug-ins Preferences

The Plug-ins preferences pane (see Figure 2-7) shows the plug-ins (add-on software items) installed for AppleScript Editor on your Mac.

If you (or whoever administers your Mac) haven't installed any plug-ins yet, the Plug-ins preferences pane will be empty. That's just fine—you don't need to install any plug-ins to start harnessing the power of AppleScript.

# Putting the Script Menu on the Menu Bar in Leopard

As you've seen earlier in this chapter, AppleScript Editor in Snow Leopard lets you put the Script menu on the menu bar directly from General Preferences. In Leopard, you have to use AppleScript Utility to put the Script menu there (if it's not there already). Follow these steps:

1. Activate the Finder by clicking the Finder icon on the Dock or clicking open space on your Desktop.

2. Choose Go | Applications to open a Finder window showing the Applications folder. Alternatively, press ⌘-SHIFT-A.

3. Display the contents of the AppleScript folder by clicking its icon (in Columns view) or double-clicking its icon (in any of the other three views).

4. Double-click the AppleScript Utility icon to launch AppleScript Utility (see Figure 2-8).

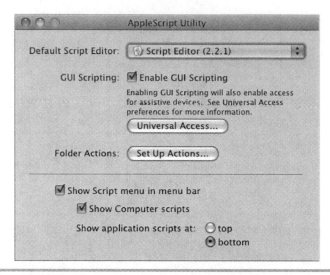

**Figure 2-8** AppleScript Utility lets you control whether the Script menu appears on the menu bar in Leopard and earlier versions of Mac OS X.

5. Select the Show Script Menu In Menu Bar check box. The Script menu icon appears on the menu bar.

6. Select the Show Computer Scripts check box if you want the scripts stored in your Mac's /Library/Scripts/ folder to appear in the Script menu. This is usually helpful until you pack the Script menu with scripts of your own.

### NOTE
The /Library/Scripts/ folder is referred to either as the "computer scripts folder" or the "local scripts folder." Your own scripts folder is the "user scripts folder."

7. In the Show Application Scripts At area, select the Top option button or the Bottom option button to choose where to display application scripts on the Script menu. Most people find placing these scripts at the top makes them easier to access, but you may be the exception.

8. Press ⌘-Q or choose AppleScript Utility | Quit AppleScript Utility to quit AppleScript Utility.

## Ask the Expert

**Q:** What are the other settings in AppleScript Utility in Leopard for?

**A:** Apart from the Script menu–related settings discussed in the main text, AppleScript Utility in Leopard also provides the following settings:

- **Default Script Editor**    In this pop-up menu, pick the script editor you want to use for AppleScript. Make sure Script Editor is selected, unless you've installed another AppleScript-capable script editor, such as Smile, Script Debugger, or Xcode. As you've seen, the General preferences of AppleScript Editor now include this pop-up menu.

- **Enable GUI Scripting**    Select this check box if you want to be able to use AppleScript to control applications that aren't directly accessible to AppleScript. Instead of controlling such an application by reaching into its objects, you control it by using its graphical user interface (GUI)—for example, by making AppleScript click a button in the GUI just as you would click it with your mouse. The Enable GUI Scripting check box is cleared by default unless you've selected the Enable Access For Assistive Devices check box at the bottom of the Universal Access pane in System Preferences. Unless you've turned on assistive devices, leave the Enable GUI Scripting check box cleared for the moment.

- **Set Up Actions**    Click this button to display the Folder Actions Setup window, which you use to create folder actions by attaching a script to a particular folder. The script can then run when you add an item to that folder (or when you remove an item).

# Running a Script from the Script Menu

Now that you've put the Script menu on the menu bar, try running one of Mac OS X's sample scripts from it. Follow these steps:

1. Click the Script Menu icon on the menu bar to display the Script menu.

2. Highlight the Info Scripts item, and then click the Font Sampler item (see Figure 2-9).

3. Mac OS X runs the Font Sampler script, which displays the informational dialog box shown here.

Font Sampler

This script will use the TextEdit application to create a document containing a sample of each installed typeface.

Cancel    Continue

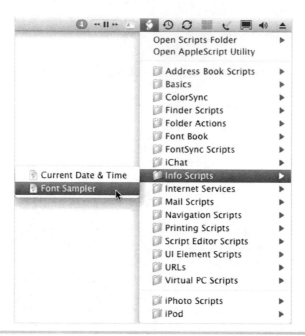

**Figure 2-9** You can quickly run a script from the Script menu on the Mac OS X menu bar.

4. Click the Continue button. The script launches TextEdit (or activates TextEdit, if it is already open), creates a new document, inserts sample paragraphs, and then formats them with different fonts.

5. Close the document without saving changes, and then quit TextEdit, unless you were using it.

You're now read to start creating scripts with AppleScript. Turn the page.

# Chapter 3

## Creating Your First Script

## Key Skills & Concepts

- Creating, editing, and saving a script

- Creating **tell** statements and **tell** blocks

- Adding comment lines and comment blocks

- Recording actions into a script

- Dealing with errors

- Wrapping lines of code

- Using a dictionary file to find the AppleScript terms you need

- Creating an application from a script

In this chapter, you'll create your first script. You'll learn how to work in AppleScript Editor, create and save a script, build **tell** statements and **tell** blocks, and compile and run the script. In creating the script, you'll also learn how to open and arrange Finder windows and how to launch, manipulate, and close other applications, using the TextEdit text editor that comes with Mac OS X as the example.

The script you create opens a Finder window, resizes and repositions the window, and changes it to show your preferred view and the contents of the Applications folder. The script then launches TextEdit, makes it create a document, enters some standard text in it, and displays the Save As dialog box so that you can name and save the document.

The chances that this script performs exactly the actions you want are slim and none (and Slim's out of the country just now), but you can use the techniques you learn in this chapter to create a script that opens the folders and applications you want and positions the windows where you prefer to have them on your Mac's Desktop. So treat this script as just a start, and modify it to meet your needs.

## Opening AppleScript Editor

To get started creating the script, open AppleScript Editor. If you've added the AppleScript Editor icon to the Dock, click the icon; otherwise, open the Applications folder, expand the contents of the AppleScript folder, and then double-click the AppleScript Editor icon.

# Creating tell Statements

To take an action in AppleScript, you use **tell** statements. A **tell** statement starts with the verb **tell**, identifies the application or object, and then tells it what to do.

For example, the following statement tells the application Microsoft PowerPoint to create a new document (a new presentation):

```
tell the application "Microsoft PowerPoint" to make new presentation
```

### *TIP*

One peculiarity of AppleScript is that it allows you to use the word "the" freely in your scripts. For example, the tell statement **tell the application "Finder" to open the desktop** has the same effect as **tell application "Finder" to open desktop**. AppleScript ignores the word "the," so you can add it wherever you want if you find it helps you structure the commands. (You can even go wild—the statement **tell the application the "Finder" the to the open the desktop** has the same effect.) Technically, AppleScript uses "the" as a *syntactic no-op keyword*—in other words, a keyword that does nothing except make the syntax more natural.

You can also tell the application or object you're addressing first to tell another application or object to do something. For example, the following statement makes the Finder apply column view in the front (foremost) Finder window:

```
tell application "Finder" to tell the front Finder window to set the
current view to column view
```

### *NOTE*

The "front" Finder window is the one that's foremost. If you click the Finder icon on the Dock, Mac OS X displays all the open Finder windows that aren't minimized. The window that has the focus is the front window. If the windows overlap one another, you can see that the front window is at the front.

### *TIP*

AppleScript isn't case-sensitive, so it doesn't matter if you capitalize the commands and names correctly. Generally, though, most people find scripts easier to read and edit if they use standard capitalization or something close to it.

**Try This** ## Opening a Finder Window
## Showing the Documents Folder

In AppleScript Editor, enter a **tell** statement that opens the Documents folder. Follow these steps:

1. Type the following and then pause:

   ```
   tell the ap
   ```

2. When Script Assistant suggests "application" for "ap," press ESC or F5 (whichever you find easier) to accept the suggestion.

3. Continue typing the following statement:

   ```
   tell the application "Finder" to open home
   ```

4. Click the Compile button on the toolbar or press ⌘-K to compile the script. (You can also choose Script | Compile if you prefer to use the menus.) You'll see the text of the statement change from the New Text (Uncompiled) font and color (which by default is magenta Courier) to the fonts and colors for compiled text. By default, the language keywords ("tell," "the," and "to") appear in blue Verdana Bold, the application keywords ("application," "open," and "home") appear in blue Verdana, and the value ("Finder") appears in black Verdana.

5. Click the Run button or press ⌘-R to run the script. AppleScript Editor opens a Finder window displaying the contents of your home folder. Admire the window briefly, and then close it.

6. Edit the **tell** statement by adding the text shown in bold here so that it opens the Documents folder in your home folder:

   ```
   tell the application "Finder" to open folder "Documents" of home
   ```

7. Click the Run button on the toolbar or press ⌘-R to run the script. This time, the script opens a Finder window showing the contents of your Documents folder. When you run an uncompiled script like this, AppleScript Editor automatically compiles it.

8. Run the script again. Notice that AppleScript Editor doesn't open another window to the Documents folder because the window you opened before is already showing this folder.

9. Now add another **tell** statement that closes all the open Finder windows. Press RETURN to create a new line in AppleScript Editor, and then type this statement:

   ```
   tell the application "Finder" to close every window
   ```

10. Click the Run button or press ⌘-R to run the script. AppleScript Editor closes all the Finder windows that are open.

# Saving a Script

As with most applications, you need to save your work in AppleScript Editor. The first time you save a script, you choose the folder in which to save it, give the script a name, and choose the file format and other options.

We'll look at the file formats later in this chapter, but for now, save your script as described in the Try This section.

## Try This Saving Your Script

Follow these steps to save your script:

1. Choose File | Save or press ⌘-S to display the Save As dialog box (see Figure 3-1).

2. In the Save As text box, type the name for the script: **Arrange Desktop**.

3. Make sure the Where pop-up menu is set to your Scripts folder. If you need to check, you may have to expand the dialog box by clicking the button to the right of the Save As text box.

4. Choose Script in the File Format pop-up menu.

5. Make sure the Run Only check box is cleared. (It should be cleared by default.)

6. Click the Save button to save the script.

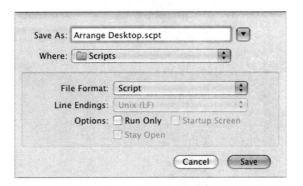

**Figure 3-1**   AppleScript Editor's Save As dialog box lets you choose from among different file formats. You can also choose to save a script as run-only (discussed later in this chapter).

# Creating tell Blocks

When you need to tell the same application or object to take two or more actions, as your script does with the Finder, you can use a *tell block* rather than a series of **tell** statements. A **tell** block is simply an easier way of giving a sequence of commands to the same application or object.

## Creating a tell Block Manually

A **tell** block starts with the **tell** verb and the application or object to which you're giving the instructions, and ends with the statement **end tell**:

```
tell application "Finder"

end tell
```

Between the **tell** statement and the **end tell** statement, you enter each command on its own line. You've already told AppleScript which application or object you're working with, so you don't need to tell it again. You also don't need to include the "to" part of the instruction. For example, this **tell** block tells the Finder to open a window showing the contents of your Documents folder and then tells it to close every Finder window:

```
tell the application "Finder"
    open folder "Documents" of home
    close every window
end tell
```

### NOTE
Often, it's handy to turn a **tell** statement into a **tell** block by pressing RETURN after the name of the application or object and then adding the **end tell** statement at the end. If AppleScript Editor gives the message "Syntax Error: Expected end of line but found end of script" when you try to compile or run a script, it usually means you've missed out an **end tell** statement.

**Try This** Using a tell Block

Change the two **tell** statements in your script into a **tell** block. You can edit the statements however you prefer, but here's an example:

1. To start with, the statements look like this:
    ```
    tell the application "Finder" to open folder "Documents" of home
    tell the application "Finder" to close every window
    ```

2. Double-click the word **to** in the first statement to select it.

3. Press RETURN to replace the selected word with a carriage return so that the statements look like this:

```
tell the application "Finder"
open folder "Documents" of home
tell the application "Finder" to close every window
```

4. In the second statement, select **tell the application "Finder" to**, and then press DELETE.

```
tell the application "Finder"
open folder "Documents" of home
close every window
```

5. On a new line after the second statement, type **end tell**.

```
tell the application "Finder"
open folder "Documents" of home
close every window
end tell
```

6. Press ⌘-K to compile the script. AppleScript Editor automatically indents the statements in the **tell** block to make it easily readable:

```
tell the application "Finder"
    open folder "Documents" of home
    close every window
end tell
```

## NOTE

You can place one **tell** block inside another tell block as needed. This is called *nesting* **tell** blocks, and is useful for structuring your scripts clearly. AppleScript Editor automatically indents each nested block farther so that you can distinguish the blocks easily.

# Using the Tell Application Pop-Up Menu

In AppleScript Editor in Snow Leopard, Apple introduced a new feature for creating **tell** blocks, the Tell Application pop-up menu.

Once you have enabled this pop-up menu by selecting the Show "Tell" Application Pop-Up Menu in Editing preferences, the Tell Application pop-up menu appears in the navigation bar (see Figure 3-2).

**Figure 3-2** You can place the Tell Application pop-up menu in the navigation bar by selecting the Show "Tell" Application Pop-Up Menu in Editing preferences.

You can then click this pop-up menu and choose the application to which you want to direct the script (see Figure 3-3). This saves you from having to write a **tell** block around your whole script while you're working in AppleScript Editor.

### NOTE

The Tell Application pop-up menu shows the applications you have added to the Library window.

# Adding Comments to Your Code

Often, it's helpful to add notes to your code as you write a script—for example, noting what works and what doesn't, what you need to do next, and other approaches you're considering to getting the job done. When a script is complete, it's a good idea to write notes that make the script easy to understand for someone who's never seen it before.

AppleScript calls such notes *comments* and lets you add them to your scripts in two ways: as end-of-line comments and block comments.

**Figure 3-3**  Choose the application to which you want the script to apply.

## Creating End-of-Line Comments

The first way of creating a comment is to tell AppleScript that it has reached the end of the line of code. This type of comment is called an *end-of-line comment.*

To create an end-of-line comment, type two hyphens at the beginning of a comment line; add a space, if you like, to keep your code easy to read. For example:

```
-- this line is a comment
```

You can also use two hyphens to "comment out" a statement that you don't want AppleScript to execute. This is useful when you're experimenting with code and need to be able to prevent a command from running without actually deleting it from your code. In the following example, everything after "Finder" is commented out because you've told AppleScript that the end of the line occurs there.

```
tell application "Finder" -- to open folder "Documents" of home
```

`Try This` Commenting Out a Line

Comment out the **close every window** statement in your script.

1. Click to place the insertion point at the beginning of the second line inside the **tell** block.

2. Type two hyphens and a space:

   ```
   -- close every window
   ```

3. Press ⌘-K or click the Compile button to compile the script. AppleScript Editor changes the line to the comments color set in the Formatting preferences; by default, this color is gray.

4. Press ⌘-R or click the Run button to run the script. The script opens a Finder window showing the Documents folder. Because the **close every window** statement is commented out, it does not run.

## Creating Block Comments

Instead of an end-of-line comment, you can create a block comment. A *block comment* is a comment that appears as its own block—normally on multiple lines rather than a single line, although you can create single-line block comments if you want. Block comments are good for presenting chunks of information without the distraction of having the two hyphens at the beginning of each line.

To create a block comment, type an opening parenthesis and an asterisk, the text of the comment, and another asterisk and a closing parenthesis. For example:

```
(* Start a tell block to the Finder.
 Open a window to the Documents folder.
 Set the view to Cover Flow. *)
```

## Ask the Expert

**Q:** Is it okay to use several end-of-line comments instead of a block comment?

**A:** Yes, it's fine—although purists may look down at you.
   If you prefer to use several end-of-line comments in sequence rather than create a block comment, by all means do so. Generally, though, a block comment is easier to read.
   One other thing while we're talking about comments—you can start a block comment after a statement of code on the same line if you like, but usually it's much clearer if you start the block comment on its own line.

**Try This** Creating a Comment Block

In your sample script, create a comment block at the beginning of the script.

1. Click before the beginning of the **tell** block and type this comment:

```
(* Start a tell block to the Finder.
Open a window to the Documents folder.
Set the view to Column view. *)
```

2. Press ⌘-K or click the Compile button to compile the script. AppleScript Editor changes the line to the comments color set in the Formatting preferences.

3. Press ⌘-R or click the Run button to run the script. AppleScript Editor ignores the comment and executes only the **open folder "Documents" of home** statement.

## Recording Actions into a Script

To quickly create parts of a script, you can record actions into AppleScript Editor. You open the script to which you want to add the actions, turn on recording, and then perform the actions in the relevant application. AppleScript Editor writes down the AppleScript commands for the actions.

Recording sounds like the perfect way to create scripts quickly, as it enables you to perform the actions the usual way—interactively in the application—and either simply use the resulting commands in AppleScript Editor or learn them easily and adapt them to your needs. The problem is that only a few applications generate the necessary Apple Events for recording to work.

Finder is one application that is recordable, and you'll use it in a moment. Another recordable application is BBEdit, the powerful text editor from Bare Bones software (www.barebones.com).

## Ask the Expert

**Q:** **How can I find out whether an application is recordable by AppleScript Editor?**

**A:** If you suspect an application may be recordable but don't know for sure, you can find out quickly enough: Just turn on recording in AppleScript Editor, and then perform a few actions in the application—for example, clicking buttons on the toolbar or choosing menu commands. If AppleScript Editor doesn't notice that you're performing actions in the other application, you'll know that you can't record the actions.

**Try This** Recording Actions: Repositioning and Resizing the Finder Window

Record actions into AppleScript Editor by turning on recording and then resizing and repositioning the Finder window. Follow these steps:

1. In AppleScript Editor, click on a new line after the **end tell** statement.

2. Click the Record button on the toolbar to start recording. You can also press ⌘-SHIFT-R or choose Script | Record.

3. Click the Finder window to activate it. You'll see AppleScript Editor begin a **tell** block and register commands for activating Finder, selecting the window, and establishing where the Finder window is:

```
tell application "Finder"
    activate
    select Finder window 1
    set position of Finder window 1 to {899, 152}
```

4. Drag the Finder window so that its upper-left corner is positioned where you want it. This example uses the upper-left corner of the Mac's screen, just below the menu bar.

5. Drag the resize handle in the lower-right corner of the Finder window to make the window the size and shape you prefer.

6. Click the View button on the toolbar for whichever view you want to apply. This example uses Column view. (Click the button even if the Finder window is already showing the view you want.)

7. Click the Applications folder in the sidebar (or choose Go | Applications) to display the Applications folder.

8. In the AppleScript Editor window, click the Stop button on the toolbar to stop recording. You can also press ⌘-. (⌘ and the PERIOD key) or choose Script | Stop. When you issue the Stop command, AppleScript Editor adds the **end tell** statement to close the **tell** block.

9. The **tell** block you've recorded should look something like this:

```
tell application "Finder"
    activate
    select Finder window 1
    set position of Finder window 1 to {899, 152}
    set position of Finder window 1 to {1, 44}
```

```
      set bounds of Finder window 1 to {1, 44, 800, 605}
      set current view of Finder window 1 to column view
      set target of Finder window 1 to folder "Applications" of
startup disk
end tell
```

**10.** Delete any extra statements that you've recorded accidentally. AppleScript Editor tries
    to follow everything you do, so any extra click shows up as a command.

# Examining the Recorded Code

Let's look quickly at what happens in the code you recorded so that we know which parts
to keep and which parts to delete.

## Activating an Application

The **activate** statement activates the Finder in AppleScript. This is the AppleScript
equivalent of you clicking the Finder button on the toolbar.

Because the Finder will already be activated by this point in the script, you can get rid
of this statement. (You'll make this change in the next Try This section.)

## Selecting the Finder Window

The **select Finder window 1** statement selects the first Finder window. AppleScript
considers the open Finder windows to be arranged in a stack from front to back, numbered
by their index position. That means the frontmost Finder window is the first window, the
one behind it is the second, the next the third, and so on.

When you select a Finder window, you bring it to the front of the stack, making it the
first window; the previously first window is now second, and so forth. Similarly, if you
open a new Finder window, the Finder automatically puts that window at the front. So it's
easy for things to get complicated when selecting Finder windows in scripts.

Because your script opens a Finder window, that window will already be at the top of
the stack, so you can delete this statement too.

## Setting the Position of the Window

The **set position of Finder window 1 to {899,152}** statement positions the Finder window
by defining where its upper-left corner appears: 899 pixels from the left edge of the screen
and 152 pixels from the top edge (but see the nearby Caution for a complication).

**CAUTION**

There are two complications when positioning Finder windows. First, the vertical measurement is not from the top edge of the Finder window itself, as you'd expect, but from the bottom edge of the Finder window's title bar. This means you must add 22 pixels (the depth of the title bar) to the top measurement to place the Finder window correctly. Second, if you're placing the Finder window on the Mac's primary screen, you must also allow another 22 pixels at the top of the screen for the Mac OS X menu bar. So normally you need to add 44 pixels (22 + 22) to the vertical offset measurement to place a Finder window at the top of the screen.

In fact, that first **set position** statement is the Finder registering the window's initial position in case you want to be able to duplicate it; you can delete this statement. The second **set position** statement (**set position of Finder window 1 to {1, 44}**) is the one that positions the Finder window where you want it.

## Ask the Expert

**Q:** **What happens to the positioning if my Mac has a second monitor attached?**

**A:** The coordinates start from the upper-left corner of your Mac's primary monitor—the monitor on which the menu bar and the Dock appear. You can change which monitor is the primary monitor by dragging the menu bar from one monitor to the other on the Arrangement tab of Displays preferences.

If you have a secondary monitor positioned to the left of the primary monitor, use negative horizontal values to position windows on it (for example, −800 is 800 pixels to the left of the 0 position). If you have a secondary monitor positioned above the primary monitor, use negative vertical values to position windows on it.

## Resizing the Window

To resize a window, you tell the Finder to set its bounds. So the **set bounds of Finder window 1 to {1, 44, 800, 605}** statement positions the window like this:

- The window's left border appears 1 pixel from the left edge of the screen.
- The window's top border appears just below the bottom edge of the Mac OS X menu bar (allowing 22 pixels for the menu bar and 22 pixels for the Finder window's title bar).
- The window's right border appears 800 pixels across the screen from the left edge.
- The window's bottom border appears 605 pixels down the screen from the top edge.

| View | Finder Command | Finder Shortcut | Term |
|------|----------------|-----------------|------|
| Icon view | View \| As Icons | ⌘-1 | **icon view** |
| List view | View \| As List | ⌘-2 | **list view** |
| Column view | View \| As Columns | ⌘-3 | **column view** |
| Cover Flow view | View \| As Cover Flow | ⌘-4 | **flow view** |

**Table 3-1**    AppleScript Terms for the Finder's Four Views

## Changing the View

Each Finder window can be in any of four views: Icon view, List view, Column view, or Cover Flow view. To set the view, you use a **set current view to** statement and the appropriate view term from Table 3-1. For example, a **set current view to column view** statement sets the view to Column view.

### NOTE

Setting a window's bounds lets you both resize and reposition the window. Just position the borders in the appropriate places.

### Try This    Editing the Script

Now edit your script to integrate the recorded statements from the second **tell** block into the first **tell** block and to create a nested **tell** block that works with the front Finder window. Follow these steps:

1. To start with, your script should look like this, with minor variations for the window positions and the view you chose:

```
(*Start a tell block to the Finder.
Open a window to the Documents folder.
Set the view to Column view. *)
tell the application "Finder"
    open folder "Documents" of home
    --close every window
end tell
tell application "Finder"
    activate
    select Finder window 1
    set position of Finder window 1 to {899, 152}
    set position of Finder window 1 to {1, 44}
```

*(continued)*

```
    set bounds of Finder window 1 to {1, 44, 800, 605}
    set current view of Finder window 1 to column view
    set target of Finder window 1 to folder "Applications" of
startup disk
end tell
```

2. Delete the lines shown in boldface (from the **--close every window** comment to the first **set position of Finder window 1** statement) to collapse the script to a single **tell** block:

```
(*Start a tell block to the Finder.
Open a window to the Documents folder.
Set the view to Column view. *)
tell the application "Finder"
    open folder "Documents" of home
    set position of Finder window 1 to {1, 44}
    set bounds of Finder window 1 to {1, 44, 800, 605}
    set current view of Finder window 1 to column view
    set target of Finder window 1 to folder "Applications" of
startup disk
end tell
```

3. Delete the **set position of Finder window 1** statement as well. You don't need this statement because the **set bounds of Finder window 1** statement both resizes and positions the window.

4. Create a nested **tell** block to deal more neatly with all the statements that manipulate **Finder window 1**. The boldfaced statements are the ones that have changed:

```
(*Start a tell block to the Finder.
Open a window to the Documents folder.
Set the view to Column view. *)
tell the application "Finder"
    open folder "Documents" of home
tell the front Finder window
set bounds to {1, 44, 800, 605}
set current view to column view
set target to folder "Applications" of startup disk
end tell
end tell
```

5. Press ⌘-K or click the Compile button on the toolbar to compile the script. AppleScript Editor automatically indents the nested **tell** block so that it is easy to read:

```
(*Start a tell block to the Finder.
Open a window to the Documents folder.
Set the view to Column view. *)
tell the application "Finder"
```

```
open folder "Documents" of home
tell the front Finder window
    set bounds to {1, 44, 800, 605}
    set current view to column view
    set target to folder "Applications" of startup disk
end tell
end tell
```

6. Save the script (press ⌘-**s**), but don't run it just yet.

# Dealing with Errors

When you tell AppleScript exactly what to do, and it is able to interpret each of your commands correctly, your script runs perfectly. But all too often, you'll run into a problem that causes an error. When you do, AppleScript displays an error message telling you that a problem has occurred. You'll then need to correct the code to make the script run correctly.

**Try This** Resolving an Error in Your Code

Try dealing with an error that occurs in a script. Follow these steps:

1. Click the Run button or press ⌘-**R** to run your script. The Finder window opens, moves to the specified position, and changes to your chosen view—but then an error occurs (see Figure 3-4).

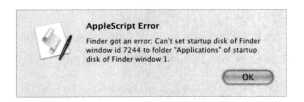

**Figure 3-4**   AppleScript warns you when an error occurs in a script you're running.

*(continued)*

2.  Read the error message—for example: *Can't set startup disk of Finder window id 7429 to folder "Applications" of startup disk of Finder window 1*. Note its contents and where it occurs. The problem is that the **tell** statement needs to go to the Finder rather than to the front window.

3.  Click the OK button to dismiss the dialog box.

4.  Edit the problem statement. You will often need to look up the solution to errors; Chapter 10 offers suggestions on where to look. For now, move the **set target to folder "Applications" of startup disk** statement out of the nested **tell** block, put it in the outer **tell** block, and spell out the window that it is to affect. The moved and revised statement is shown in boldface in the next listing.

```
(*Start a tell block to the Finder.
Open a window to the Documents folder.
Set the view to Column view. *)
tell the application "Finder"
    open folder "Documents" of home
    tell the front Finder window
        set position to {1, 44}
        set bounds to {1, 44, 800, 605}
        set current view to column view
    end tell
    set target of the front Finder window to folder "Applications"
of startup disk
end tell
```

5.  Compile the script, run it, and make sure it works without raising an error.

6.  Save the changes to the script (for example, press ⌘-s).

# Wrapping a Line of Code

Lines of code can easily grow longer than the width of the AppleScript Editor window—but AppleScript Editor gives you an easy way to avoid scrolling left and right to see your statements in their entirety.

If you've selected the Wrap Lines check box in Editing preferences, AppleScript Editor automatically wraps lines of code to fit within the window. And if you selected the Indent Wrapped Lines By check box, AppleScript Editor automatically indents the wrapped lines by however many spaces you chose. This enables you to see instantly which lines of code are wrapped.

If you've cleared the Wrap Lines check box, you can break a line of code manually by placing the insertion point where you want to break the line and then pressing OPTION-RETURN. AppleScript Editor inserts the *continuation character* to show that the line has been broken visually but continues logically. The continuation character appears as a "not sign" symbol, a horizontal line with a downward hook at the right end: the ¬ character. If you want to insert this character without breaking the line, press OPTION-L instead.

### TIP
Even if you've turned wrapping on, you can break lines of code manually as needed. For example, you may find it better to break a line of code at the most logical point rather than have AppleScript Editor break it at the point dictated by the window width.

## Try This  Breaking Lines of Code Manually

Try breaking the long **set target** statement near the end of the script onto two lines.

Position the insertion point at a handy place, such as after **the front Finder window**, and then press OPTION-RETURN. AppleScript Editor inserts the continuation character and breaks the line, indenting it to the same level:

```
    end tell
    set target of the front Finder window ¬
    to folder "applications" of startup disk
end tell
```

Press ⌘-K or click the Compile button to compile the script, and AppleScript Editor indents the continued line to the next level so that you can more easily see that it is continued:

```
    end tell
    set target of the front Finder window ¬
        to folder "applications" of startup disk
end tell
```

So far, the script opens a Finder window, resizes and repositions it, changes the view, and then displays the contents of another folder. Now let's make the script open TextEdit, create a new document, add some text to it, and save it automatically. To find the commands needed, we'll open the AppleScript dictionary file for TextEdit.

# Opening a Dictionary File

To find out the AppleScript verbs, classes, and properties you need to control an application, you open the application's AppleScript dictionary. The dictionary explains the AppleScript structure of the application and how to use it.

You can open an application's dictionary file in either of two ways:

- **Use the File | Open Dictionary command from AppleScript Editor.** This is the normal and more formal way. You'll probably want to use this way most of the time.
- **Drag the application's icon and drop it on the AppleScript Editor icon.** This way works well when the AppleScript Editor icon appears on the Dock (as it does when AppleScript Editor is open) and you've got a Finder window open to the Applications folder.

## Try This Opening the Dictionary File for TextEdit

To open the dictionary file for TextEdit, follow these steps:

1. In AppleScript Editor, choose File | Open Dictionary or press ⌘-SHIFT-O to display the Open Dictionary dialog box (see Figure 3-5).

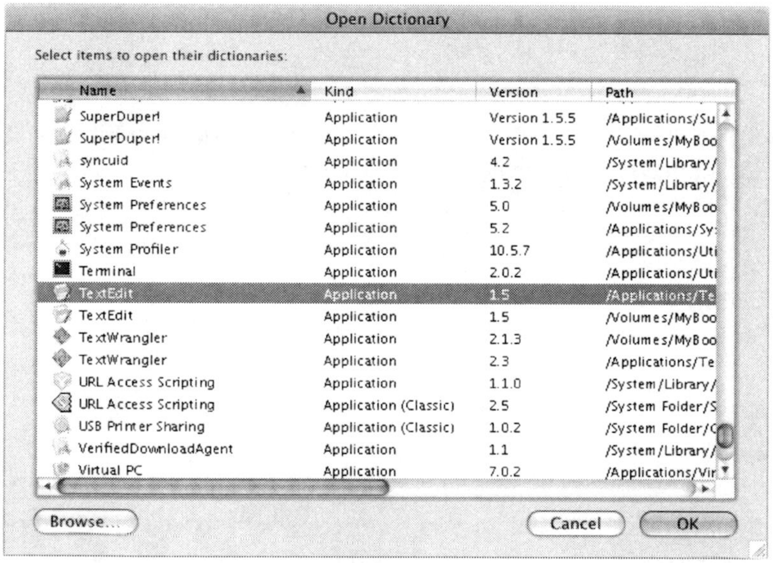
Open Dictionary
Select items to open their dictionaries:
Name
Kind
Version
Path
SuperDuper! Application Version 1.5.5 /Applications/Su
SuperDuper! Application Version 1.5.5 /Volumes/MyBoo
syncuid Application 4.2 /System/Library/
System Events Application 1.3.2 /System/Library/
System Preferences Application 5.0 /Volumes/MyBoo
System Preferences Application 5.2 /Applications/Sy
System Profiler Application 10.5.7 /Applications/Uti
Terminal Application 2.0.2 /Applications/Uti
TextEdit Application 1.5 /Applications/Te
TextEdit Application 1.5 /Volumes/MyBoo
TextWrangler Application 2.1.3 /Volumes/MyBoo
TextWrangler Application 2.3 /Applications/Te
URL Access Scripting Application 1.1.0 /System/Library/
URL Access Scripting Application (Classic) 2.5 /System Folder/S
USB Printer Sharing Application (Classic) 1.0.2 /System Folder/C
VerifiedDownloadAgent Application 1.1 /System/Library/
Virtual PC Application 7.0.2 /Applications/Vir
Browse...
Cancel
OK

**Figure 3-5** In the Open Dictionary dialog box, either pick the application from the list or click the Browse button to locate it elsewhere.

### *NOTE*

If you find two or more listings for the application, choose the one with the highest version number (in the Version column). If two or more versions have the same number, pick the one in your Applications folder over any others.

**2.** Select the entry for TextEdit, and then click the OK button. The TextEdit dictionary file opens in a AppleScript Editor window that bears the application's name, so you can easily see which dictionary it is (see Figure 3-6).

### *TIP*

You can open multiple dictionary files at once from the Open Dictionary dialog box. Click the first dictionary file, and then ⌘-click each of the others you want; click the OK button when you've finished choosing. Alternatively, click the first dictionary file and then SHIFT-click the last to select a range of files.

Like iTunes, the Dictionary Viewer window has three columns in the upper part of the window for browsing through its contents. The main section of the window is the dictionary pane, which shows the definition for the selected term.

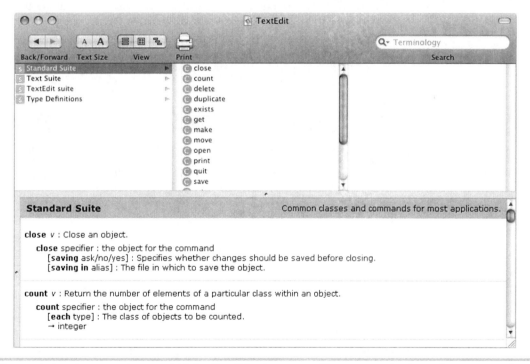

**Figure 3-6**   Once you've opened the TextEdit dictionary file, you can look up the commands, classes, and properties you need.

*(continued)*

If AppleScript Editor opens the dictionary file in a small window, expand it to a decent size so that you can see what you're doing. Zoom it to fill the screen if you prefer.

You can resize the different areas of the window by dragging the divider bars that separate them. For example, if you want to have more space in the browsing area, click the separator bar above the dictionary pane and drag it downward.

## Finding the Terms You Need

As you'll probably remember from the PowerPoint example near the beginning of this chapter, all you need to do to launch an application and create a new document is give the command to make a new document—for example:

```
tell application "TextEdit" to make new document
```

Sure enough, when you run this command in a script, AppleScript activates TextEdit, if it's already running; if TextEdit isn't running, AppleScript launches TextEdit and then activates it.

But to get beyond this, we'll use the dictionary. Let's start by looking up the **make** command.

### Try This  Using the Dictionary File

We'll look at dictionary files in more detail in the upcoming chapters. For now, follow these steps to find the commands needed and to enter them in the script:

1. Make sure Standard Suite is selected in the left column of the three and that the leftmost of the three View buttons on the toolbar is selected.

2. In the second column, click the **make** command to display its information in the dictionary pane (see Figure 3-7), which tells us this:

    ● The **new** parameter is what we need to make a new object, such as the new document we want to create. This parameter has no brackets around it, which means that it's required.

    ● The **at** parameter lets you choose where to insert the new object—for example, at the front or at the back of the TextEdit stack of windows. This parameter appears in brackets, which means it's not required; we'll just let TextEdit place the new document in a window at the front.

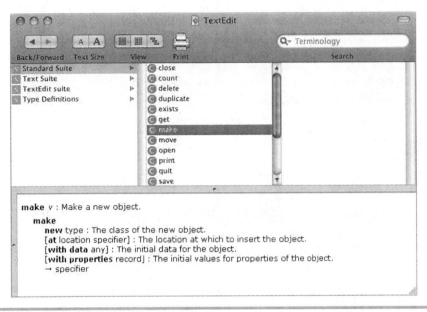

**Figure 3-7**   The dictionary viewer shows the selected item's information in the dictionary pane.

- The **with data** parameter lets you place initial data in the object. This parameter is optional, too, and we won't use it either.

- The **with properties** parameter lets you set properties for the new object. This parameter is also optional and one we won't use right now.

3. Click in the main AppleScript Editor window and comment out all the Finder commands by entering (* (an opening parenthesis and an asterisk) before the first **tell** statement and *) (an asterisk and a closing parenthesis) after the last **end tell** statement. You're commenting out these statements so that they don't run while you're creating and testing the TextEdit part of the script.

4. Now create a **tell** block for TextEdit at the end of your script:

```
tell the application "TextEdit"

end tell
```

5. Inside the **tell** block, add a **make new document** statement, as shown in boldface here:

```
tell the application "TextEdit"
    make new document
end tell
```

(continued)

6. Now click the TextEdit Suite item in the left column of the dictionary viewer, and then click the **document** item in the second column to display information about the **document** class. Figure 3-8 shows the information you'll see.

7. The property we're interested in here is the **text** property, which contains the text of the document. Set the **text** property to assign text to the front document. The text you assign is a string that includes two **return** characters, which break the text into three paragraphs.

```
set the text of the front document to "Latest Report" & return ¬
    & "Here is the latest news from the front." & return & "Sales
have doubled!"
```

8. Next we need to look up the properties for the **paragraph** class to see how TextEdit lets us manipulate it. Click in the Search box in the upper-left corner of the dictionary viewer window and type **parag**. The dictionary viewer window displays results as you type.

9. In the list of results, click the **paragraph** class—the one with the white C in a purple box to its left. The dictionary pane displays the information on the class (see Figure 3-9). As you can see, there's a **color** property that sets the font's color, a **font** property that sets the font's name (for example, Arial or Times New Roman), and a **size** property that sets the font size in points.

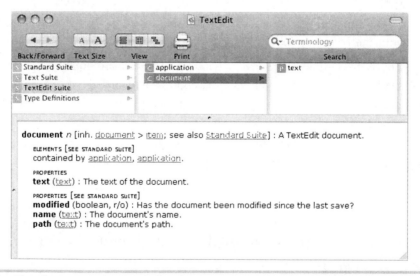

**Figure 3-8** The document class includes a text property that contains the text of the document.

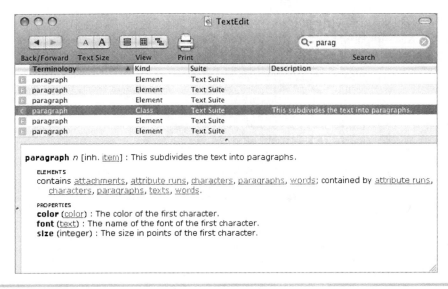

**Figure 3-9**  The paragraph class contains information on the properties of the paragraph in TextEdit.

10. Start a **tell** block to the front document like this:

```
tell application "TextEdit"
    make new document
    set the text of the front document to "Latest Report" & return ¬
        & "Here is the latest news from the front." & return ¬
        & "Sales have doubled!"
    tell the front document
    end tell
```

11. Within the **tell** block to the front document, insert a nested **tell** block to the first paragraph that sets the **font** property and the **size** property, as shown in boldface here:

```
tell application "TextEdit"
    make new document
    set the text of the front document to "Latest Report" & return ¬
        & "Here is the latest news from the front." & return ¬
        & "Sales have doubled!"
    tell the front document
        tell the first paragraph
            set the font to "Arial Bold"
            set the size to 18
        end tell
    end tell
end tell
```

*(continued)*

12. After the **end tell** statement for the first paragraph, insert another nested **tell** block to the second paragraph that sets the **font** property and the **size** property, as shown in boldface here:

```
tell application "TextEdit"
    make new document
    set the text of the front document to "Latest Report" & return ¬
        & "Here is the latest news from the front." & return ¬
        & "Sales have doubled!"
    tell the front document
        tell the first paragraph
            set the font to "Arial Bold"
            set the size to 18
        end tell
        tell the second paragraph
            set the font to "Arial"
            set the size to 12
        end tell
    end tell
end tell
```

13. Set the bounds of the front TextEdit window by using the same technique you learned earlier in this chapter for the Finder window, as shown in boldface here:

```
tell application "TextEdit"
    make new document
    set the text of the front document to "Latest Report" & return ¬
        & "Here is the latest news from the front." & return ¬
        & "Sales have doubled!"
    tell the front document
        tell the first paragraph
            set the font to "Arial Bold"
            set the size to 18
        end tell
        tell the second paragraph
            set the font to "Arial"
            set the size to 12
        end tell
    end tell
    set the bounds of the front window to {800, 22, 1400, 822}
end tell
```

14. Now all that remains is to save the document. Type **save** into the Search box in the dictionary viewer window to find the information about the **save** verb. As you can see in Figure 3-10, **save** takes an optional **as** parameter to specify which file type to use and an optional **in** parameter to specify the filename (and the folder path).

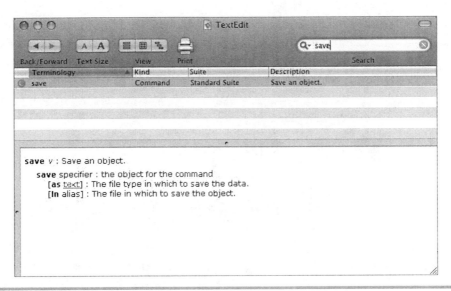

**Figure 3-10**    The TextEdit dictionary shows that the save verb takes two parameters, both of which are optional.

15. Both of these parameters are optional, so you can use the **save** verb without either, in which case TextEdit prompts the user to enter the filename and choose the folder path if the document has never been saved. That's the behavior we'll use here, so add a **save the front document** statement before the final **end tell** statement in the script, as shown in boldface here:

```
tell application "TextEdit"
    make new document
    set the text of the front document to "Latest Report" & return ¬
        & "Here is the latest news from the front." & return ¬
        & "Sales have doubled!"
    tell the front document
        tell the first paragraph
            set the font to "Arial Bold"
            set the size to 18
        end tell
        tell the second paragraph
            set the font to "Arial"
            set the size to 12
        end tell
    end tell
    set the bounds of the front window to {800, 22, 1400, 822}
    save the front document
end tell
```

*(continued)*

16. Uncomment the Finder part of the script by removing the (* from before the first **tell** statement and the *) from after the last Finder-related **end tell** statement. Your script should now look like this (with minor variations in the bounds of the windows and the view used in the Finder):

```
tell the application "Finder"
    open folder "Documents" of home
    tell the front Finder window
        set bounds to {1, 44, 836, 605}
        set current view to column view
    end tell
    set target of the front Finder window to ¬
        folder "Applications" of startup disk
end tell
tell application "TextEdit"
    make new document
    set the text of the front document to "Latest Report" & return ¬
        & "Here is the latest news from the front." & return ¬
        & "Sales have doubled!"
    tell the front document
        tell the first paragraph
            set the font to "Arial Bold"
            set the size to 18
        end tell
        tell the second paragraph
            set the font to "Arial"
            set the size to 12
        end tell
    end tell
    set the bounds of the front window to {800, 22, 1400, 822}
    save the front document
end tell
```

17. Press ⌘-S to save your changes to the script.

18. Press ⌘-R to run the script. When TextEdit displays the Save As dialog box, type a name for the document and choose the folder in which to save it.

### NOTE
If you click the Cancel button in the Save As dialog box, AppleScript displays an error message. We'll look at how to handle errors in Chapter 10.

# Turning a Script into an Application

To make your script easy to run, you can turn it into a usable application and put an icon for it somewhere handy—for example, on the Dock.

AppleScript Editor enables you to save a script in the five different formats explained in Table 3-2.

| Script Format | Explanation | Use This Format When |
|---|---|---|
| Script | This is the basic format for scripts you run in AppleScript Editor or from the Scripts menu. | You're creating a script, or you have a finished script that you want to run from the Scripts menu. |
| Application | This creates an executable application that you can run on any Mac. You can include a startup screen showing the script's description, make the script read-only, and choose to leave it open after it finishes running. | You've created a script that doesn't use any external components (such as documents or graphics) and are ready to distribute it. |
| Script Bundle | This creates a script that includes any external components needed, such as graphics, sounds, or movies. | You've created a script that needs external components but that you want to run from the Script menu rather than as an executable application. |
| Application Bundle | This creates an executable application that you can run on any Mac. The application includes any external components needed, such as graphics, movies, or sounds. | You've created a script that uses external components, and you're ready to distribute it. |
| Text | This contains the uncompiled text of the script. | You need to create a text-only version of the script so that you can edit it in a word processor or text editor. |

**Table 3-2**   File Formats in Which AppleScript Editor Can Save Scripts

## Ask the Expert

**Q:** When I'm saving a script in the Script format, what happens if I select the Run Only check box?

**A:** The code vanishes into thin air…

More seriously: When you save a script in the Script format, select the Run Only check box if you want to prevent the commands in the script from being visible.

This sounds odd, but it's useful when you need to distribute a script but you don't want anybody to be able to see how it works. Use this run-only option only for versions of scripts that are ready for distribution, not for working versions or reference versions that you need to be able to read and edit.

**Try This** ## Making an Application from Your Script and Adding It to the Dock

Follow these steps to add a description to your script, make an application from it, and add the application to the Dock so that you can run it easily:

1. In AppleScript Editor, click the Description button at the bottom (unless it's selected already) to display the Description pane.

2. Type a description of what the script does, such as this:

```
This application opens, positions, and resizes a Finder window, and
then creates a document in TextEdit.
```

3. Press ⌘-s or choose File | Save to save the script with the description.

4. Press ⌘-SHIFT-S or choose File | Save As to display the Save As dialog box.

5. Open the File Format pop-up menu and choose Application.

6. Select the Startup Screen check box.

7. Make sure that the Run Only check box and the Stay Open check box are both cleared. (These check boxes will normally be cleared by default.)

8. If you want, choose the folder in which to save your scripts. AppleScript Editor automatically suggests the current folder, which will normally be your ~/Library/ Scripts/ folder, but you may prefer to use another folder.

9. Click the Save button. AppleScript Editor closes the Save As dialog box and creates the application.

10. Open a Finder window to the folder in which you saved the script.

11. Drag the icon for the script to the applications area of the Dock (the area to the left of the divider bar, or above the divider bar if you've positioned the Dock on the left side or right side of the screen).

12. Click the new Dock icon to run the application. The application displays its startup screen (see Figure 3-11).

13. Click the Run button to run the application.

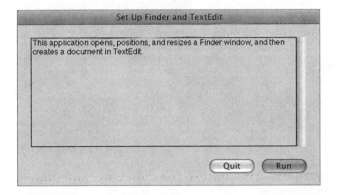

**Figure 3-11**   The startup screen for a script application lets the user choose whether to run the script or quit it.

# Part II

## Learning Essential AppleScript Programming Techniques

# Chapter 4

## Working with Variables, Classes, Operators, and Coercions

## Key Skills & Concepts

- ⊛ Working with variables

- ⊛ Understanding AppleScript's data types

- ⊛ Using operators to perform operations and comparisons

- ⊛ Understanding AppleScript's classes

- ⊛ Changing data from one type to another

Often, you'll need to store data temporarily in your scripts so that you can use it later. To do so, you use variables. For example, instead of asking the user to input his or her name at each point you need it in the script, you can ask for the user's name one time via an input box, store the result in a variable, and then insert that variable throughout the script.

In this chapter, you'll learn how to declare variables, assign data to them, and use them in your code. You'll also learn how to use AppleScript's operators to perform operations (such as addition or division) or to make comparisons (such as checking whether one value is greater than or equal to another value). Finally, I'll explain about the different classes of objects that AppleScript provides and teach you to change data from one type to another.

# Working with Variables

A *variable* is a named area in memory in which you can store an item of data—for example, your company's name, the date two months ago, or the hundreds of thousands of dollars your company has lost since that date.

When you need to store data during a script, use a variable. You can then retrieve the contents of the variable whenever you need to use the information, or overwrite the contents of the variable with new information if needed.

## Understanding the Seven Data Types

When you create a variable, you can assign to it any of seven types of data. Table 4-1 explains these data types with examples.

| Data Type | Data in the Variable | Example or Explanation |
|---|---|---|
| Boolean | Only **true** or **false** | true |
| Integer | A whole number (with no decimal places) | 10 |
| Real | A double-precision number (with decimal places) | 39282.87270 |
| Date | A floating-point number that has the date before the decimal point and the time after it | AppleScript lets you retrieve various parts of the date—for example, the year, the month, the day, or the time. |
| List | Any quantities that you enter between braces and separate with commas | **{"San Francisco", "Oakland", "Hayward", "San Jose"}** |
| Record | A list of pairs of keys and values | **set client to {name:"Industrial Amalgams", city:"City of Industry"}** |
| String | Text enclosed within double quotation marks ("") | **set prompt to "Save the document?"** |

**Table 4-1**   AppleScript Data Types for Variables

When you're working with AppleScript, you don't normally need to specify the data type of a variable explicitly. Instead, AppleScript automatically works out the data type from the data you assign to the variable and assigns the appropriate data type.

For example, say you create a variable like this:

```
set IsUserSane to true
```

From the **true** value that you assign to the variable, AppleScript infers that the variable should be Boolean—either **true** or **false**—and so gives the variable the Boolean type.

### NOTE

If you want to assign the literal string "True" or "False" to a variable, put the string in quotes. AppleScript then infers that the variable should be a string variable.

Similarly, if you assign a string of text to a variable, AppleScript automatically makes it a string variable:

```
set myUsername to "Bill"
```

## Creating a Variable

All you have to do to create a variable is to use a **set** command to specify a name for it and assign the data to it. For example, the following statement creates the variable named **myGreeting** and assigns the string **"Good morning!"** to it:

```
set myGreeting to "Good morning!"
```

After you create a variable in a script, the variable retains its contents—the data you assign it—unless you change the contents by assigning other data. You can do this in several ways, as you'll see later in this chapter.

## Understanding the Difference Between the set Command and the copy Command

The examples shown so far in this chapter have used the **set** command to create a variable and assign data to it. But there's also another command you can use to create a variable and shovel data into it—the **copy** command.

For most purposes, the **copy** command has the same effect as the **set** command, but it has a different syntax—in effect, it's the **set** command's syntax in reverse. For example, instead of using **set myGreeting to "Hello"**, you can use the **copy** command, like this:

```
copy "Hello" to myGreeting
```

The result of this **copy** command is to create a variable named **myGreeting** whose contents are the string **"Hello"**. For general instances like these, you can use the **set** command and the **copy** command more or less interchangeably.

But the difference between the two commands becomes important when you're creating a variable that contains a date, a list, a record, or a script object. Here's the difference:

- If you use a **set** command, AppleScript assigns to the variable a reference to the object. The reference is a pointer that means the variable contains whatever the object contains.

- If you use a **copy** command, AppleScript assigns to the variable a separate copy of the object. This copy is independent of the original—so if the original object changes after you use the **copy** command, the variable contains an object with different values than the original object.

This can lead to confusion if you set two or more variables to point to the same object. For example, the following code snippet creates a variable named **CompanyOffices** and assigns a list of three cities to it: Little Rock, Paris, and Albuquerque. It then creates a variable named **Destinations** and uses a **set** command to assign to it the **CompanyOffices** object. It then changes the first item in the **Destinations** variable and displays a dialog box showing the first item in the **CompanyOffices** variable. You'll learn about dialog boxes in detail in Chapter 8.

```
set CompanyOffices to {"Little Rock", "Paris", "Albuquerque"}
set Destinations to CompanyOffices
tell Destinations to set {item 1} to {"Cincinnati"}
display dialog item 1 of CompanyOffices
```

When you run this code, the dialog box shows Cincinnati rather than Little Rock. Changing the **Destinations** variable also changes the **CompanyOffices** variable, because both variables point to the same object as a result of the **set** command.

To prevent the **Destinations** variable from trampling the **CompanyOffices** variable like this, use a **copy** command to create a separate copy of the **CompanyOffices** variable rather than a **set** command. The code (shown here with the change in boldface) then displays Little Rock in the dialog box, as you would expect.

```
set CompanyOffices to {"Little Rock", "Paris", "Albuquerque"}
copy CompanyOffices to Destinations
tell Destinations to set {item 1} to {"Cincinnati"}
display dialog item 1 of CompanyOffices
```

## Understanding the Rules for Naming Variables

AppleScript has several rules for creating the names for variables. These rules aren't very restrictive, so you can create a wide variety of variable names without running afoul of them. Here are the details:

- **Start with a letter**   Each variable name must start with a letter.

- **Use letters, numbers, and underscores only**   After the first letter, you can use any combination of letters, numbers, and underscores. Many people use underscores to separate different words in variable names, as you can't use spaces or other punctuation. For example, the variable name **first_name** is easier to read than the variable name **firstname**. You can also use capital letters to separate the parts (for example, **FirstName**) or both (for example, **First_Name**)—it's your choice.

- **Don't worry about capitalization**   Names are not case-sensitive, but AppleScript enforces the first capitalization you use. The first time you enter a variable name, AppleScript takes that to be the way you want to capitalize the variable. So if you create a variable with the name **myCompany**, you can enter the name thereafter as **mycompany** (or any other variation of capitalization—for example, **MYCOmpaNY**), and AppleScript will apply the original capitalization when you compile the script.

### TIP

AppleScript's trick of enforcing the first capitalization you use for variables is usually helpful, but it can be awkward when you realize you want to improve on that initial capitalization after you've compiled the code. In these cases, you need to quit and restart AppleScript Editor before you can persuade it to accept your new capitalization.

● **Avoid reserved words**   Don't use any of AppleScript's reserved words—any of the words defined as terms in AppleScript. For example, don't call a variable **result** or **error**, because AppleScript uses those words. This is one of those things that's apparently forehead-slapping obvious but in practice easy enough to trip up on, because most people can't reel off every single AppleScript keyword. If AppleScript gives you an unexpected syntax error, see whether you've inadvertently stepped on a reserved word.

### NOTE

If you truly must, you can use a reserved word as a variable name by putting it between vertical bar characters (| characters). For example, if you feel compelled to name a variable **error**, use |error| to do so. There's normally no good reason to do this. You can also use this syntax to create a variable name that contains characters you otherwise can't use, such as spaces or symbols. There's no good reason to do this either unless you take joy in doing so.

## Creating a Variable That Refers to Another Object

Instead of assigning to a variable the contents of an object, you can assign a reference to the object. Doing this lets you get the current contents of the object whenever you use the variable rather than what the contents were when you created the variable. This is useful when the object you're referring to may change value during the course of a script.

To create a reference, create the variable using the **a reference to** operator. For example, the following **tell** block makes the Finder create a variable named **myWin** as a reference to the front Finder window. It then sets the **position** property of **myWin** to position the front Finder window.

```
tell the application "Finder"
    set myWin to a reference to the front window
    set the position of myWin to {800, 44}
end tell
```

That's all straightforward. But where using the reference makes a difference is when the object changes. The following expanded **tell** block (with changes in boldface) opens another Finder window, this one to the startup disk. Because this new window is now the front window, the **myWin** variable now refers to it, so the second **set the position of myWin** command repositions the new window rather than the first window.

```
tell the application "Finder"
    set myWin to a reference to the front window
    set the position of myWin to {800, 44}
    open startup disk
    set the position of myWin to {0, 44}
end tell
```

# Understanding the Scope and Persistence of Variables

AppleScript lets you use two different types of variables: local variables and global variables.

The normal way of using variables is to simply create them as you need them in your scripts, as the examples so far in this chapter have done. When you create a variable like this, you get a *local variable,* one that is available only in the part of the script that creates the variable and that retains its value only as long as the script is executing.

When you create scripts that consist of only a single part, local variables are all you need to store data. But when you create scripts that contain multiple subroutines (a *subroutine* is a separate section of code that performs a specific function), you may also need global variables. A *global variable* is one that is available to all the subroutines in the script and to the main body of the script. By contrast, a local variable that you create in one subroutine is available only in that subroutine, not in any of the other subroutines or in the main body of the script.

The area within which a variable is available is called its *scope,* so global variables have global scope and local variables have local scope.

To create a global variable, you need to declare it ahead of time so that your script knows about it. You declare it by using the term **global** and the name you want to give the variable. For example, the following statement declares the global variable **myCity**:

```
global myCity
```

Normally, you declare each global variable at the top level of a script rather than in one of the subroutines, as in the following example, where the declaration of the global variable **myUserName** appears in boldface. This makes the global variable available to the main body of the script and to each subroutine, which is what you normally want. The script first calls the **get_user_name** subroutine, which displays a dialog box prompting the user to enter his or her name and stores it in **myUserName**, and then calls the **show_user_name** subroutine, which displays the contents of **myUserName** in a dialog box.

```
global myUserName

get_user_name()
show_user_name()

on get_user_name()
    display dialog "Please type your name:" default answer ""
    set myUserName to text returned of the result
end get_user_name

on show_user_name()
    display dialog myUserName
end show_user_name
```

An approach you may need to use sometimes is to declare a global variable in only the subroutines that need it. The following script declares the global variable **myUserName** in the **get_user_name** subroutine (again, in boldface), making it available to that subroutine and to the main body of the script but not to the **show_user_name** subroutine:

```
get_user_name()
show_user_name()

on get_user_name()
    global myUserName
    display dialog "Please type your name:" default answer ""
    set myUserName to text returned of the result
end get_user_name

on show_user_name()
    display dialog myUserName
end show_user_name
```

In this case, moving the declaration to the **get_user_name** subroutine isn't a good idea, as it causes the **show_user_name** subroutine to fail with an error. This is because the **show_user_name** subroutine doesn't know about the variable **myUserName** whose contents the **display dialog** command tells it to display.

To fix this problem, you need to declare the global variable **myUserName** in the **show_user_name** subroutine as well, as shown here in boldface:

```
get_user_name()
show_user_name()

on get_user_name()
    global myUserName
    display dialog "Please type your name:" default answer ""
    set myUserName to text returned of the result
end get_user_name

on show_user_name()
    global myUserName
    display dialog myUserName
end show_user_name
```

### NOTE

Within a script, each global variable name must be unique. Each local variable name must be unique within its scope, but you can use the same local variable names in different scopes if you want. Generally speaking, it's best not to reuse local variable names in the same script because having multiple variables with the same name tends to be confusing.

You can also declare local variables ahead of time by using the term **local** and the name you want to give the variable. For example, the following statement declares the local variable **Boss**:

```
local Boss
```

Each local declaration must appear in the part of the script in which you will use it—in the main body of the script (if it's not in a subroutine) or in the subroutine that uses it.

## Ask the Expert

**Q:** Do I need to declare local variables ahead of time using the local term?

**A:** In a word: No.

Even when you start declaring global variables, you don't need to declare local variables ahead of time by using the **local** term: You can continue to create your local variables by using **set** statements at any point in your code.

But—you sensed a "but" coming, didn't you?—when you use global variables, you may find it helpful to use local declarations so that your code is absolutely clear about the scope of each variable.

You may also benefit from declaring local variables ahead of time so that you can place all the local variable declarations for a subroutine together in the same place, where you can easily see all the variables the subroutine uses. This is helpful both when you revisit your code after a while and when someone else is trying to come to grips with your code.

## Try This Using a Global Variable

In this example, you use a global variable to make information available to different subroutines in a script. This example uses a script shown earlier in the chapter. The script includes several features you haven't learned about in detail, including creating and calling subroutines and displaying dialog boxes, but you'll find it easy to work through.

To create the script, follow these steps:

1. In AppleScript Editor, press ⌘-N or choose File | New to create a new script.

2. Create the global variable **myUserName** at the beginning of the script by typing the **global** term and the variable's name:

```
global myUserName
```

*(continued)*

3. Call the **get_user_name** subroutine by typing its name and putting empty parentheses after it, as shown in boldface here. This makes AppleScript run the **get_user_name** subroutine.

```
global myUserName
get_user_name()
```

4. On the next line, call the **show_user_name** subroutine in the same way, as shown in boldface here:

```
global myUserName
get_user_name()
show_user_name()
```

5. Create the **get_user_name** subroutine by typing an **on** command, the subroutine's name, and a pair of parentheses. Then, on a new line, type the **end** keyword to end the subroutine. These changes appear in boldface here:

```
global myUserName
get_user_name()
show_user_name()

on get_user_name()

end
```

6. Press ⌘-K or click the Compile button on the toolbar to compile the script. You'll notice that AppleScript automatically adds the **get_user_name** subroutine's name to the **end** statement, as shown in boldface here:

```
global myUserName
get_user_name()
show_user_name()

on get_user_name()

end get_user_name
```

7. Inside the **get_user_name** subroutine, add a **display dialog** command that prompts the user to type his or her name in a text-entry field that is empty at first (the **default answer ""** parameter). Set the **myUserName** global variable to the text returned by the text-entry field. The changes appear in boldface here:

```
global myUserName
get_user_name()
show_user_name()

on get_user_name()
```

```
        display dialog "Please type your name:" default answer ""
        set myUserName to text returned of the result
end get_user_name
```

8. Create the **show_user_name** subroutine and give it a **display dialog** command that displays the contents of the **myUserName** variable. The changes appear in boldface here:

```
global myUserName
get_user_name()
show_user_name()

on get_user_name()
    display dialog "Please type your name:" default answer ""
    set myUserName to text returned of the result
end get_user_name

on show_user_name()
    display dialog myUserName
end show_user_name
```

9. Press ⌘-R or click the Run button on the toolbar to run the script. When the first dialog box appears, type a name in the text-entry field, and then click the OK button. Verify that the text you typed appears in the second dialog box.

10. Save the script under a name of your choice.

# Using Script Properties to Store Data Permanently in the Script

When you need to store data from one time you run a script to the next time, use a script property rather than a variable. A *script property* is a piece of data stored in the script that you can get and set as needed.

Script properties largely follow the same naming rules you learned for variables earlier in this chapter:

- Each name must be unique within the script. (Script properties are global to the script; you can't restrict them to certain areas of it.)

- Each name must start with a letter.

- After that first letter, you can use letters, numbers, and underscores as you wish, but no spaces or symbols.

● You should avoid stepping on AppleScript's reserved words. But if you really want, you can use a reserved word by cordoning it off with vertical bar characters (for example, |dialog| if you want to name a property "dialog"). You can also use vertical bars to create property names featuring spaces and symbols.

To declare a script property, you use the term **property**, the name you want to assign the property, a space, a colon, another space, and then the property's initial value. You can't declare a property without assigning an initial value—a notable difference from variables. But that initial value can be empty—for example, an empty string ("") or an empty list ({}).

## NOTE

You can initialize a property with any AppleScript data type or object. For example, you can initialize a property with a list, a window, or a document.

For example, the following statement declares the script property **committee_name** and assigns the string **"Management Steering Committee"** to it.

```
property committee_name : "Management Steering Committee"
```

The best place to declare your script properties is right at the beginning of a script, where anyone reading your code will notice the declarations immediately. There's no obligation to put property declarations here, though—you can place them anywhere in the top level of the script. You can't put them in a **tell** block or in a subroutine handler.

If you like, you can use script properties for storing information that doesn't change, but in many cases, you're better off simply hard-coding the information into the script. What you'll usually find more useful is using script properties to store information that *does* change. For example, you can store the folder in which the user last ran the script, and then use that folder as the default folder the next time, as shown here. This example uses the **choose folder** command, which you'll meet in detail in Chapter 8.

```
property starting_folder : "/"
set starting_folder to choose folder default location starting_folder
```

## CAUTION

Here's one thing you need to be careful about with script properties—once you've set a property correctly in a script and compiled the script, don't run the script so that you change the value before distributing the script—otherwise, the script will start with the data you left in it. Instead, compile the script, and check to make sure it's fine. Then make a trivial change (for example, edit a comment) and compile the script again so that it remains as you wrote it.

**Try This** Using a Script Property

In this example, you declare a script property that contains a committee name, display a dialog box that prompts the user to confirm the name, and then set the property to the result of the dialog box. You'll learn all the details of how to use dialog boxes in Chapter 8, but you'll find this preview straightforward.

Follow these steps to create the script:

1. In AppleScript Editor, press ⌘-N or choose File | New to create a new script.

2. Declare a property named **committee_name** and set its initial value to **"Management Steering Committee"**:

   ```
   property committee_name : "Management Steering Committee"
   ```

3. Add the **display dialog** statement shown in boldface here, which displays the value of the **committee_name** property as its default value and prompts the user to change or accept it:

   ```
   property committee_name : "Management Steering Committee"
   display dialog "Please confirm the committee name:" default answer
   committee_name
   ```

4. Add a **set** statement that sets the **committee_name** property to the text returned from the dialog box's text-entry field, as shown in boldface here:

   ```
   property committee_name : "Management Steering Committee"
   display dialog "Please confirm the committee name:" default answer
   committee_name
   set committee_name to text returned of the result
   ```

5. Press ⌘-S or click the Run button on the toolbar to run the script. The dialog box shown in Figure 4-1 appears.

**Figure 4-1**   Change the committee name displayed in the dialog box to change the property's value in the script.

*(continued)*

6. Type a different name in the text entry field, and then click the OK button to close the dialog box. AppleScript stores the name you entered in the script.

7. Run the script again. This time, the name you entered appears in the dialog box.

8. Save the script under a name of your choice.

# Performing Operations with Operators

An *operator* in AppleScript is an expression or a character that performs an operation on specified data. Some operators are peculiar to AppleScript, but you'll already be familiar with others that have more general usage. For example, in the expression 100–50, the – sign is a subtraction operator that tells you (or AppleScript) to subtract the second value (50) from the first value (100).

Like that subtraction operator, most operators work on two values, or *operands*. These operators are known as *binary operators*. The other kind of operator is a *unitary operator*, one that works on a single operand.

Table 4-2 explains AppleScript operators by category and gives examples of them in use.

| Operator | Explanation or Details | Example |
|---|---|---|
| **Arithmetic Operators** | | |
| + | Addition | **5 + 3 = 8** |
| – | Subtraction | **5 – 3 = 2** |
| – | Unary negation (making a number negative) | **–3** |
| * | Multiplication | **5 * 3 = 15** |
| / | Division | **6 / 3 = 2** |
| Div | Integral division (returning the integer value from division and ignoring any remainder) | **27 div 7** returns **3** **28 div 7** returns **4** |
| Mod | Modulus (returning the remainder from dividing the first number by the second number) | **9 mod 2** returns **1** **10 mod 2** returns **0** **24 mod 7** returns **3** |
| ^ | Exponentiation (raising to the power) | **2^3** returns **8** **2^4** returns **16** **2^5** returns **32** |

**Table 4-2** AppleScript's Operators

| Operator | Explanation or Details | Example |
|---|---|---|
| **Logical Operators** | | |
| And | Inclusion (this one *and* that one) | **name begins with "T" and size is greater than 10000000** |
| Or | Alternation (this one *or* that one) | **name begins with "T" or name begins with "W"** |
| Not | Exclusion (this one but *not* that one) | **name begins with "T" not name begins with "W"** |
| **Concatenation Operator** | | |
| & | Concatenation (joining two strings of data together into a single string) | **"Good morning, " & "Universe!"** creates the string **Good morning, Universe!** |
| **Containment Operators** | | |
| begin[s] with/start[s] with | Finds the specified item at the beginning of the target | **name begins with "A"** |
| end[s] with | Finds the specified item at the end of the target | **name ends with "tion"** |
| contains | Finds the specified item in the target | **name contains "test"** |
| does not contain/ doesn't contain | Finds a target without the specified item | **name does not contain "Project"** |
| is in | Finds a target that matches one of the specified items | **name extension is in {"doc", "docx"}** |
| is not in | Finds a target that doesn't match any of the specified items | **name extension is not in {"doc", "docx"}** |
| is contained by | Checks whether an item is contained by another item | **{"Tokyo", "Paris"} contains {"Paris"}** returns **true** |
| is not contained by/ isn't contained by | Checks whether an item is not contained by another item | **{"Tokyo", "Paris"} does not contain {"Seoul"}** returns **true** |
| **Comparison Operators for Equality** | | |
| is equal to | You can also use =, **equal**, **equals**, or **equal to**. AppleScript automatically changes any of the text variations to **is equal to** when you compile the script. | **1 is equal to 2** returns **false** |
| is not equal to | You can also use /=, **does not equal**, **doesn't equal**, or **is not equal** (without "to"). AppleScript automatically changes /= to ≠ (the not-equal sign) and the text variations to **is not equal to** when you compile the script. | **"cheese" is not equal to "burger"** returns **true** |
| is | Returns **true** if the first item is the same as or equal to the second item; otherwise, returns **false** | **object1 is object2** |

**Table 4-2**   AppleScript's Operators *(continued)*

| Operator | Explanation or Details | Example |
|---|---|---|
| is not | Returns **true** if the first item is not the same as or equal to the second item; otherwise, returns **false** | **object1 is not object2** |
| **Comparison Operators for Precedence** | | |
| is less than | You can also use < or **less than**. AppleScript automatically changes **less than** to **is less than** when you compile the script. Returns **true** if the first item is less than the second item. | **1 is less than 2** |
| is greater than | You can also use > or **greater than**. AppleScript automatically changes **greater than** to **is greater than** when you compile the script. | **"bun"is greater than "burger"** returns **false** |
| is greater than or equal to | You can also use ≥ or **is greater than or equal**. AppleScript automatically changes the text version to **is greater than or equal to** when you compile the script. | **4 is greater than or equal to 5** returns **false** |
| is not greater than or equal to | You can also use **is not greater than or equal, isn't greater than or equal,** or **isn't greater than or equal to**. AppleScript automatically changes the text versions to **is not greater than or equal to** when you compile the script. | **4 is not greater than or equal to 5** returns **true** |
| is less than or equal to | You can also use ≤ or **is less than or equal**. AppleScript automatically changes **is less than or equal** to **is less than or equal to** when you compile the script. | **10 is less than or equal to 10** returns **true** |
| is not less than or equal to | You can also use **is not less than or equal, isn't less than or equal,** or **isn't less than or equal to**. AppleScript automatically changes the text versions to **is not less than or equal to** when you compile the script. | **10 is not less than or equal to 10** returns **false** |
| comes before | Tests whether a number or a string comes before another number or string | **1 comes before 2** returns **true** |
| does not come before | Tests whether a number or string doesn't come before another number or string. You can also use **doesn't come before**. AppleScript automatically changes this to **does not come before** when you compile the script. | **1 does not come before 2** returns **false** |
| comes after | Tests whether a number or string comes after another number or string | **"steak" comes after "fries"** returns **true** |
| does not come after | Tests whether a number or string does not come after another number or string You can also use **doesn't come after**. AppleScript automatically changes this to **does not come after** when you compile the script. | **"fries" does not come after "ice cream"** returns **true** |

**Table 4-2** AppleScript's Operators *(continued)*

**NOTE**

To enter the √ symbol, type >=; AppleScript substitutes the symbol when you compile the script. Similarly, type <= to enter the ∏ symbol, and type /= to produce the ≠ symbol.

# Understanding Classes

In AppleScript, a *class* is a category for objects that have similar characteristics. For example, the **file** class consists of a reference to an object in the file system—a file, a folder, or a volume. Each object of the **file** class is typically different because it points to a different file (or folder, or volume), but each object is the same kind of thing.

Table 4-3 explains the classes built into AppleScript. Each scriptable application also has its own classes. For example, as you saw in the previous chapter, the TextEdit application has a **document** class that represents document objects and a **paragraph** class that represents paragraph objects.

| Class | Explanation | Example or Details |
|---|---|---|
| alias | A reference to an existing file, folder, or volume in the Mac's file system. You can't create an alias to an object that doesn't exist. | **set myAlias to "Macintosh HD:Users:" as alias** |
| application | An application on the Mac or on a server to which the Mac is connected | **tell application "TextEdit" to quit** |
| boolean | A Boolean value, either **true** or **false** | **set docExists to true** |
| class | The class of an object or a value | **class of 123.45** returns **real** |
| constant | A term with a value predefined by AppleScript or by an application. You can't create your own constants in scripts. | AppleScript includes text constants, such as **tab**, **space**, **return**, **linefeed**, and **quote**, for working with text. |
| date | The day of the week, the date (month, day, year), and the time (hours, minutes, seconds) | **current date** returns the current date—for example, date **"Thursday, April 1, 2010 9:48:16 AM"** |
| file | A reference to a file, folder, or volume in the Mac's file system. You can create a **file** object that refers to an object that doesn't exist. | **set myFile to choose file name** uses the **choose file name** command (see Chapter 8) to let the user specify a filename |
| integer | A whole number (a number without any fraction) | **set myInteger to 7** |
| list | A collection of items in order | **set myList to {"bacon", "eggs", "kidneys"}** |
| number | Either an integer number or a real number | This is an abstract class; any number's actual class must always be either **integer** or **real**. |

**Table 4-3** AppleScript's Built-in Classes

| Class | Explanation | Example or Details |
|---|---|---|
| POSIX file | A pseudo-class that returns a **file** object. This is not a class; rather, it enables you to evaluate a POSIX file specifier. | **set fileName to POSIX file "/System"** returns a file object such as **file "Macintosh HD: System"** |
| real | A number that can include a fractional part | **set myReal to 1.43** |
| record | A collection of labeled properties that you access by label rather than by position | **set myDog to {name:"Roofer", animal:"Dog", breed:"Terrier"}** |
| reference | An object that refers to another object | **set docWin to a reference to the front window of the application "TextEdit"** |
| RGB | A three-item list of integer values in the range 0–65535 giving the red, green, and blue components of a color | **{65535, 0, 0}** produces a full-intensity red |
| script | An AppleScript script | This script shows the current date: **script DateScript display dialog (current date) as string end script** |
| text | A string of Unicode characters | **set headline to "Special Offers"** |
| unit types | A collection of unit type classes for working with measurements—for example, the **feet** class and the **miles** class | **set distance to 200 as miles** |

**Table 4-3**   AppleScript's Built-in Classes *(continued)*

# Converting Data with Coercions

In most of life, coercion is such a bad thing it's often illegal, but it's not only a positive thing, but also a highly welcome one in AppleScript, where a *coercion* is an expression that changes one type of data to another type. For example, when you need to change a real number or an integer number to a string, you use a coercion to make the change.

In many cases, AppleScript performs any necessary coercion for you automatically, drawing your attention to it only if an error occurs—for example, because your code needs to coerce data into a data type in which it will not fit.

You can also coerce data manually to a particular data type whenever you need to. To apply a coercion, you use the **as** operator and the data type you want. For example, the following commands create an integer variable named **myInteger** with the value **100**, and then use **as string** to coerce the value of **myInteger** to a string. The result is **"100"** (including the double quotation marks that indicate a string).

```
set myInteger to 100
myInteger as string
```

Table 4-4 shows the full list of coercions you can perform, with explanations and examples.

| Original Class | Coerce to Class | Explanation or Notes |
|---|---|---|
| alias | List | Returns a single-item list |
| alias | Text | Returns a text string |
| boolean | Integer | Returns **1** for **true** and **0** for **false** |
| boolean | List | Returns a single-item list, either **{true}** or **{false}** |
| boolean | Text | Returns a string, either **"true"** or **"false"** |
| class | List | Returns a single-item list |
| class | Text | Returns a string |
| constant | List | Returns a single-item list |
| constant | Text | Returns a string |
| date | List | Returns a single-item list using the format shown in International preferences—for example, **{date "Thursday, April 1, 2010 6:44:03 AM"}** |
| date | Text | Returns a string using the format shown in International preferences—for example, **"Thursday, April 1, 2010 6:44:03 AM"** |
| file | List | Returns a single-item list |
| file | Text | Returns a text string |
| integer | List | Returns a single item list—for example, **{150}** |
| integer | Real | Returns a real number—for example, **150.0** |
| integer | Text | Returns a string containing the integer's value—for example, **"150"** |
| item from list | [various] | You can coerce the list item to any class to which you can coerce an individual item of that class. For example, if you have a list of aliases, you can coerce them to text. |
| list | Text | **{"Morning", "Afternoon", "Night"}** as string returns **MorningAfternoonNight** |
| number | Integer | Returns the integer portion of the number |
| number | List | Returns a single-item list containing the number—for example, **{178.24}** |
| number | Real | Returns a real number—for example, **178.24** |
| number | Text | Returns a string containing the number—for example, **"178.24"** |
| POSIX file | List | Returns a single-item list |
| POSIX file | Text | Returns a string |
| real | Integer | Returns the integer part of the number—for example, **178.24 as integer** returns **179** |
| real | List | Returns a single-item list—for example, **{178.24}** |
| record | List | Returns a list with the labels removed. For example, **{name:"Roofer", animal:"Dog", breed:"Terrier"} as list** returns **{"Roofer", "Dog", "Terrier"}**. |

**Table 4-4** AppleScript Coercions

| Original Class | Coerce to Class | Explanation or Notes |
|---|---|---|
| reference | [various] | You can coerce the reference to any class to which you can coerce the object referenced. |
| script | List | Returns a single-item list |
| text | Integer | Returns an integer from a string that contains a number. For example, **"150.5" as integer** returns **150**. |
| text | List | Returns a single-item list containing a string—for example, **"Yellowstone" as list** returns **{"Yellowstone"}** |
| text | Real | Returns a real number from a string that contains a number. For example, **"150.5" as real** returns **150.5**. |
| unit types | Integer | Returns an integer containing the integer part of the number of the specified item (for example, **liters**) |
| unit types | List | Returns a single-item list containing the number of the specified item (for example, **miles**) |
| unit types | Real | Returns a real number containing the number of the specified item (for example, **centimeters**) |
| unit types | Text | Returns a string containing the number of the specified item (for example, **degrees Celsius**) |

**Table 4-4** AppleScript Coercions *(continued)*

## Try This Creating a Variable and Applying a Coercion

In this example, you create a variable using one of AppleScript's classes and assign data to it. You then apply a coercion to return the data in a different format.

1. In AppleScript Editor, press ⌘-N or choose File | New to create a new script.

2. Use a **set** command to create a variable named **ThisDay** and assign the current date to it:

   ```
   set ThisDay to current date
   ```

3. Add a **display dialog** command to display the contents of the **ThisDay** variable in a dialog box, coercing it to a string so that the dialog box can display it:

   ```
   display dialog ThisDay as string
   ```

4. Press ⌘-R or click the Run button on the toolbar to run the script. AppleScript displays a dialog box showing the current date.

5. Save the script under a name of your choice.

# Chapter 5

## Working with Text, Numbers, and Dates

## Key Skills & Concepts

- Working with Text
- Working with Numbers
- Working with Dates

In this chapter, you learn a core set of skills for working with three essential types of content: text, numbers, and dates.

Text is the most complicated of the three. We'll start by entering normal text in a **text** object, and then move along to joining two text strings together, adding white space, and adding special characters. We'll then look at how to return different parts of a text object (for example, a word or a paragraph), how to trim white space off a text string, and how to find a text string within a **text** object. Finally, for text, I'll show you how to move text from one application to another.

Compared to text, numbers are straightforward—but you still need to know the difference between AppleScript's **real** numbers and **integer** numbers, when to use each, and how to convert data to and from numeric data types.

Dates are vital to many procedures, and AppleScript deals with them in a smart way that enables you to enter dates easily, return exactly the parts of them you need (for example, the year or the month), and perform arithmetic with them.

# Working with Text

For dealing with text, AppleScript provides the **text** object, which contains a series of Unicode characters in a particular order. This series of characters is often referred to as a *string* of text.

## Entering Normal Text in a Text Object

To enter a string of text in a **text** object, you put it between double-quote characters. For example, the following statement creates the variable **myCity** and assigns the text **San Francisco** to it:

```
set myCity to "San Francisco"
```

You can also create a **text** object by passing to it a **text** object from a document. For example, the following code tells TextEdit to create the variable **myString** and assign to it the text from the front document:

```
tell the application "TextEdit"
    set myString to text of front document
end tell
```

You can then return different parts of the **text** object as needed—for example, you can return the first character, the second word, or the third paragraph. We'll look at how to do this later in this chapter.

## Joining Two or More Strings of Text

To join two or more strings of text together, you use **&**, the concatenation operator. For example, the following statements declare two string variables, myopically named **String1** and **String2**, and then join them together into a third string variable logically named **String3**:

```
set String1 to "Five boxing wizards"
set String2 to " jump quickly"
set String3 to String1 & String2
```

As a result, **String3** contains **Five boxing wizards jump quickly**, one of the all-alphabet phrases for testing keyboards whose fidelity you doubt.

Notice that the second string variable includes a leading space to produce a readable result. Without the leading space, AppleScript smashes the two strings together, because that's what you've told it to do.

## Adding Spaces, Tabs, Line Feeds, and Returns

When you're entering a string of text, you can include any spaces, tabs, or returns it needs to make sense. Just press SPACEBAR, TAB, or RETURN as you would in a text document. When you press RETURN, AppleScript Editor actually enters a linefeed character rather than a carriage return.

For example, the following statement creates the variable **strTC** and assigns four lines of text to it, the second line being blank space:

```
set strTC to "New terms and conditions:

    1.    The bank now owns all your money.
    2.    The country owns all the banks."
```

If you've selected the Escape Tabs And Line Breaks In Strings check box in Editing Preferences, AppleScript Editor automatically changes a tab from a chunk of white space to the **\t** value and a line feed to the **\n** value when you compile the script. So after compilation, the preceding example looks like this:

```
set strTC to "New terms and conditions:\n\n\t1.\tThe bank now owns all
your money.\n\t2.\tThe country owns all the banks."
```

With the tab and line feed values, the statements are harder to read, but they still work just the same. For example, if you display the **strTC** variable in a dialog box, you see the four lines (see Figure 5-1).

If you prefer, you can type the values directly into a string in AppleScript Editor. You can also use the constants shown in Table 5-1. These are useful when you're putting together a string from different components.

For example, the following statements declare string variables for the different components of an address, build from them a string containing the full address, and then display the string in a dialog box:

```
set FirstName to "Megg"
set MiddleInitial to "A"
set LastName to "Byte"
set strAddress1 to "8192 Giggs St."
set strAddress2 to "Apt. AF"
set strCity to "City of Industry"
set Zip to "CA 91745"

set FullAddress to FirstName & space & MiddleInitial & space & ¬
    LastName & linefeed & strAddress1 & linefeed & strAddress2 & ¬
        linefeed & strCity & tab & Zip

display dialog FullAddress
```

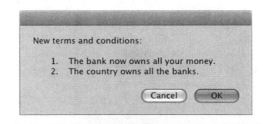

**Figure 5-1**   You can use spaces, tabs, and carriage returns in strings.

| White Space Character | Constant | Value |
|---|---|---|
| Space | Space | " " |
| Tab | Tab | "\t" |
| Carriage return | return | "\r" |
| Linefeed | linefeed | "\n" |

**Table 5-1**   AppleScript Constants for White Space Characters

## Ask the Expert

**Q:** Okay, I'll bite: What *is* the "carriage return" character that Table 5-1 mentions?

**A:** Quick warning: You may regret that you asked this…

When you press RETURN in AppleScript Editor, you get a linefeed character—so what's a carriage return character?

In ASCII, a linefeed character has the value 10, and a carriage-return character has the value 13. In many applications, these two characters have the same effect, and you can use the two interchangeably—which is handy but continues the confusion.

But you'll find that other applications treat a carriage return differently from a linefeed—so if your code isn't able to identify the end of a paragraph, you may need to use the other character. Some Windows programs even use both a carriage return and a linefeed at the end of paragraphs.

## Using Backslash and Double-Quote Characters

Because AppleScript uses the backslash character (\) to denote the tab character (\t), linefeed character (\l), and carriage-return character (\r), you can't use a backslash on its own in text. Instead, use \\ to represent a single backslash.

Similarly, AppleScript uses the double-quote character (") to mark the beginning or end of a string, so you can't use a double-quote character as itself. Instead, use the constant **quote** or the two-character sequence \" to represent a double-quote character. For example, each of the following statements displays a dialog box showing the sentence *He said "How do you pronounce the \ symbol?"*:

```
display dialog "He said " & quote & "How do you pronounce the \\
symbol?" & quote
display dialog "He said \"How do you pronounce the \\ symbol?\""
```

Both work; neither is pretty.

## Returning Parts of a Text Object

What's often useful is getting just part of a **text** object. For example, if you store the contents of a TextEdit document in a variable, as shown earlier in this chapter, you may need to pull out parts of it.

To do so, you can use the different elements of the **text** object—**text** itself, **paragraph**, **character**, and **word**. Table 5-2 explains these elements.

Before we get into examples of how to pull the different elements out of a **text** object, we need to go over the reference forms shown in Table 5-2. The next table, Table 5-3, explains the five reference forms shown there (Arbitrary, Every, Index, Middle, and Range), together with the other five reference forms AppleScript supports.

| Element | Reference Forms | Explanation |
|---|---|---|
| **Text** | Every, Name | All of the text in the text object, including characters such as spaces, tabs, and returns. You can use this item when you need to return a range of contiguous characters in the **text** object. |
| **paragraph** | Arbitrary, Every, Index, Middle, Range | A paragraph of text as most of us understand it: All the text from the beginning of the document to the character that ends the first paragraph, from the character after the end of a paragraph to the character that ends the next paragraph, or from the character after the end of a paragraph to the end of the document. |
| **character** | Arbitrary, Every, Index, Middle, Range | A character in the text. AppleScript uses Unicode characters, which means that even combining characters (such as à) count as one character. This is unremarkable, but in some encodings, combining characters count as two characters (the base character—here, a—and the combining mark). |
| **Word** | Arbitrary, Every, Index, Middle, Range | A word in the text. This seems straightforward, but you need to be careful with words because the setting in the Word Break pop-up menu on the Language tab of International Preferences can trip you up. For example, if Word Break is set to Standard, **word 1 of "Steak:Fries"** returns **"Steak:Fries"** because the separator between the words isn't a space. But if Word Break is set to English (United States, Computer), **word 1 of "Steak:Fries"** returns only **"Steak"** the Atkins version of the classic meal. |

**Table 5-2**   Elements of AppleScript Text Objects

| Reference Form | Keywords or Usage | Explanation |
|---|---|---|
| Arbitrary | **some** | Returns a random object from whatever you're referring to—for example, some word or other in the document. This is seldom useful for working with text, but can be useful for other objects (for example, numbers). |
| Every | **every** | Returns a list containing every object from the collection. For example, **every word of "How are you?"** returns the list **{"How", "are", "you"}**. |
| Filter | **whose, where, that** | Returns a list of items that match the specified condition. For example, **tell the application "Finder" folders of home whose name starts with "D"** returns a list of folders with names that start with *D*. |
| ID | [*the ID property*] | Returns the object specified by the **id** property. This works only with application objects that have an **id** property. |
| Index | A cardinal integer (**1, 2**), an ordinal integer (**1ˢᵗ, 2ⁿᵈ**), an ordinal word (**first, second,** up to **tenth**), or a positional word (**last, front, back**) | Returns the object specified by the index position. For example, **the first character of the 2nd word of paragraph 3 of the front document of application "TextEdit"**. Cardinal integers are usually easiest to understand, but AppleScript Editor automatically corrects any bogus ordinal integers you produce—for example, it changes **25ˢᵗ** to **25ᵗʰ**. |
| Middle | **middle** | Returns the middle item in the object. This is sometimes useful with lists that contain an odd number of objects. (If the object contains an even number of objects, **middle** returns the object before the middle—for example, the fourth object out of eight objects.)<br><br>If you use **middle** with a string, specify the item you want (for example, **middle word of "one two three"**); otherwise, AppleScript gives you the middle character, which is seldom helpful. |
| Name | **named** | Returns the item specified by name. Use this reference form with objects that have names. For example, **tell the application "Finder" folder named "Documents" of home** returns the Documents folder. You can usually refer to an object more simply by its name (for example, **folder "Documents" of home**). |
| Property | A property of the object | Returns the property or properties you specify of the object. For example, **tell the application "TextEdit" properties of the front window** returns a list of the properties for the front window. |
| Range | **from** *start* **to** *finish,* *start* **through** *finish* | Returns a list containing the specified range of objects contained by the target object. For example, **words 1 through 3 of "The quick brown fox jumped over the lazy dog"** returns **{"The", "quick", "brown"}**. You can use **thru** instead of **through**. |
| Relative | **before, in front of, after, behind, in back of** | Returns the object you specify in relation to another object (the *base object*) in the same container. For example, **tell the application "TextEdit" to set doc_process to text of the document behind the front document** assigns the text of the second document in the stack (the document behind the front document) to the variable **doc_process**. |

**Table 5-3**   AppleScript's Reference Forms

**NOTE**

You can also use the plural of the class instead of using the **every** keyword. For example, you can use **tell application "Finder" every folder of home** or **tell application "Finder" folders of home** to return a list of the folders in the current user's home folder.

With that in mind, here are examples of using the **text**, **paragraph**, **character**, and **word** elements of the **text** object. Each example uses the **text** object **doc_process**:

- To get the whole of the text, use the **text** element:

  ```
  set allText to text of doc_process
  ```

- To get the first paragraph, use **the first paragraph** or a similar formulation (for example, **paragraph 1**):

  ```
  set firstPara to the first paragraph of doc_process
  ```

- To get a list containing the first five characters, use **characters 1 through 5**:

  ```
  set fiveChars to characters 1 through 5 of doc_process
  ```

- To get the second word, use **the second word**:

  ```
  set secondWord to the second word of doc_process
  ```

To find out how many of an item a text object contains, get the **count** of the item. For example, use **count of paragraphs in doc_process** to return the number of paragraphs in **doc_process**.

# Trimming a String

Sometimes, a string may have leading spaces or trailing spaces that you need to get rid of, especially if you receive the string from another application (for example, a database application). For example, if you get the string **"     Minneapolis     "** (with several spaces before it and several more after it), you may need to trim it down to **"Minneapolis"** so that you can use it without inserting extra spaces in text.

AppleScript doesn't provide a command for trimming off leading spaces or trailing spaces (as some other programming languages do), so you need to create a subroutine to remove them. Chapter 10 gives an example of using a subroutine to remove leading spaces and trailing spaces from a string.

# Finding a String Within Another String

When you need to find where one string is within another string, use the **offset** command. This command takes two parameters, as you'd expect: the string you're looking for, preceded by the **of** keyword, and the string in which you're looking for it, preceded by the **in** keyword.

The **offset** command returns the position of the first character in the search string within the target string. For example, the following statement return the offset position of the string **"back"** in the string **"I'll be back"**:

```
offset of "back" in "I'll be back"
```

This statement returns **9**, because the word **back** starts at the ninth character in the string **I'll be back**—in lay terms, the *b* of *back* is the ninth letter. (If AppleScript doesn't find the search string in the target string, it returns **0**.)

### CAUTION
In Mac OS X 10.3 (Panther) and later versions, the **offset** command ignores case when searching for one string inside another string. Usually, this is what you want—but it's as well to know what you're getting rather than to be surprised. If you need your comparisons to be case-sensitive, add **considering case**, as discussed later in this chapter.

Often, finding out whether the search string is within the target string (and, if so, where it starts) is enough. But what if the search string occurs two or more times in the target string? In this case, AppleScript returns only the first instance. To find the next instance, you need to search again from after the end of the first string found.

## Finding Out Whether One Text Object Contains Another Text Object

AppleScript makes it easy to find whether one **text** object contains another **text** object. To find out whether the text string **"quick"** is in the **text** object **myString**, just check like this:

```
"quick" is in myString
```

If the text string is in the **text** object, AppleScript returns **true**; if it's not, AppleScript returns **false**.

If you want to make the comparison the other way around, check whether the **text** object contains the text string. For example, to find out whether **"quicksilver"** contains **"silver"**, use the **contains** operator like this:

```
"quicksilver" contains "silver"
```

This example returns **true**; if the first string doesn't contain the second, the comparison returns **false**.

## Choosing What to Ignore When Comparing Text

When you're comparing **text** objects, you may need to tell AppleScript to ignore some attributes of the text to perform the comparison—or to consider some attributes that it automatically ignores.

To control which attributes AppleScript uses, you add an **ignoring** statement, a **considering** statement, or both to the comparison.

Table 5-4 explains the attributes you can use.

To use a **considering** statement, set up a **considering** block like this:

```
considering case
    -- make the comparison here
end considering
```

Similarly, to use an **ignoring** statement, create an **ignoring** block like this:

```
ignoring diacriticals
    -- make the comparison here
end ignoring
```

| Attribute | Explanation | Default Setting | Considering Example | Ignoring Example |
|---|---|---|---|---|
| Case | Uppercase and lowercase letters | ignoring | *A* is different from *a* | *T* is the same as *t* |
| diacriticals | The accent marks over letters | considering | *õ* is different from *o* | *ë* is the same as *e* |
| hyphens | – characters | considering | *dog-food* is different from *dogfood* | *play-pen* is the same as *playpen* |
| numeric strings | Whether text strings (such as "1.4.3") are evaluated as text or by their character values | ignoring | **"2.20.3" is greater than "2.8.4"** returns **true** | **"2.20.3" is greater than "2.8.4"** returns **false** |
| punctuation | Punctuation marks such as , . ; : + " ' ? | considering | *won't* is different from *wont* | *can't* is the same as *cant* |
| White space | Spaces, tabs, linefeeds, and carriage returns | considering | *stand alone* is different from *standalone* | *no one* is the same as *noone* |

**Table 5-4**  AppleScript Attributes for Considering Statements and Ignoring Statements

To use two **considering** items or two **ignoring** items together, use **and** like this:

```
considering case and numeric strings
    -- make the comparison here
end considering
```

To combine **considering** and **ignoring** statements, put the **considering** statement first, then **but**, and then the **ignoring** statement. End the block with **end considering**, as shown here:

```
considering case and diacriticals but ignoring hyphens
    --make the comparison here
end considering
```

### NOTE
You can also nest **considering** and **ignoring** statements.

## Transferring Text from One Application to Another
The easiest way to transfer text from one application to another in a script is to store the data in a variable from the first application and then use the data from the variable in the other application.

The following example grabs the text from a TextEdit document, stores it in a variable, chops it down to the first paragraph, and then slaps that paragraph into a new Microsoft Word document:

```
tell the application "TextEdit"
    set myText to the text of the front document
end tell

set myText to the first paragraph of myText

tell the application "Microsoft Word"
    make new document at the front
    set the content of the text object of the first paragraph ¬
    of the front document to myText
end tell
```

You can also place text on the clipboard from one application and then insert it from the clipboard in the other application.

To place text on the clipboard, use the **set the clipboard to** command. This command takes a single required parameter, **anything**, which is the data you're placing on the clipboard.

For example, the following statement places the text *Vital Mac Software* on the clipboard:

```
set the clipboard to "Vital Mac Software"
```

To return text from the clipboard, use the command **the clipboard**. The following statement assigns the contents of the clipboard to myClip:

```
set myClip to the clipboard
```

## Try This   Using the Clipboard

In this example, you place a string of text on the clipboard, and then insert it in a TextEdit document. Follow these steps:

1. In AppleScript Editor, press ⌘-N or choose File | New to create a new script.

2. Create a **tell** block to the TextEdit application:

```
tell the application "TextEdit"
end tell
```

3. Inside the **tell** block, add text to the clipboard, as shown in boldface here:

```
tell the application "TextEdit"
    set the clipboard to "Essential Mac Software"
end tell
```

4. Tell TextEdit to make a new document at the front, as shown in boldface here:

```
tell the application "TextEdit"
    set the clipboard to "Essential Mac Software"
    make new document at the front
end tell
```

5. Assign the contents of the clipboard to the **text** property of the front document, as shown in boldface here:

```
tell the application "TextEdit"
    set the clipboard to "Essential Mac Software"
    make new document at the front
    set the text of the front document to the clipboard
end tell
```

6. Press ⌘-R or click the Run button on the toolbar to run the script. You'll see TextEdit create a new document and add the text to it.

7. Close the document without saving it (unless you happen to need a list of essential Mac software—in which case, start typing).

8. Save the script under a name of your choice.

# Working with Numbers

As you saw in the previous chapter, AppleScript uses two types of numbers: **integer** numbers (with no fractional part) and **real** numbers (with fractional parts as needed). Both **integer** numbers and **real** numbers belong to the abstract **number** class, though in practice the class of every number is either the **integer** class or the **real** class.

## Performing Arithmetic with Numbers

You can perform arithmetic by using the arithmetic operators discussed in Chapter 3. Here is a brief summary:

- Use **+** for addition and **−** for subtraction.
- Use **\*** for multiplication and **/** for straightforward division.
- Use **div** for integral division (ignoring the remainder).
- Use **mod** for modulus (returning the remainder).
- Use **^** for exponentiation.

You can use these operators with either **integer** numbers or **real** numbers. The type of result depends on the numbers you use. For example, if you multiply two integers, you get an integer; but if you multiply an integer by a real number, or a real number by another real number, you get a real number.

If necessary, you can coerce the result of a calculation to another data type, as discussed next.

## Coercing Numbers to Other Data Types

You can easily coerce a number to the other type—**real** number to **integer** number, or vice versa—or to a list or a string.

- To coerce a **real** number to an **integer** number—in effect, rounding it to the nearest number—use **as integer**. For example, **1.5 as integer** returns **2**.
- To coerce an **integer** number to a **real** number, use **as real**. AppleScript adds a decimal point and a 0 to the end of the **integer** number to create the **real** number. For example, **100 as real** returns **100.0**.
- To coerce an **integer** number or **real** number to a string, use **as string**. The string contains the same number as the **integer** number or **real** number used. For example, **254 as string** returns **"254"**; **255.693 as string** returns **"255.693"**.
- To coerce an **integer** number or **real** number to a list, use **as list**. The result is a single-item list. For example, **189 as list** returns the list **{189}**.

## Coercing Other Data Types to Numbers

You can coerce two data types to numbers.

● **boolean** You can coerce a **boolean** value to an **integer** number by using **as integer**. The result is **1** for **true** or **0** for **false**.

### NOTE

AppleScript doesn't let you coerce a **boolean** value directly to a **real** value, but there's nothing to stop you from coercing the **boolean** value to an **integer** value and then coercing the result to a **real** value (for example, **myBool as integer as real**). You'll end up with **1.0** for a **true** value and **0.0** for a **false** value.

● **string** If you have a string that contains a number, you can coerce it to either an **integer** number or a **real** number. Unless you know that the string contains no fractional part, or you want the result to be an **integer** number, coercing the string to a **real** number is usually the safer choice.

If you try to coerce a string that contains non-numeric data to a number, AppleScript returns an error.

# Working with Dates

In your scripts, you'll often need to work with dates, doing everything from returning the current date and time to calculating the number of days or weeks between two dates.

In this section, you'll come to grips with the powerful set of tools that AppleScript provides for working with dates.

## Understanding How AppleScript Handles Dates

To work with dates, AppleScript uses the **date** object. The **date** object is a floating-point number with the integer portion representing the date and the fractional portion representing the time within the day.

### NOTE

The **date** object puts the Pope firmly above Caesar, using the Gregorian calendar and ignoring the Julian calendar.

Treating dates as numbers enables AppleScript (and computers in general) to calculate them easily. But AppleScript lets you return any of the components of the date—the year, the month, the hour, and so on—simply enough.

The **date** object returns the date in a standard format such as this:

```
date "Thursday, April 1, 2010 6:14:47 AM"
```

What you'll normally want to do is get at one or more of the separate parts of the date. To do so, use the properties of the **date** object. Table 5-5 explains these properties.

As you can see in the table, the properties return three types of data: **text** strings, **integer** numbers, and weird things (**weekday** and **month**).

The text strings are great for when you need to insert a date as text (for example, in a document) or display it in a dialog box. For example, the following statement returns the day and date from a **date** object:

```
date string of date "1 December 2010"
```

When you compile a script, AppleScript changes a date entered like this into its standard format, including the time, which it sets to midnight if you haven't specified any other time. Here's what the compiled statement looks like:

```
date string of date "Wednesday, December 01, 2010 12:00:00 AM"
```

| Property | Data Type | Explanation | Example Using 4/15/2010 2:23:45 PM |
|---|---|---|---|
| date string | text | The day and date as a string | "Thursday, April 15, 2010" |
| short date string | text | The date as a string | "4/15/2010" |
| time string | text | The time as a string | "2:23:45 PM" |
| Day | integer | The day of the month as a number | 15 |
| weekday | weekday | The name of the day of the week | Thursday |
| Month | month | The month | April |
| Year | integer | The year as a four-digit number | 2010 |
| Time | integer | The number of seconds elapsed since midnight | 51825 |
| Hours | integer | The hour of the date's time | 14 |
| minutes | integer | The minutes of the date's time | 23 |
| seconds | integer | The seconds of the date's time | 45 |

**Table 5-5**    Properties of the AppleScript Date Object

**NOTE**

AppleScript lets you enter dates in a variety of formats as strings after the **date** keyword. For example, **date "2/2/11"**, **date "2 feb 11"**, **date "February 02 11"**, and **date "2-feb-2011"** all compile to **"Wednesday, February 02, 2011 12:00:00 AM"**. This friendly flexibility means you don't need to worry about how you enter dates—you can simply hammer in dates using whichever format you find most natural.

When you need to perform date and time arithmetic, the strings are about as much use as a cheerful grin in an earthquake. Instead, use the integer numbers provided by the **day**, **year**, **time**, **hours**, **minutes**, and **seconds** properties of the **date** object. For example, the following statements use the **year of (current date)** integer to calculate an item's age in years:

```
set YearNow to year of (current date)
set YearThen to 2000
set AgeInYears to YearNow - YearThen
```

**TIP**

When you enter a time in a script, always enter the date as well. If you don't, AppleScript automatically adds the current date for you when you compile the script. This can be useful, but for clarity, you should enter the dates explicitly.

# Working with the month Property of the Date Object

Calculating with integers is easy enough, but you'll have noticed that the **month** property doesn't return an integer between 1 and 12: Instead, it returns a **month** class that contains a **month** constant, such as **June** for the month of June.

Each **month** constant has a corresponding integer value, so you can perform arithmetic with the **month** constants. For example, if you subtract a date that returns the **month** constant **February** from a date that returns the **month** constant **June**, as in the following example, you get **4**, the number of months between February and June.

```
set month1 to month of date "Monday, February 22, 2010 12:00:00 AM"
set month2 to month of date "Thursday, June 24, 2010 12:00:00 AM"
set monthDiff to month2 - month1
```

But what you'll often want to do is coerce a **month** constant to an integer so that you can see what you're working with. For example, the following statement returns **6**, the integer value for **June**:

```
set intMonth to month of date "Tuesday, June 22, 2010 12:00:00 AM" as
integer
```

## Working with the weekday Property of the Date Object

Just as the **month** property of the **date** object returns a **month** constant, so the **weekday** property of the **date** object returns a **weekday** constant containing the name of the day of the week—**Saturday**, **Sunday**, or one of the five less friendly days.

You can use the **weekday** constants to perform calculations if you want. For example, **(Saturday) – (Wednesday)** returns **3**, the number you get if you subtract 4 (Wednesday's integer value) from 7 (Saturday's integer value).

You can also coerce the **weekday** constants to their corresponding integers. For example, **Sunday as integer** returns **1**, **Monday as integer** returns **2**, and **Tuesday as integer** returns **3**.

## Coercing a Date Object to a String

If you need the full date and time, you can coerce a **date** object to a string. For example, the following statement displays a dialog box showing the full current date and time, as shown in Figure 5-2:

```
display dialog (current date) as string
```

## Changing a Date

Once you've stored a date in a **date** object, you can alter the date by setting its properties. For example, the following statements declare the variable **myDate** and assign to it the current date, but then move the date out to 14 November 2025:

```
set myDate to current date
set month of myDate to November
set year of myDate to 2025
set day of myDate to 14
```

### *CAUTION*

You can't set the **weekday** property of a date object, because that would involve damage to the space-time continuum.

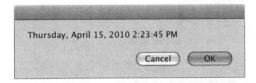

**Figure 5-2**    On the rare occasions you need the full date and time, you can coerce a date object to a string.

## Calculating Hours, Minutes, Days, and Weeks

As you saw earlier in this chapter, the **time** property of the **date** object returns the number of seconds since midnight. This is nice and precise, but most of us fuzzy-brained humans find hours and minutes easier units to deal in.

To break down a time in seconds into hours, minutes, or larger units, use the date constants shown in Table 5-6. For example, the following statement returns the number of hours that have passed so far in the day:

```
(time of (current date)) div hours
```

## Finding Out How Far Off GMT Your Mac Is

Finding the current date and time is useful, but in many cases, you also need to know where your Mac's clock is set in relation to Greenwich Mean Time (GMT). To do so, use the **time to GMT** command, which returns the time in seconds between your Mac's time zone and GMT.

For example, if you're stuck outside of Memphis with a mobile Mac, **time to GMT** typically returns **–18000**, which is five hours behind GMT, whereas if you're in New Zealand, **time to GMT** typically returns **43200**, or twelve hours ahead of GMT.

To get the number of hours, divide the result of **time to GMT** by the **hours** constant:

```
set ZuluHours to time to GMT / hours
```

## Comparing Dates and Times

You can use the standard operators discussed in Chapter 4 to compare dates and times. For example, each of the following comparisons works for finding out whether the current date lies before Independence Day 2012:

```
(current date) comes before date "Wednesday, July 04, 2012 12:00:00 AM"
(current date) < date "Wednesday, July 04, 2012 12:00:00 AM"
(current date) is less than date "Wednesday, July 04, 2012 12:00:00 AM"
```

| Date Constant | Returns | Number of Seconds |
|---|---|---|
| Minutes | The number of minutes | 60 |
| Hours | The number of hours | 3600 |
| Days | The number of days | 86,400 |
| Weeks | The number of weeks | 604,800 |

**Table 5-6**   Date Constants for Converting Seconds to Larger Units of Time

AppleScript's natural-language formulations (**comes before**, **does not come before**, **comes after**, and **does not come after**) are usually the easiest way of making date comparisons, but you can use the regular operators instead if you prefer. For example, the **does not come before** operator gives the same result as the **is not less than or equal to** operator.

## Try This Working with Dates and Times

In this example, you create a short script that calculates the number of hours and minutes that have passed so far in the day and displays the results in a dialog box.

1. In AppleScript Editor, press ⌘-N or choose File | New to create a new script.

2. Type a statement that creates a variable named **mySeconds** and assigns to it the number of seconds in the **time** property of the **current date** object:

```
set mySeconds to time of (current date)
```

3. On the next line, type a statement that creates a variable named **myHours** and assigns to it the value of **mySeconds** divided by the **hours** constant (using **div**, which ignores the remainder). The new statement appears in boldface here:

```
set mySeconds to time of (current date)
set myHours to mySeconds div hours
```

4. On the next line, type a statement that creates a variable named **myMinutes** and assigns to it the value of the remainder from dividing **mySeconds** by the **hours** constant (**mySeconds mod hours**) and then converting the result to minutes (**mySeconds mod hours div minutes**). The new statement appears in boldface here:

```
set mySeconds to time of (current date)
set myHours to mySeconds div hours
set myMinutes to mySeconds mod hours div minutes
display dialog "Hour:" & tab & myHours & return & Minutes:" ¬
   & tab & myMinutes
```

5. On the next line, type a statement (shown in boldface here) that displays a dialog box showing the hours and minutes stored in the variables:

```
set mySeconds to time of (current date)
set myHours to mySeconds div hours
set myMinutes to mySeconds mod hours div minutes
display dialog "Hour:" & tab & myHours & return & Minutes:" ¬
   & tab & myMinutes buttons {"OK"}
```

*(continued)*

Hours: 16
Minutes: 55

OK

**Figure 5-3** This dialog box shows the number of hours and minutes that have elapsed since midnight.

6. Press ⌘-R or click the Run button on the toolbar to run the script. A dialog box such as that shown in Figure 5-3 appears.

7. Click the OK button to close the dialog box.

8. Save the script under a name of your choice.

# Chapter 6

## Working with the Finder, Files, and Folders

## Key Skills & Concepts

- Referring to files and folders
- Opening and manipulating Finder windows
- Working with folders
- Working with files
- Mounting and unmounting volumes

Pretty much everything you do on your Mac involves files and folders, so the chances are that you'll need to work with both of them in your scripts. As when working interactively, your main tool for manipulating files and folders in AppleScript is the Finder.

This chapter starts by explaining how to refer to the files and folders you need by using AppleScript's various types of references. You will then learn how to open, configure, and close Finder windows; create, rename, move, and delete folders; and perform essential actions with files, such as creating aliases, copying and duplicating files, and renaming them.

You will also learn how to mount a network volume on a Mac's file system via AppleScript—and how to unmount the volume when you no longer need it.

# Working with Finder Windows

You saw some basic maneuvers for Finder windows in Chapter 3, when you created your first script. In this section, we'll dig more deeply into how to control Finder windows. First, though, we need to go over how to refer to the objects you want in your Mac's file system.

## Referring to the Objects You Need

To reach files and folders in your Mac's file system, you need to describe where they are. AppleScript gives you several ways to reach the objects you need, starting with directly accessible objects (such as your home folder) and special folders whose location Mac OS X tracks for you.

### Using Directly Accessible Objects

The easiest way to get into your Mac's file system is to use one of the handy reference points that AppleScript provides. Table 6-1 provides a list of the reference points that are most widely useful in scripts.

| Folder or Item | AppleScript Name | Notes |
|---|---|---|
| Your Mac | computer container | This reaches the contents of your Mac as you see them if you click your Mac's entry in the Devices list in the sidebar of a Finder window. The computer container contains your Mac's internal hard disk or disks, any external hard disks, your iDisk (if you have one), the Network item, and any mounted network drives. |
| Your Mac's current startup disk | startup disk | The disk from which your Mac has started on this boot. You can change startup disk from Startup Disk preferences in System Preferences. |
| Your home folder | home | The folder represented by ~ (a tilde)—for example, if your short user name is joan, the /Users/joan/ folder. |
| Your Desktop folder | desktop | Your Desktop folder is the ~/Desktop folder (the Desktop folder in your home folder). |
| Trash | trash | The Trash folder |

**Table 6-1**   Useful Mac OS X Locations You Can Open Directly from AppleScript

## Using the path to Command to Reach Special Folders

Each Mac has various special folders, many of which you'll be familiar with from using the operating system (OS) interactively—the System folder, the various Library folders, the Applications folder, your Documents folder, and so on. Mac OS X keeps track of where these folders are, even if the operating system is customized, and you can get the path to these folders by using the **path to** command.

These special folders fall into four different *domains,* or areas of the operating system.

- **user**   This domain contains folders that belong in the user account—for example, the user's own Documents folder or Movies folder.

- **local**   This domain contains files and preferences that are available to all users—for example, the Applications folder is in the local domain.

- **system**   This domain contains operating system components.

- **network**   This domain contains items Mac OS X uses over networks.

### NOTE

Older versions of Mac OS X also recognize a fifth domain, the **classic** domain. Leopard and Snow Leopard no longer use this domain. Follow their lead.

Some folders belong to only a single domain, but most of them belong to two or three domains; some folders even belong to all four domains.

When a folder belongs to more than one domain, one of the domains is almost always the default domain—the domain that AppleScript gives you if you don't specify one of the other domains. For example, the Library folder belongs to the user domain, the local domain, and the system domain. The system domain is the default domain, so if you give the **path to library folder** command without specifying the user domain or the local domain, you get the system domain. To get the Library folder from the user domain (the ~/Library folder), add **from user domain** to the command like this:

```
path to library folder from user domain
```

Each special folder has a name, which is usually the name under which it appears in the operating system (for example, Applications). Each folder also has a four-character code that you can use to identify the folder uniquely—for example, **apps** for the Applications folder. Some of the more widely used folders also have constants that you can use instead of the codes to refer to them in more natural language—for example, you can refer to the Applications folder as **applications folder**.

Table 6-2 lists the special folders that are normally most useful in scripts. The table breaks down the folders by default domain for the user domain, local domain, and system domain, but also shows which other domains they belong to. No special folders belong to the network domain by default, so the table has no section for the network domain.

For example, the following command tells the Finder to open a window showing the contents of the Applications folder:

```
tell the application "Finder" to open (path to Applications folder)
```

### TIP

To type the mu (μ) character used in paths such as the Music path (**μdoc**), press OPTION-M.
To type the *f* character used in paths such as the Desktop Pictures path (**dtp*f***),
press OPTION-F.

You can also use the **path to** command to return the path to the reference points explained in Table 6-2. For example, the following command tells the Finder to open a window showing the contents of the **computer container** object:

```
tell the application "Finder" to open (path to computer container)
```

| Folder Name | Folder Constant | Folder Code | Explanation | Sample Location | Other Domains |
|---|---|---|---|---|---|
| **Special Folders That Default to the User Domain** | | | | | |
| Desktop | Desktop | desk | The Desktop folder in the current user's account | ~/Desktop/ | — |
| Documents | documents folder | docs | The Documents folder in the current user's account | ~/Documents/ | — |
| Downloads | downloads folder | down | The Downloads folder in the current user's account | ~/Downloads/ | local |
| Favorites | favorites folder | favs | The Favorites folder in the Library folder in the current user's account | ~/Library/Favorites/ | local |
| Home | Home folder | cusr | The home folder in the current user's account | ~ | local, system, network |
| Movies | Movies folder | mdoc | The Movies folder in the current user's account | ~/Movies/ | — |
| Music | Music folder | μdoc | The Music folder in the current user's account | ~/Music/ | — |
| Pictures | pictures folder | pdoc | The Pictures folder in the current user's account | ~/Pictures/ | — |
| Preferences | preferences folder | pref | The Preferences folder in the current user account's library | ~/Library/Preferences/ | local |
| Public | public folder | pubb | The Public folder in the current user account | ~/ | — |
| Sites | sites folder | site | The Sites folder in the current user's account | ~/Sites/ | — |
| Users | users folder | usrs | The Users folder on the Mac | /Users/ | local, system, network |

**Table 6-2**   Mac OS X Special Folders You Can Reach with the path to Command

| Folder Name | Folder Constant | Folder Code | Explanation | Sample Location | Other Domains |
|---|---|---|---|---|---|
| **Special Folders That Default to the Local Domain** | | | | | |
| Applications | applications folder | apps | The Applications folder on the Mac | /Applications/ | user, system |
| Desktop Pictures | desktop pictures folder | dtp$f$ | The Desktop Pictures folder on the Mac | /Library/Desktop Pictures/ | user |
| Startup Items | startup items | empz | The Mac's StartupItems folder | /Library/StartupItems/ | user, system |
| Utilities | utilities folder | uti$f$ | The Utilities folder on the Mac | /Applications/Utilities/ | user, system |
| **Special Folders That Default to the System Domain** | | | | | |
| Fonts | fonts | font | The Fonts folder on the Mac | /System/Library/Fonts/ | user, local |
| Library | library folder | dlib | The Library folder on the Mac | /Library/ | user, local |
| Printers | — | impr | The Printers folder in the System library | /System/Library/Printers/ | user, local |
| Root | — | root | The System folder (the root folder) | /System/ | user, local |
| System | system folder | dtop | The System folder on the Mac's startup disk | /System | user, network |
| System Preference panes | system preferences | sprf | The PreferencePanes folder in the System library | /System/Library/PreferencePanes/ | user, local |

**Table 6-2** Mac OS X Special Folders You Can Reach with the path to Command *(continued)*

*TIP*

To identify the foreground application, use the **path to foremost application** command. To refer to the application running the script or to the script itself, use the **path to me** command.

From these special folders, you can easily reach other folders by using nested references, as described in the next section.

**Try This**  Using Special Folders

In this example, you open Finder windows to two special folders. Follow these steps:

1. In AppleScript Editor, press ⌘-N or choose File | New to create a new script.

2. Create a **tell** block to the Finder application:

```
tell the application "Finder"

end tell
```

3. In the **tell** block, add a statement to open the Public folder in your user account by using its constant, as shown in boldface here:

```
tell the application "Finder"
    open (path to public folder)
end tell
```

4. Add a statement to open the Utilities folder in the local domain (the default domain) by using its folder code, as shown in boldface here:

```
tell the application "Finder"
    open (path to public folder)
    open (path to "utiɟ")
end tell
```

5. Press ⌘-R or click the Run button on the toolbar to run the script.

6. Save the script under a name of your choice.

## Referring to Objects with Nested References and Path References

In AppleScript, you reach the objects you need by using references to them. This works the same for all scriptable objects, so you can use it in the Finder. For example, to refer to the /Library/Audio/Apple Loops/Apple/Apple Loops for GarageBand/ folder on your Mac's hard disk, you can use a reference such as this:

```
folder "Apple Loops for GarageBand" of folder "Apple" ¬
    of folder "Apple Loops"
    of folder "Audio" ¬
of folder "Library" of startup disk
```

If you can stand the relentless repetition of the word "of," the reference is completely clear, as it goes all the way from the startup disk to the folder. This type of reference is called a *nested reference,* because each folder specified is within the next: The Apple

Loops for GarageBand folder is inside the Apple folder, which is inside the Apple Loops folder, and… I'll spare you the rest. The nested reference starts at the end of the chain of references—in this case, with the Apple Loops for GarageBand folder.

In the Finder, you can also use path references to access objects more concisely. A *path reference* is one that starts at the beginning of the chain of objects to the object you want to reach. For example, to refer to that same Apple Loops for GarageBand folder with a path reference:

```
folder "Macintosh HD:Library:Audio:Apple Loops:Apple:Apple Loops for
    GarageBand:"
```

You place the path reference within double quotation marks to indicate that it's not a command, and identify the class of object before it (in this case, **folder**). A path reference to a folder ends with a colon, like the previous example, whereas a path reference to a file ends with the file's extension, like this:

```
document file "Macintosh HD:Library:Audio:Apple Loops:Apple:
    Apple Loops for GarageBand:70s Ballad Drums 01.caf"
```

### NOTE
When you're referring to an object in AppleScript like this, include its class—for example, **folder** or **document file**. If you don't know the class, use the generic class name **item** instead.

## Referring to Objects with Alias References
Nested references and path references work great in the Finder, but not in most other applications, which simply don't understand them. You also can't pass a nested reference from one application to another.

So to refer to files and folders in most applications, or to pass references from one application to another, you need to use a different type of reference. This is the *alias reference,* and all applications understand it. An alias reference is nothing more complicated than a path reference with the word **alias** before it, like this:

```
alias "Macintosh HD:Users:angela:Music:"
```

You can create an alias reference by putting the path together yourself or by reading it from the path bar at the bottom of a Finder window, but what's easier is to use AppleScript Editor to make the Finder create an alias reference for you. To do so, add the **as alias** coercion to a command that returns the object like this:

```
tell application "Finder" to get folder "Mail" of folder "Library" of
    startup disk as alias
```

This command returns this alias:

```
alias "Macintosh HD:Library:Mail:"
```

## CAUTION

In Tiger (Mac OS X 10.4) and earlier versions of AppleScript, each alias reference must refer to an existing item; a script won't compile if it refers to an object that doesn't exist. In Leopard, an alias reference can refer to an object that doesn't yet exist (for example, one that you're about to create) until the point at which you run the code, when you will get an error if the object doesn't exist.

# Understanding and Using POSIX References

With AppleScript, you can also use POSIX references, ones that are constructed as POSIX paths delimited with forward slash (/) characters rather than colons. (POSIX is the contraction for Portable Operating System for Unix.) In POSIX, the first forward slash refers to the startup disk. For example, the following POSIX path refers to the Users:jane:Documents:Reference:BeatingSpyware.pdf file:

```
"/Users/jane/Documents/Reference/BeatingSpyware.pdf"
```

To get a POSIX path from an alias reference, use the **get POSIX path** command like this:

```
tell application "Finder"
    get POSIX path of (folder "Mail" of folder "Library" of startup
        disk as alias)
end tell
```

This command returns the following POSIX path:

```
"/Library/Mail/"
```

To get an alias reference from a POSIX path, add **as POSIX file** after the path reference like this:

```
"/Library/Audio" as POSIX file as alias
```

This command returns the following alias:

```
alias "Macintosh HD:Library:Audio:"
```

## Opening a Finder Window

To open a Finder window, you use the **open** command and a reference to the folder you want the Finder window to show. Here are four examples:

- To open the startup disk in the simplest way possible:

```
tell the application "Finder"
    open the startup disk
end tell
```

- To open the /Library/Fonts/ folder by using a nested reference:

```
tell the application "Finder"
    open the folder "Fonts" of the folder "Library" of the
        startup disk
end tell
```

- To open the /Library/Fonts/ folder by using a path reference:

```
tell the application "Finder"
    open folder "Macintosh HD:Library:Fonts:"
end tell
```

- To open the /Library/Fonts/ folder by using an alias reference:

```
tell the application "Finder" to open alias "Macintosh HD:Library:
    Fonts:"
```

## Try This Using Nested References, Path References, and Alias References

In this example, you use a nested reference, a path reference, and an alias reference to open folders and files. Follow these steps:

1. With the previous script you created still open, press ⌘-**SHIFT-S** or choose File | Save As to open the Save As dialog box. Specify a different name for the new script, and then click the Save button.

2. Delete the two **open** commands from the script.

3. Add an **open** command that uses a nested reference to open the /Library/Desktop Pictures/Nature/ folder, as shown in boldface here:

```
tell the application "Finder"
    open folder "Nature" of folder "Desktop Pictures" ¬
        of folder "Library" of startup disk
end tell
```

4. Add an **open** command that uses a path reference to open the document file named Aurora.jpg in the /Library/Desktop Pictures/Nature/ folder, as shown in boldface here:

```
tell the application "Finder"
    open folder "Nature" of folder "Desktop Pictures" ¬
        of folder "Library" of startup disk
    open document file ¬
        "Macintosh HD:Library:Desktop Pictures:Nature:Aurora.jpg"
end tell
```

5. Add an **open** command that uses an alias reference to open the document file named Mojave.jpg in the /Library/Desktop Pictures/Black & White/ folder, as shown in boldface here:

```
tell the application "Finder"
    open folder "Nature" of folder "Desktop Pictures" ¬
        of folder "Library" of startup disk
    open document file ¬
        "Macintosh HD:Library:Desktop Pictures:Nature:Aurora.jpg"
    open document file alias ¬
        "Macintosh HD:Library:Desktop Pictures:Black & White:
            Mojave.jpg"
end tell
```

6. Press ⌘-R or click the Run button on the toolbar to run the script. The Finder opens a Finder window showing the Desktop Pictures folder and then opens the Aurora. jpg desktop picture and the Mojave.jpg desktop picture in your default JPG viewer application (for example, Preview).

7. Close the windows the script has opened.

8. Save the script under a name of your choice.

## Changing the View in a Finder Window

When you open a Finder window, you'll often want to make sure it's in the best view for whoever is using it.

To find out which view a Finder window is in, check the **current view** property of the window. As you'll remember from Chapter 3, there are four views (see Table 6-3).

For example, the following **tell** block tests whether the current view is Column view. If it is, the code changes the view to Cover Flow view.

```
tell the application "Finder"
    tell the front window
        if the current view is column view then
```

| View | Finder Command | Finder Shortcut | Term |
|---|---|---|---|
| Icon view | View | As Icons | ⌘-1 | icon view |
| List view | View | As List | ⌘-2 | list view |
| Column view | View | As Columns | ⌘-3 | column view |
| Cover Flow view | View | As Cover Flow | ⌘-4 | flow view |

**Table 6-3**  AppleScript Terms for the Finder's Four Views

```
        set the current view to flow view
    end if
  end tell
end tell
```

## Changing the Position of a Finder Window

To find out where a Finder window is positioned, get its **position** property. AppleScript returns a list showing the horizontal and vertical coordinates from the upper-left corner of the primary monitor (the monitor on which the menu bar appears)—for example:

```
{800, 44}
```

**NOTE**

As discussed in Chapter 3, the reference point isn't actually the upper-left corner of the Finder window—it's the leftmost point below the title bar. Ideally, you should allow 22 pixels for the depth of the Finder window's title bar. You should also allow 22 pixels for the depth of the menu bar if you're positioning the Finder window near the top of a Mac's primary monitor. However, if you try to position a Finder window on top of the menu bar (for example, by using a vertical position of 0), Mac OS X forces the Finder window below the title bar without comment.

To change the position of a Finder window, set its **position** property and provide a list of the coordinates of where you want to put the upper-left corner. For example, the following statement positions the front Finder window in the upper-left corner of the primary monitor:

```
tell the application "Finder"
    set the position of the front Finder window to {0, 44}
end tell
```

You can also change the position of a Finder window by setting its bounds, as described next.

## Changing the Size of a Finder Window

To discover how big a Finder window is, get its **bounds** property. AppleScript returns a list showing the positions of the left edge, top edge (below the title bar), right edge, and bottom edge of the window—for example:

```
{0, 44, 752, 870}
```

To change the size of a Finder window, set its bounds to the appropriate positions. For example, the following **tell** block positions the Finder window named Documents in the upper-left corner of the primary monitor and makes it 800 pixels high by 800 pixels wide:

```
tell the application "Finder"
    set the bounds of the Finder window "Documents" to {0, 44, 800, 822}
end tell
```

## Minimizing and Restoring a Finder Window

To minimize a Finder window to an icon on the Dock, you set its **collapsed** property to **true**. For example, the following statement minimizes the front Finder window:

```
tell application "Finder" to set collapsed of front Finder window to
    true
```

### NOTE

The property for minimizing a Finder window is called "collapsed" because Mac System 9 used to allow you to collapse a window to just its title bar. Most other applications use the **miniaturized** property for minimizing windows. For example, the statement **tell application "iPhoto" to set miniaturized of window 1 to true** minimizes the first iPhoto window.

To restore a minimized Finder window to its previous position, set the **collapsed** property to **false** like this:

```
tell application "Finder" to set collapsed of front Finder window to
    false
```

## Changing the Width of the Sidebar

To find out how wide the sidebar is in a Finder window, get the **sidebar width** property of the window. AppleScript returns an integer showing the number of pixels. The minimum width is 135 pixels; AppleScript ignores any smaller value you care to suggest.

To change the width of the sidebar, set the **sidebar width** property of the window. For example, the following **tell** block makes the sidebar in the front Finder window 160 pixels wide:

```
tell the application "Finder"
    set the sidebar width of the front Finder window to 160
end tell
```

### NOTE

*Two quick things here. First, if you need to hide the sidebar, hide the toolbar as described next; the sidebar disappears at the same time. Second, after you set the sidebar width, Mac OS X uses that width for each new Finder window you open—so don't set the sidebar as wide as the flares you're hiding in your closet.*

## Showing and Hiding the Toolbar

To find out whether the toolbar is visible in a Finder window, get the **toolbar visible** property of the window. This is a Boolean property, so AppleScript returns **true** if the toolbar and the sidebar are displayed and **false** if they're hidden.

## Hiding the Front Application or All Background Applications

You can use the System Events application to hide either the front application or all other applications apart from the front application. To do so, you tell System Events to issue the keystrokes you use for hiding when working interactively.

● Hide the front application    ⌘-H

```
tell application "System Events" to keystroke ¬
    "h" using command down
```

● Hide all other applications    ⌘-OPTION-H

```
tell application "System Events" to keystroke ¬
    "h" using {command down, option down}
```

To hide the toolbar and the sidebar, set the **toolbar visible** property to **false**, as in this example:

```
tell the application "Finder"
    set toolbar visible of the front Finder window to false
end tell
```

To show the toolbar and the sidebar again, set the **toolbar visible** property to **true**.

# Hiding All Finder Windows

You can't hide a single Finder window, but you can hide the entire application. You need to use the System Events application to hide the application in question rather than simply telling the application straight to its face.

For example, the following statement hides all open Finder windows:

```
tell application "System Events" to tell ¬
    process "Finder" to set visible to false
```

To display the Finder windows again, set the **visible** property to **true** like this:

```
tell application "System Events" to tell ¬
    process "Finder" to set visible to true
```

### NOTE
This technique of hiding an application works for other applications as well as the Finder. For example, to hide all the open Microsoft Word windows, you can use **tell application "System Events" to tell process "Microsoft Word" to set visible to false**.

# Closing Finder Windows

To close a Finder window, use a **close** command and identify the window. For example, the following **tell** block closes the Finder window at the back of the stack:

```
tell the application "Finder"
    close the back Finder window
end tell
```

If you want to close every open Finder window, you need only specify **every window**:

```
tell the application "Finder"
    close every Finder window
end tell
```

**Try This** Opening, Configuring, and Closing Finder Windows

In this example, you open a Finder window, reposition and resize it, make sure the toolbar is visible, and then close the window after a pause.

To create this script, follow these steps:

1. In AppleScript Editor, press ⌘-N or choose File | New to create a new script.

2. Create a **tell** block to the Finder application:

```
tell the application "Finder"

end tell
```

3. Add an **open** command to open the Documents folder in the current user's account, as shown in boldface here:

```
tell the application "Finder"
    open folder "documents" of home
end tell
```

4. Create a nested **tell** block that works with the front Finder window (the window the **open** command opens), as shown in boldface here:

```
tell the application "Finder"
    open folder "documents" of home
    tell the front Finder window

    end tell
end tell
```

5. Inside the nested **tell** block, set the **current view** property to **column view**, the **position** property to **{0, 44}**, and the **bounds** property to **{0, 44, 800, 844}**, as shown in boldface here:

```
tell the application "Finder"
    open folder "documents" of home
    tell the front Finder window
        set the current view to column view
        set the position to {0, 44}
        set the bounds to {0, 44, 800, 844}
    end tell
end tell
```

6. Still inside the nested **tell** block, set the **sidebar width** property to **150** pixels and the **toolbar visible** property to **true**, as shown in boldface here:

```
tell the application "Finder"
    open folder "documents" of home
```

```
    tell the front Finder window
        set the current view to column view
        set the position to {0, 44}
        set the bounds to {0, 44, 800, 844}
        set the sidebar width to 140
        set toolbar visible to true
    end tell
end tell
```

7. After the nested **tell** block, but still within the outer **tell** block, add a **delay 5** statement to insert a five-second pause when the script runs, and then add a **close** command to close the front Finder window. The additions are shown in boldface here:

```
tell the application "Finder"
    open folder "documents" of home
    tell the front Finder window
        set the current view to column view
        set the position to {0, 44}
        set the bounds to {0, 44, 800, 844}
        set the sidebar width to 150
        set toolbar visible to true
    end tell
    delay 5
    close the front Finder window
end tell
```

8. Press ⌘-R or click the Run button on the toolbar to run the script. You'll see a Finder window open; change to the position, size, and configuration you specified; pause to take a curtain call; and then close.

9. Save the script under a name of your choice.

# Working with Folders

Mac OS X's Spotlight feature is a wonderful technology for hunting down lost files and folders, but it's still no excuse for not keeping tight organization of the file system of your Mac—or whoever's Mac your script is running on.

To keep the file system in apple-pie order, your scripts will often need to create, modify, or delete folders. In this section, we'll look at the essential maneuvers you'll need to be able to perform with folders—creating them, renaming them, moving them, lobbing them in the Trash, and so on.

## Creating a Folder

To create a folder using AppleScript, use a **make** command. The **make** command is a widely used command that takes two required parameters.

● **new** *type*   You use the **new** parameter to tell AppleScript which class of object you want to create. So to create a new folder, you use a **make new folder** command.

● **at** *location*   You use the **at** parameter to tell AppleScript where you want to create the new object. For example, when you use a **make new folder** command, you can use the parameter **at desktop** to tell Mac OS X to create the new folder on the Desktop. If you need to reach a folder within the Mac's file system, use one of the means discussed earlier in this chapter. For example, use the **alias** keyword and provide the path to the folder—such as **"Macintosh HD:Users:ben:Documents"** or a similar path.

When you're using the **make** command to create a folder, you also use the **with properties** parameter to provide essential information for the folder you're creating. The essential nugget of information you need to give AppleScript is the **name** item. If you don't provide a name for the new folder, Mac OS X obligingly gives it the default name of *untitled folder* for you. (If that name is already taken—which does happen, especially if you mess around with scripts—Mac OS X uses *untitled folder 2, untitled folder 3,* or the next available name.)

The following example creates a folder named *Test Folder* on the Desktop:

```
tell application "Finder"
    make new folder at desktop with properties {name:"Test Folder"}
end tell
```

This example creates a folder named *Sample Files* within the Temp subfolder of the user's Documents folder. The Documents folder is a standard Mac OS X system folder, but you will need to create the Temp subfolder (or verify that it already exists) if you want to make this example work on your Mac.

```
tell application "Finder"
    make new folder at folder "Temp" ¬
        of folder "Documents" of home ¬
        with properties {name:"Sample Files"}
end tell
```

If you want to open the folder you've just created, all you need do is add an **open the result** command to the **tell** block like this:

```
tell application "Finder"
    make new folder at folder "Temp" ¬
        of folder "Documents" of home ¬
```

```
        with properties {name:"Sample Files"} ¬
        open the result
end tell
```

## Copying a Folder

To copy a folder, use the **copy** command, identify the folder to copy, and tell AppleScript where to place the copy. For example, the following **tell** block copies the ~/Documents/Shift/ folder to the Loading Zone folder on the Desktop:

```
tell application "Finder"
    copy folder "Shift" of folder "Documents" of home ¬
        to folder "Loading Zone" of desktop
end tell
```

## Duplicating a Folder

Instead of copying a folder, you can duplicate it by using the **duplicate** command. As when you use the command interactively, **duplicate** is like a single-minded version of the **copy** command: It creates a copy of the folder in the same containing folder and gives the copy the same name as the original but with *copy* added (or *copy 2* if *copy* is already taken). For example, when you duplicate a folder named Samples, Finder names the duplicate Samples copy.

The following statement duplicates the folder named Loading Zone on the desktop:

```
tell application "Finder" to duplicate folder "Loading Zone" of desktop
```

## Renaming a Folder

To rename a folder, use the **set** command to change the **name** property of the folder. The following **tell** block changes the name of the folder named Current, which is located on the Desktop, to Old:

```
tell application "Finder"
    set name of folder "Current" of desktop to "Old"
end tell
```

## Moving a Folder

To move a folder, use the **move** command, identify the folder you're moving, and tell AppleScript where to move it. For example, the following **tell** block moves the ~/Desktop/Video/ folder to the ~/Movies/Files/ folder:

```
tell application "Finder"
    move folder "Video" of desktop to folder "Files" ¬
        of (path to movies folder)
end tell
```

## Deleting a Folder

To delete a folder, use the **delete** command and specify the victim folder. For example, the following statement deletes the ~/Documents/Temp/Sample Files/ folder:

```
tell application "Finder"
    delete folder "Sample Files" of folder "Temp" ¬
        of folder "Documents" of home
end tell
```

## Try This    Creating, Renaming, and Moving a Folder

In this example, you create a folder, rename it, and then move it to a different location. The script opens a Finder window so that you can see the folder has been created and then changes the window's target so that you can verify that the folder has been moved. You get to delete the folder manually, unless it happens to be just what you need.

Follow these steps to create the script:

1. In AppleScript Editor, press ⌘-N or choose File | New to create a new script.

2. Create a **tell** block to the Finder application:

   ```
   tell the application "Finder"

   end tell
   ```

3. Inside the **tell** block, add a **make new folder** command to create a folder named **Temp1** in the current user account's Documents folder. Follow up with an **open the result** command to open the new folder in a Finder window. The commands appear in boldface here:

   ```
   tell application "Finder"
       make new folder at folder "Documents" of home ¬
           with properties {name:"Temp1"}
       open the result
   end tell
   ```

4. Next, add a two-second delay to give you a breath to see the new folder in place, and then follow with a **set name** command to change the new folder's name to **Temp2**. Then add another two-second delay for you to see the change. The new commands appear in boldface here:

   ```
   tell application "Finder"
       make new folder at folder "Documents" of home ¬
           with properties {name:"Temp1"}
       open the result
       delay 2
   ```

```
        set name of folder "Temp1" of folder "Documents" ¬
            of home to "Temp2"
        delay 2
    end tell
```

5. Now add a **move** command to move the Temp2 folder from the Documents folder to the Desktop, and then set the front Finder window's target to show the Desktop so that you can see the moved folder. Again, the new commands appear in boldface:

```
tell application "Finder"
    make new folder at folder "Documents" of home ¬
        with properties {name:"Temp1"}
    open the result
    delay 2
    set name of folder "Temp1" of folder "Documents" ¬
        of home to "Temp2"
    delay 2
    move folder "Temp2" of folder "Documents" of home to desktop
    set the target of the front Finder window to folder "Desktop"
of home
end tell
```

6. Press ⌘-R or click the Run button on the toolbar to run the script. When the Finder window opens, look for the Temp 1 folder, marvel as its name changes to Temp2, and then sigh with satisfaction as it migrates to the desktop.

7. Save the script under a name of your choice.

8. Delete the Temp2 folder from your Desktop.

# Working with Files

To work with files, you can use techniques similar to those for working with folders. This section shows you how to create files from the Finder; copy, duplicate, and move files; and rename and delete files.

## Creating Files from the Finder

To create a file via AppleScript, you use a **make new** command, as you did when creating a new folder earlier in this chapter. The **make new** command works in most scriptable applications, and normally you'll want to create a file by using the application with which you'll manipulate it. For example, to create a Microsoft Excel workbook, you use Excel, which handles the details of the file format for you. You don't tell the Finder to "make a new file of the Excel workbook type" or something like that.

From the Finder, you can create folders (as you've seen) and three different types of files: aliases, Internet link files, and text files. Aliases tend to be the most useful of these file types, so we'll start with them.

## Creating an Alias File

Another type of file you may want to create using Finder is an alias file—a file that the user can double-click to open an object that's located elsewhere in the Mac's file system. For example, you can create an alias to a file or folder that's hard to reach, or place an alias for an obscure application within easy view.

To create an alias file, use the **make new** command like this:

1. Specify the **alias file** type and provide the path to the file or folder.

2. Use the **at folder** parameter to tell the Finder which folder to create the alias in.

3. Set the **name** property to the name you want the alias file to have.

Here's an example of creating an alias file to the Public folder on the volume named Server:

```
tell application "Finder"
    make new alias file to folder "Server:Public:" ¬
        at folder "Test Folder" of desktop ¬
        with properties {name:"Public Folder on Server"}
end tell
```

## Creating an Internet Link File

Often, it's useful to create an Internet link file—a file that the user can double-click to open a website using his or her default browser. To create an Internet link file, use the **make new** command like this:

1. Specify the **internet location file** type and supply the URL.

2. Use the **at folder** parameter to tell the Finder where to create the link.

3. Set the **name** property to the name you want the link file to bear.

Here's an example of creating an Internet link file to the www.mhprofessional.com website:

```
tell application "Finder"
    make new internet location file to "http://www.mhprofessional.com" ¬
```

```
        at folder "Key Links" of desktop ¬
        with properties {name:"McGraw-Hill Professional website"}
end tell
```

### Creating a Plain-Text File

The third type of file you can create from the Finder is a plain-text file—one that contains only text, with no formatting and no objects (such as graphics). This capability is occasionally useful, but you may prefer to create your text files from TextEdit or another application, or to create rich-text format documents rather than plain-text ones.

To create a plain-text file, use the **make new** command like this:

1. Specify the **document file** type.

2. Use the **at folder** parameter to tell the Finder the folder in which to create the text file.

3. Set the **name** property to the name you want to give the text file.

For example, the following **tell** block creates a text file named Log File.txt in the ~/Desktop/Loading Zone/ folder:

```
tell application "Finder"
    make new document file at folder "Loading Zone" of desktop ¬
        with properties {name:"Log File.txt"}
end tell
```

## Copying a File

To copy a file, use the **copy** command, identify the target file by name and folder, and tell AppleScript where to place the copy. For example, the following **tell** block copies the ~/Desktop/Stuff/Sample.tiff file to the user's Pictures folder:

```
tell application "Finder"
    copy file "Picture 1" of folder "Stuff" of desktop ¬
        to folder (path to pictures folder)
end tell
```

## Duplicating a File

As with a folder, you can duplicate a file by using the **duplicate** command. The Finder creates a copy of the original file in the same folder and gives the copy the original's name with *copy* added (or *copy 2* if *copy* is already in use).

The following example duplicates the file named Picture 1 on the Desktop, creating a file named Picture 1 copy:

```
tell application "Finder"
    duplicate file "Picture 1" of desktop
end tell
```

## Deleting a File

To delete a file, use the **delete** command and specify your target file (by using **document file** and the file's name) and the folder that contains it. For example, the following statement deletes the file named *Red Bull.doc* stored in the ~/Documents/Temp/ folder:

```
tell application "Finder"
    delete document file "Red Bull.doc" of folder "Temp" ¬
        of folder "Documents" of home
end tell
```

# Renaming a File

You can rename a file in the same way as you rename a folder, by using a **set name** command, telling the Finder which folder the file is in, and specifying the new name. For example, the following **tell** block renames the file named Bills in the ~/Documents/Money/ folder to Invoices:

```
tell application "Finder"
    set name of file "Bills" of folder "Money" ¬
        of folder "Documents" of home to "Invoices"
end tell
```

## Moving a File

To move a file, use the **move** command, identify the file you're moving by its name and folder, and tell AppleScript where you want to put it. For example, the following **tell** block moves the file named Invoices from the ~/Documents/Money/ folder to the ~/Desktop/Sort/ folder:

```
tell application "Finder"
    move file "Invoices" of folder "Money" of folder "Documents" ¬
        of home to folder "Sort" of desktop
end tell
```

**Try This**  Creating a File and Opening It

In this short example, you create a new Internet location file and then tell Safari to open it. Follow these steps:

**1.** In AppleScript Editor, press ⌘-N or choose File | New to create a new script.

**2.** Create a **tell** block to the Finder:

```
tell the application "Finder"

end tell
```

**3.** Declare a variable named **myWebLoc** and assign to it the result of a **make new internet location file** command. This example (shown in boldface) uses Amazon.com, since the site seems likely to survive the Credit Crunch, but substitute your preferred URL if you like:

```
tell application "Finder"
    set myWebLoc to make new internet location file ¬
        to "http://www.amazon.com" ¬
        at desktop ¬
        with properties {name:"Amazon.com"}
end tell
```

**4.** Add a **tell** statement that tells Safari to open **myWebLoc**, as shown in boldface here:

```
tell application "Finder"
    set myWebLoc to make new internet location file ¬
        to "http://www.amazon.com" ¬
        at desktop ¬
        with properties {name:"Amazon.com"}
end tell
tell the application "Safari" to open myWebLoc
```

**5.** Press ⌘-R or click the Run button on the toolbar to run the script. You'll see Safari launch (or become active) and open the Internet location file.

**6.** Save the script under a name of your choice.

**7.** Delete the Internet location file from your Desktop.

# Mounting and Unmounting Volumes

To give users of your scripts access to all the files they need, you may have to mount volumes located in servers. When the users have finished using files on a volume, you can eject the volume to unmount it from the Mac's file system.

## Mounting a Volume

To mount a network volume in a script, use the **mount volume** command. This command takes the following parameters:

- *volume_name* This required parameter gives the name or URL of the volume—for example, **smb://10.0.0.7/** or **afp://server/public/**.

- **on server** This optional parameter gives details of the server that contains the volume. If *volume_name* contains the full network path or URL to the server, you can omit the **on server** parameter.

- **in AppleTalk zone** This optional parameter specifies the AppleTalk zone in which to find the server. As with **on server**, if *volume_name* contains the full network path, you can omit **in AppleTalk zone**.

- **as user name** This optional parameter specifies the user name under which to log on to the server. If you omit this parameter, Mac OS X tries to log on as a guest user; if the server doesn't allow guest access, Mac OS X will be unable to mount the volume.

- **with password** This parameter specifies the password to use for authenticating the user name. This parameter is optional in the sense that when you use the **as user name** parameter, you use this parameter with it to supply the password; if you don't supply the password, the server prompts the user for it, as shown in Figure 6-1.

If you specify a server but not which volume on it to mount, Mac OS X prompts the user to choose from among the available volumes (see Figure 6-2).

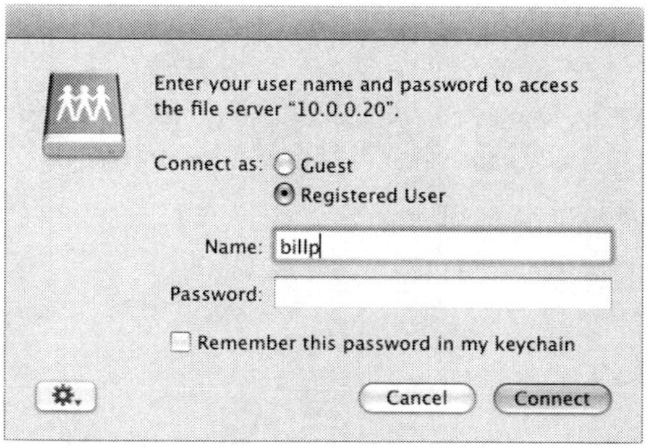

**Figure 6-1** If you don't include the password when mounting a volume, the user has the choice of entering the password or trying to connect as a guest user.

## Ask the Expert

**Q:** I'm using the with password parameter, but the server is still bugging the user for the password. What can I do to get around this?

**A:** When you're mounting a server with the **mount volume** command, you may find that the server demands a password even if you use the **with password** parameter to supply the correct password.

To avoid being prompted for the password, place the name and password in the URL like this: smb://*username:password@server.domain.com/volume,* where each of the italic items is a placeholder for the details you'll supply.

For example, the following command mounts the volume named Shared on the server with the IP address 10.0.0.7 using the Server Message Block (SMB) protocol:

```
mount volume "smb://10.0.0.7/Shared"
```

The following command mounts the volume named Spreads on the server with the IP address 10.0.0.20, authenticating with the user name *dfinkel* and the password *drowssap:*

```
mount volume "afp://10.0.0.20/spreads" as user name "dfinkel" with
password "drowssap"
```

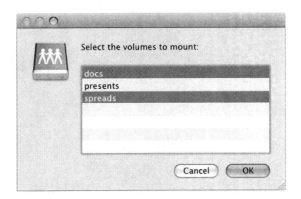

**Figure 6-2**   If necessary, Mac OS X prompts the user to choose from among the available volumes on the server.

## Unmounting a Volume

When you no longer need to have a volume mounted on the Mac's file system, unmount it by telling the Finder to eject it. For example, the following statement ejects the volume named "spreads":

```
tell application "Finder" to eject alias "spreads"
```

# Chapter 7

## Making Decisions
## in Your Scripts

# Key Skills & Concepts

* Making a decision with an **if… then** statement

* Using **if… then… else** statements

* Using **if… then… else if… else** statements

In some scripts, you'll always need to take the same actions—for example, running the same application, creating the same document, or manipulating the same files in a particular way. But more often, you'll need to make decisions in your scripts and take action accordingly.

This short chapter shows you how to make decisions by using the three If structures that AppleScript provides.

* **if… then**   This structure lets you test whether a condition is **true** and take actions if it is. If the condition is **false**, the script takes no actions.

* **if… then… else**   This structure lets you test whether a condition is **true**, take actions if it is, and take other actions if it is not.

* **if… then… else if… else**   This structure lets you test whether multiple conditions are true, taking actions for whichever of the conditions turns out to be **true**. If all the conditions return **false**, the **else** code runs.

The various kinds of **if** statements are so vital to programming in AppleScript that you've already seen some of them in action earlier in this book.

## NOTE
The **if** statements are great for taking decisions in your scripts, but AppleScript also provides other ways of taking decisions. For example, the next chapter shows you how to display dialog boxes that enable the user to choose from among different courses of action or to pick one or more choices from a list that you present to them.

# Checking a Single Condition with an if... then Statement

To check a single condition, use an **if... then** statement. You normally write it as a block of code like this, starting with the **if** statement and its condition, and ending with the **end if** statement:

```
if condition then
    statements
end if
```

### NOTE

You can also use a single-line **if** statement that reads **if** *condition* **then** *statement*—for example, **if myNumber = 10 then display dialog "The value of myNumber is 10."**. This type of **if** statement is more compact and has no **end if** line. But laying your code out in block **if** statements makes it easier to read and to debug, so it's usually a better idea.

Here's an example of an **if... then** statement:

```
tell application "Finder"
    if (count of Finder windows) = 0 then
        open folder "Documents" of home
    end if
end tell
```

Inside the **tell** block that addresses the Finder, the **if** statement compares the **count of Finder windows** to 0 to see if no Finder windows are open. If that's the case, the **open folder "Documents" of home** statement runs, opening a Finder window showing the contents of the Documents folder.

## Try This Using an if... then Statement to Launch an Application If It's Not Running

In this example, you write a script that checks whether TextEdit is running, and launches and activates it if it is not. Follow these steps:

1. If TextEdit is open, quit it. Save any unsaved changes that you want to keep.

2. In AppleScript Editor, press ⌘-N or choose File | New to create a new script.

*(continued)*

**3.** Type in the following **if... then** block:

```
if (get running of application "TextEdit") is false then
    activate application "TextEdit"
end if
```

**4.** Press ⌘-R or click the Run button on the toolbar to run the script. The script launches and activates TextEdit so that TextEdit is the frontmost window.

**5.** Run the script again with TextEdit still open. Verify that the script doesn't open another TextEdit document window.

# Deciding Between Two Courses of Action with an if... then... else Statement

Often, you'll need to decide between two paths in your code: If a condition is **true**, do this; if it's not **true** (in other words, if it's **false**), do something else instead.

In AppleScript, you use an **if... then... else** statement to make this kind of decision:

```
if condition then
    statements1
else
    statements2
end if
```

If the condition is **true**, AppleScript runs *statements1*, the statements before the **else** keyword. If the condition is **false**, AppleScript runs *statements2*, the statements after the **else** keyword. Both these sets of statements are optional, though you'll always want to have one or the other (with neither, the **if** statement does nothing), and usually you'll want to have both (if you have only one, you might as well use an **if... then** statement instead).

Here's a brief example of an **if... then... else** statement. If the number stored in the variable **myHour** is less than 12, the script sets the text in the **myGreeting** variable to **Good morning!**; otherwise (if the number is 12 or greater), the script sets the text in **myGreeting** to **Good afternoon!**.

```
if myHour is less than 12 then
    set myGreeting to "Good morning!"
else
    set myGreeting to "Good afternoon!"
end if
```

## Try This Using an if... then... else Statement

In this example, you write a script that checks the hour of the day, assigns an appropriate greeting ("Good morning!", "Good afternoon!", or "Good evening!", depending on the time) to the variable **myGreeting**, and then displays **myGreeting** in a dialog box. You'll meet dialog boxes in detail in the next chapter, but in this example, you'll use the **display dialog** command in its simplest form.

Follow these steps to create the script:

1. In AppleScript Editor, press ⌘-N or choose File | New to create a new script.

2. Type the following statement that assigns the **hours** property of the **current date** class to the variable **myHour**:

```
set myHour to hours of (current date)
```

3. Create the **if... then... else** statement from the previous example, as shown in boldface here:

```
set myHour to hours of (current date)
if myHour is less than 12 then
    set myGreeting to "Good morning!"
else
    set myGreeting to "Good afternoon!"
end if
```

4. Adapt the **else** section by adding another **if... then... else** statement to make it distinguish between the afternoon and the evening, as shown in boldface here:

```
set myHour to hours of (current date)
if myHour is less than 12 then
    set myGreeting to "Good morning!"
else
    if myHour is less than 18 then
        set myGreeting to "Good afternoon!"
    else
        set myGreeting to "Good evening!"
    end if
end if
```

5. Add a **display dialog** statement at the end to display a dialog box containing the text in **myGreeting**, as shown in boldface here:

```
set myHour to hours of (current date)
if myHour is less than 12 then
    set myGreeting to "Good morning!"
```

*(continued)*

```
    else
        if myHour is less than 18 then
            set myGreeting to "Good afternoon!"
        else
            set myGreeting to "Good evening!"
        end if
    end if
display dialog myGreeting
```

6. Press ⌘-R or click the Run button on the toolbar to run the script. Make sure the dialog box that appears shows the appropriate greeting for the time.

7. Save the script under a name of your choice so that you can work with it again later in this chapter.

## Choose Among Multiple Courses of Action with an if… then… else if… else Statement

When you need to choose among three or more courses of action in a script, you can use an **if… then… else if… else** statement. Here's how this statement looks logically:

```
if condition1 then
    statements1
else if condition2 then
    statements2
[other else if statements here as needed]
else
    statements3
end if
```

As you can see, this works in the same way as the **if… then… else** statement except that it also has one or more **else if** statements between the **if** line and the **else** line.

Here's an example of an **if… then… else if… else** statement that assigns to the variable **myGreeting** the text **Good morning!**, **Good afternoon!**, **Good evening!**, or **Goodnight!** as appropriate to the hour in many western civilizations:

```
set myHour to hours of (current date)
if myHour is less than 12 then
    set myGreeting to "Good morning!"
else if myHour is greater than or equal to 12
    and myHour is less than 18 then
    set myGreeting to "Good afternoon!"
```

```
else if myHour is greater than or equal to 12
    and myHour is less than 22 then
    set myGreeting to "Good evening!"
else
    set myGreeting to "Goodnight!"
end if
display dialog myGreeting
```

**Try This** ## Using an if... then... else if... else Statement

In this example, you adapt the script you created in the last Try This example so that it uses an **if... then... else if... else** statement as shown previously. Follow these steps:

1. In AppleScript Editor, open the script you created in the previous section if it's not still open.

2. Press ⌘-**SHIFT-S** or choose File | Save As, and then save the script under a name of your choice.

3. Edit the script so that it reads as follows:

```
set myHour to hours of (current date)
if myHour is less than 12 then
    set myGreeting to "Good morning!"
else if myHour is greater than or equal to 12 ¬
    and myHour is less than 18 then
    set myGreeting to "Good afternoon!"
else if myHour is greater than or equal to 12 ¬
    and myHour is less than 22 then
    set myGreeting to "Good evening!"
else
    set myGreeting to "Goodnight!"
end if
display dialog myGreeting
```

4. Press ⌘-**R** or click the Run button on the toolbar to run the script.

5. Press ⌘-**S** or choose File | Save to save the changes to the script.

# Chapter 8

## Using Dialog Boxes to Get User Input

## Key Skills & Concepts

- Getting user input with dialog boxes

- Communicating with the user via alerts

- Asking the user to choose a filename and location

- Letting the user choose from a list of items

- Letting the user choose files, folders, applications, and URLs

In this chapter, you'll learn how to use dialog boxes to let the user control your scripts and provide input to them.

AppleScript provides a **display dialog** command that lets you display custom dialog boxes containing a prompt, one to three action buttons, and an icon. You can also add a text-entry box to get input from the user for use in your scripts or the documents they create.

For more emphasis, you can use the **display alert** command to display an informative message and an icon. You can give alerts different buttons to allow the user to choose from among different actions.

In many scripts, you'll need to present the user with a list of items from which they can make one or more selections. To do so, you use the **choose from list** command. You may also need to have the user choose the name and folder in which to save a file you create. You can do this by using the **choose file name** command.

AppleScript also gives you commands for letting the user choose files, folders, applications, and URLs via built-in dialog boxes while a script is running. These commands make it easy to perform actions such as manipulating files and folders using the Mac OS X interface items with which the user is already familiar.

# Using Dialog Boxes

When you need to communicate information with the user of a script, or enable them to make a choice between two or three alternatives, use a dialog box.

In AppleScript, you use the **display dialog** command to display a dialog box. This command requires only one parameter: the text that appears in the dialog box as the prompt. When you give the **display dialog** command like this, as in the next example, you get

**Figure 8-1**   A basic dialog box contains a prompt and one or more buttons.

a dialog box with an empty title bar, the prompt in the body of the dialog box, and an OK button and a Cancel button (see Figure 8-1).

```
display dialog "This script will set up your Desktop for fast work."
```

# Displaying Multiple Paragraphs of Text in a Dialog Box

When you need to put a large amount of text in the prompt, you can make the dialog box easier to digest by breaking it up into multiple paragraphs. To do so, create the prompt as separate strings joined with the & concatenation operator. Place a **return** character where you want to start a new line; place two **return** characters where you want to start a new paragraph.

For example, the following command creates the dialog box shown in Figure 8-2:

```
set myPrompt to "This script helps you open a text file in the
TextEdit application." & return & return
set myPrompt to myPrompt & "First, you will see the Choose a File
dialog box. Click the text file you want and click Choose." & return &
return
set myPrompt to myPrompt & "Second, you will see the Choose an
Application dialog box. Click the TextEdit application, and then click
Choose." & return & return
set myPrompt to myPrompt & "OK to proceed?"
display dialog myPrompt
```

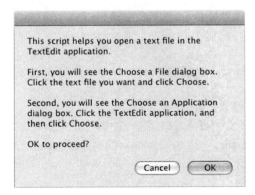

**Figure 8-2**   You can break up a dialog box's prompt into multiple paragraphs to make it easier to read.

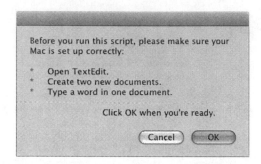

**Figure 8-3** You can also create bulleted-style lists or lay out text with tabs in your dialog boxes.

You can also use tab characters, spaces, or other characters to improve the layout of the prompt and to convey your message more clearly. The following command produces the dialog box shown in Figure 8-3:

```
set myText to ¬
    "Before you run this script, please make sure your Mac is set up
correctly:" ¬
    & return & return
set myText to myText & ¬
    "*" & tab & ¬
    "Open TextEdit." & return
set myText to myText & ¬
    "*" & tab & ¬
    "Create two new documents." & return
set myText to myText & ¬
    "*" & tab & ¬
    "Type a word in one document." & return & return
set myText to myText & tab & tab & tab & tab & ¬
    "Click OK when you're ready."
display dialog myText
```

### TIP

If you need to display a short paragraph of heading-like text before your prompt, consider using an alert rather than a dialog box. See the discussion of alerts later in this chapter.

## Adding a Title to a Dialog Box

To make your dialog boxes easier to understand, you'll usually want to use the **add title** parameter to put custom text in the title bar. The following statement displays the dialog box shown in Figure 8-4:

```
display dialog "This script will set up your Desktop for fast work." ¬
    with title "Desktop Setup: Continue?"
```

**Figure 8-4**   Add a descriptive title to make your dialog boxes easier to recognize and understand.

### TIP

Name your dialog boxes consistently to make them easy to recognize. For example, if a script displays several dialog boxes at different times, put the script's name first, followed by a short name for the dialog box—for example, "Desktop Setup: Continue?," "Desktop Setup: Choose Number of Windows," and so on. Given how many applications most people run these days, it's easy to lose track of which application a particular dialog box belongs to.

## Choosing the Buttons Displayed in the Dialog Box

The **display dialog** command's default set of buttons—OK and Cancel—are fine for many dialog boxes, but you'll often do better to customize the buttons. With AppleScript, you can have one, two, or three buttons in a dialog, and you can set their names to whatever you need.

To control which buttons the **display dialog** command displays, add the **buttons** parameter, and then provide the list of button names as strings within a pair of braces. Put a comma between each string. The buttons appear from left to right in the order in which you list them.

For example, sometimes you may need a single-button dialog box to present information, such as the fact that a script has finished running. The following statement displays the dialog box shown in Figure 8-5:

```
display dialog "The Desktop Setup script has finished running." ¬
    with title "Desktop Setup: Complete" buttons {"OK"}
```

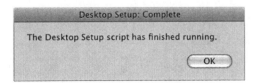

**Figure 8-5**   When presenting information without a choice, all you need is an OK button.

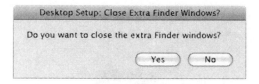

**Figure 8-6**   In a two-button dialog box, Yes and No are often clearer than OK and Cancel.

Two buttons are great for giving the user a binary choice. This example uses a Yes button and a No button (see Figure 8-6) instead of the default OK button and Cancel button:

```
display dialog "Do you want to close the extra Finder windows?" ¬
    with title "Desktop Setup: Close Extra Finder Windows?" ¬
    buttons {"Yes", "No"}
```

When the user needs to choose among three paths of action (or inaction), add three buttons to the dialog box, as in this example (see Figure 8-7):

```
display dialog "How many Word windows do you want to open?" ¬
    with title "Desktop Setup: Open Word Windows?" ¬
    buttons {"One Window", "Two Windows", "No Windows"}
```

## Setting a Default Button in a Dialog Box

As you'll probably have noticed in the last few figures, none of the dialog boxes has a default button—the one that appears with the blue highlight (or gray highlight if the Mac is using the Graphite look in Appearance preferences) and that receives the press of the RETURN key. Usually, you'll want to make one of the buttons in any dialog box the default button to shepherd the user toward the choice that's appropriate more often than the other choices. Omit a default button only when the choice between the buttons is too close to recommend one over the other.

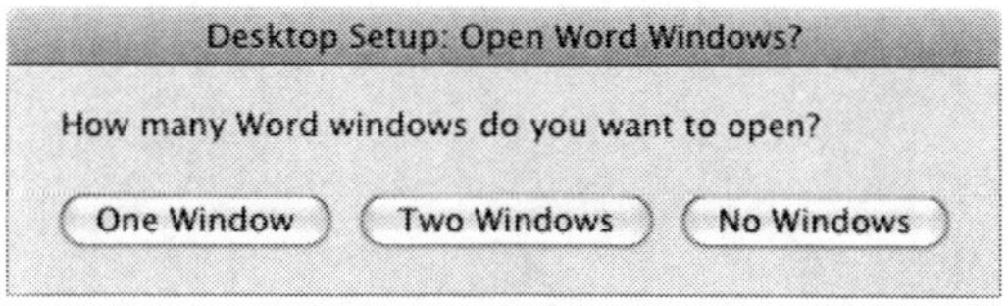

**Figure 8-7**   A three-button dialog box lets you make more complex choices in your scripts.

To set the default button, add to the **display dialog** command the **default button** parameter followed by the button's name. The following statement makes the One Window button the default, as you can see in Figure 8-8:

```
display dialog "How many Word windows do you want to open?" ¬
    with title "Desktop Setup: Open Word Windows?" ¬
    buttons {"One Window", "Two Windows", "No Windows"} ¬
    default button "One Window"
```

You can also set the default button by number, counting from left to right. For example, the following statement makes the second button (the Two Windows button) the default button:

```
display dialog "How many Word windows do you want to open?" ¬
    with title "Desktop Setup: Open Word Windows?" ¬
    buttons {"One Window", "Two Windows", "No Windows"} ¬
    default button 2
```

### TIP

In many cases, you'll want the "action" button for the dialog box to be the default button. For example, when you display an OK/Cancel dialog box, you'll often want to make the OK button the default button so that the user can proceed by simply pressing RETURN. But if the dialog box asks for confirmation of a wide-ranging or destructive action (such as deleting files or folders), it's better to make the "cancel" button the default. (The button may have a name other than "Cancel"—for example, "No," "Keep Files," or "Keep My Current Settings.")

## Creating a Cancel Button That's Not Called "Cancel"

In any dialog box with two or three buttons, it's usually a good idea to have one button be a cancel button—a button that lets the user stop running the script or refuse the action the dialog box suggests. The button isn't necessarily *called* "Cancel," but that's the function it fulfills.

### NOTE

The cancel button captures a press of the ESC key, so you'll usually want to set it to allow the user to dismiss the dialog box using the keyboard. If you don't set a cancel button, the user must press TAB (or SHIFT-TAB) to put the selection ring around the appropriate button, and then press SPACEBAR to "click" it (when using only the keyboard).

**Figure 8-8**   You'll normally want to set a default button in each dialog box to help the user make the best choice.

You can create a cancel button in three ways:

● **Use the default buttons** If you don't set the **buttons** parameter, AppleScript automatically gives you a cancel button named Cancel, which is nice and clear. You also get an OK button, which is clear, too, if not inspiring.

● **Create a button named "Cancel"** If you do set the **buttons** parameter, you can name a button "Cancel." AppleScript then treats it as a cancel button, which is handy.

● **Tell AppleScript which button is the cancel button** If you don't want to give the cancel button a different name, use the **cancel button** parameter to tell AppleScript which button to treat as the cancel button. As with the **default button** parameter, you can use either the button's name or the button's number to identify the cancel button. The following example uses the button's name:

```
display dialog "Do you want to set up your desktop?" ¬
    buttons {"Yes", "No"} ¬
    default button "Yes" ¬
    cancel button "No"
```

### NOTE

The cancel button is special in AppleScript because it returns an error that you can use to tell the user wants to cancel the action. You'll learn how to use this error (error -128) in Chapter 10.

## Seeing Which Button the User Clicked in a Dialog Box

If you use a single-button dialog box, you don't need to check which button the user clicked, because you're not giving them any choice. But when you use a two- or three-button dialog box, you must check which button the user clicked so that you can direct the flow of the script in the corresponding way.

When the user clicks a button in a dialog box, AppleScript stores the details in the dialog record. To find out the button, you check the **button returned** property of the **result**, where **result** is a predefined variable that automatically grabs the details of what the user chose in the dialog box. For example, the following **if** block checks the result of the Desktop Setup: Open Word Windows? dialog box shown in Figure 8-7 earlier in this chapter. The comments indicate where the script would take the appropriate action based on the button the user chose.

```
if the button returned of the result is "Two Windows" then
    -- open two Word windows here
else if the button returned of the result is "One Window" then
    -- open one Word window here
end if
```

## Adding an Icon to a Dialog Box

To pack more meaning into a dialog box, you can add an icon to it. AppleScript lets you use any of three built-in icons or a custom icon of your own.

### Adding a Built-in Icon to a Dialog Box

To add a built-in icon to a dialog box, add the **with icon** parameter and specify the appropriate icon. Table 8-1 shows the three built-in icons and suggests when to use them.

For example, the following statement causes the Finder to display a two-button dialog box that includes a Caution icon (see Figure 8-9):

```
tell the application "Finder" to display dialog ¬
    "Do you want to delete this document?" ¬
    & return & return & tab & docName ¬
    with title "Workflow Streamliner: Delete Document" ¬
    buttons {"Delete File", "Keep File"} ¬
    default button 2 ¬
    cancel button 2 ¬
    with icon caution
```

### Creating and Using Custom Icons

To give your scripts a custom look or to convey exactly the information required, you can make your dialog boxes display custom icons. This is great when you need to use a company logo or other standard icon in your dialog boxes.

| Icon Picture | Icon Name | Icon Number | When to Use This Icon |
|---|---|---|---|
|  | Stop | 0 | When a major problem has arisen with the script. Don't waste this icon on trivial problems, as doing so reduces the icon's effect when you genuinely need it. |
|  | Note | 1 | For general dialog boxes where nothing unexpected or dangerous is happening. The icon shown is the default icon for the application you're using. For example, if your script makes Microsoft Word display a dialog box, the Word icon appears; if you're using Finder, the Finder icon appears. |
|  | Caution | 2 | When the user needs to pay extra attention to a decision—for example, because the script is about to delete a file or folder. |

**Table 8-1** Built-in Icons for Dialog Boxes

**Figure 8-9**    Add an icon to a dialog box to make its impact clearer.

First, create an icon file using the Apple icon image format and the .icns file extension. Follow these guidelines:

- Use either an icon editor such as the Icon Composer tool included in the Apple Developer Tools or the IconBuilder plug-in for Adobe Photoshop, Adobe Photoshop Elements, or Macromedia Fireworks. Some other applications can also create Apple icon image files.
- Make the file 512 pixels high by 512 pixels wide and 72 dpi resolution.
- Use RGB color rather than CMYK color.
- If the icon occupies only part of the square (as most icons do), apply alpha to make the empty parts see-through so that the dialog box's background can appear through them.

Now save your script as a script bundle and add the icon file to it. Follow these steps:

1. In AppleScript Editor, press ⌘-SHIFT-S or choose File | Save As to display the Save As dialog box.
2. In the File Format pop-up menu, choose Script Bundle.

**NOTE**
You can also add custom icons to a script you save as an application bundle.

3. Change the filename and folder as needed, and then click the Save button to save the script bundle.
4. Click the Bundle Contents button on the toolbar. AppleScript Editor displays the Bundle Contents drawer at the side of the window (usually on the right, unless AppleScript Editor is too near the right edge of your Mac's screen).
5. Open a Finder window to the folder that contains the icon file, and then drag it to the Bundle Contents drawer (see Figure 8-10).

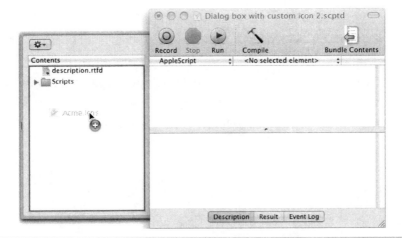

**Figure 8-10**    Drag your icon to the Bundle Contents drawer at the side of the AppleScript Editor window.

Now that the icon file is in place, use the **path to** command to specify the icon's alias in the **display dialog** command, as in the last line of the statement here:

```
display dialog "This script will set up your Desktop for fast work." ¬
    with title "Desktop Setup: Continue?" ¬
    buttons {"Yes", "No"} ¬
    default button 1 ¬
    cancel button 2 ¬
    with icon file ((path to me) & "Contents:Resources:Acme.icns" ¬
as string)
```

The **path to me** part returns the path to the script itself, and the **Contents:Resources: Acme.icns** part specifies the file named **Acme.icns** in the **Resources** folder in the **Contents** folder of the script.

## Try This Adding a Custom Dialog Box to the Set Up Finder and TextEdit Script

In this example, you'll add a custom dialog box to the Set Up Finder and TextEdit script you created in Chapter 3. The dialog box tells the user what the script will do and lets the user choose between running the script and stopping it in its tracks. Follow these steps:

1. In AppleScript Editor, press ⌘-o or choose File | Open to display the Open dialog box.

2. Choose the Set Up Finder and TextEdit script you created in Chapter 3, and then click the Open button.

*(continued)*

3. Press ⌘-**SHIFT-S** or choose File | Save As to display the Save As dialog box.

4. Change the name to "Set Up Finder and TextEdit with Opening Dialog" and then click the Save button to save the script.

5. Click at the beginning of the script (before the **tell the application "Finder"** statement), and press **RETURN** to create a new paragraph.

6. Add the **display dialog** command shown here and its prompt:

```
display dialog ¬
    "This script will set up your Desktop for fast work." ¬
    & return & return & ¬
    "Do you want to continue?"
```

7. Add a custom title to the dialog box, as shown in boldface here:

```
display dialog ¬
    "This script will set up your Desktop for fast work." ¬
    & return & return & ¬
    "Do you want to continue?" ¬
    with title "Desktop Setup"
```

8. Add the note icon to the dialog box, as shown in boldface here:

```
display dialog ¬
    "This script will set up your Desktop for fast work." ¬
    & return & return & ¬
    "Do you want to continue?" ¬
    with title "Desktop Setup" ¬
    with icon note
```

9. Specify Yes and No buttons for the dialog box, with the Yes button the default button and the No button the cancel button, as shown in boldface here:

```
display dialog ¬
    "This script will set up your Desktop for fast work." ¬
    & return & return & ¬
    "Do you want to continue?" ¬
    with title "Desktop Setup" ¬
    with icon note ¬
    buttons {"Yes", "No"} ¬
    default button "Yes" ¬
    cancel button "No"
```

10. Press ⌘-**S** to save the script.

11. Press ⌘-**R** or click the Run button to run the script. On the first run, click the No button to make sure that canceling the dialog box stops the script from running further.

12. Run the script again. This time, click the Yes button so that the script continues running and sets up the Finder window and the TextEdit window.

## Creating a Dialog Box That Closes Itself

By using the **giving up after** parameter with the **display dialog** command, you can create a dialog box that closes itself after a number of seconds. This is great for displaying progress information or for occasions when the user's input is optional rather than essential: If the user has left the script running, you can make the dialog box dismiss itself automatically after an interval, allowing the script to continue running rather than waiting for the user to return.

The **giving up after** parameter takes an integer number that specifies the number of seconds to wait. For example, the following dialog box closes itself after 2 seconds:

```
display dialog "10 files created... 10 files to go!" ¬
    with title "File Creator Script: Status" giving up after 2
```

When you use the **giving up after** parameter, the **dialog reply** record includes the **button returned** property as usual and the **gave up** parameter. The **gave up** parameter is Boolean, so it is **true** if the dialog box dismissed itself and **false** if the user clicked a button. When **gave up** is **true**, **button returned** is blank, because the user didn't click a button.

## Getting Text Input from the User

Dialog boxes are great for asking the user what to do, as you've seen so far in this chapter. But often, you'll need to get a piece of information from the user—for example, their name or the quantity of widgets their company wants to order.

To add a text-entry field to a dialog, add the optional **default answer** parameter to the **display dialog** command. If you want to provide a default answer in the text-entry field, add the appropriate string after the **default answer** parameter; if you want to leave the text-entry field blank, just place **""** (two pairs of double quotation marks indicating an empty string) after the parameter instead.

For example, the following statement produces the dialog box shown in Figure 8-11:

```
display dialog "Please enter your employee code:" ¬
    default answer "CZ 1234" ¬
    with title "Employee Code"
```

When you add the **default answer** parameter, the **dialog reply** record includes a **text returned** property containing the text in the text-entry field as well as the **button returned** property containing the button clicked. For example, the dialog box shown in Figure 8-11 returns a **dialog reply** record like this:

```
{text returned:"CZ 9288", button returned:"OK"}
```

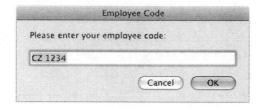

**Figure 8-11** You can add a text-entry field to any dialog box. This dialog box includes a default value to show the user a sample response.

To store the user's input, you can assign it to a variable, like this:

```
set the employee_code to the text returned of the result
```

Even if you assign an empty string to the **default answer** parameter, the OK button (or its equivalent) is still available for the user to click without entering text in the text-entry field. So if you need the user to enter text, you'll need to check that the field isn't blank. We'll look at an example of how to do this in the next chapter.

*TIP*

If the information the user is typing in the text-entry field needs to be protected from casual snooping, add the **with hidden answer** parameter to the **display dialog** statement. This parameter makes Mac OS X display the user's input as bullet characters rather than actual characters for security.

## Try This Returning Text from a Text-Entry Field

Try this example of adding a text-entry field to a dialog box and returning the user's input.

1. In AppleScript Editor, press ⌘-N to create a new script.
2. Create a **display dialog** statement that includes the **default answer** parameter with sample text as shown here:

```
display dialog "How old are you?" default answer "25"
```

3. Add a **set** statement that assigns the **text returned** property of the **result** to a variable:

```
set userAge to the text returned of the result
```

4. Display a dialog that shows a string including the variable:

```
display dialog "Your age is " & userAge & "."
```

5. Run the script and verify that it works as expected.

# Using Alerts

Instead of displaying a dialog box, you can display an *alert*—a window that notifies the user that there's a problem and offers information or different buttons for solving the problem.

There's a wide overlap between dialog boxes and alerts, so it can sometimes be hard to choose which to use. That means our first order of business is to sort out what the differences are between alerts and standard dialog boxes.

### TIP

The difference between alerts and dialog boxes may be clear to Apple's human interface design experts, but most users treat alerts in the same way as dialog boxes— as something to deal with and dismiss as quickly as possible. This means it's not worth agonizing over whether to use a dialog box or an alert in cases where either will work; just make sure your code works, and all will be well.

## Understanding How Alerts Differ from Standard Dialog Boxes

Like a standard dialog box, an alert contains one, two, or three buttons, which you can set using the **buttons** parameter. As with a standard dialog box, you use the **default button** parameter to set the default button for an alert and the **cancel button** parameter to set the cancel button. You can also use the **giving up after** parameter to automatically dismiss an alert after the number of seconds you choose.

So far, so similar. But an alert differs from a standard dialog box in five important ways:

- **An alert contains bold alert text at the top**   The alert text appears in boldface at the top of the alert window. You use this line to present a summary of the problem— preferably using few enough words that the user can grasp it at a glance. This bold text works as a kind of headline for the alert.

- **An alert's title bar is blank**   It's tempting to try to add text to the title bar of an alert window by using the **with title** parameter, but this doesn't work.

- **An alert always contains an icon**   As you'll see shortly, you can put either of two different icons in an alert. But even if you don't specify an icon, the alert window contains an icon—so your choice is limited.

- **An alert has no text-entry field**   You can't add a text-entry field to an alert.

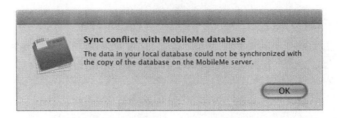

**Figure 8-12** An alert has a blank title bar, a paragraph of bold text, a prompt, and your choice of buttons. The application's icon appears on an alert to identify the perpetrator.

- **An alert doesn't register a custom button named "Cancel"** As you saw earlier in this chapter, if you create custom buttons in a dialog box, you can make one a cancel button by simply naming it "Cancel." In an alert, this doesn't work; instead, you need to use the **cancel button** parameter explicitly to turn a button into a cancel button. Figure 8-12 shows an alert for the OmniFocus organizer application.

## Choosing the Icon for an Alert

In theory, AppleScript lets you use three different icons for alerts: You can set the optional **as** parameter to **as critical**, to **as informational**, or to **as warning**. But because **critical** and **informational** both display the application's own icon (for example, the OmniFocus icon shown in Figure 8-12 if you're scripting OmniFocus), there's little point in using them, because this icon is what you get anyway if you omit the **as parameter**.

When you use the **as warning** parameter, you get the yellow-triangle-with-white-exclamation-point icon shown in Figure 8-13, with a smaller version of the application's icon superimposed on it so that you can see immediately which application is raising the alert.

**Figure 8-13** The **as warning** parameter displays an exclamation-point icon that's good for getting the user's attention. The application's icon (here, AppleScript Editor's own icon) appears in miniature to identify the perpetrator.

**Try This** Creating an Alert

In this example, you write a script that creates a folder on the Desktop, displays an alert warning (see Figure 8-14) that the script is about to delete that folder, and then deletes it.

Follow these steps:

1. In AppleScript Editor, press ⌘-N to create a new script.

2. Create a **tell** statement that tells the Finder to create a new folder named "Test Folder" on the desktop:

```
tell the application "Finder" to ¬
    make new folder at desktop with properties {name:"Test Folder"}
```

3. Start a **display alert** statement and add the prompt:

```
display alert ¬
    "Delete the Test Folder?"
```

4. Add the **as warning** parameter, as shown in boldface here:

```
display alert ¬
    "Delete the Test Folder?" as warning
```

5. Add the **message** parameter and a string giving more detail, as shown in boldface here:

```
display alert ¬
    "Delete the Test Folder?" as warning ¬
    message "The script will delete the folder named Test Folder on
your Desktop.
```

6. Add the **buttons** parameter with a confirmation button and a cancel button called Cancel. Make the cancel button the default button for the alert, as shown in boldface here:

```
display alert ¬
    "Delete the Test Folder?" as warning ¬
    message "The script will delete the folder named Test Folder on
your Desktop." ¬
    buttons {"Delete the Test Folder", "Cancel"} ¬
    cancel button "Cancel" ¬
    default button "Cancel"
```

**Figure 8-14**    The sample alert warns that the script will delete a folder.

*(continued)*

**7.** Create another **tell** statement that makes the Finder delete the Test Folder:

```
tell the application "Finder" to delete folder "Test Folder" of
desktop
```

**8.** Run the script and click the Delete The Test Folder button in the alert. The Finder deletes the folder that it has just created.

# Choosing the Name Under Which to Save a File

Chances are you'll often need to create documents in your scripts. Most scriptable applications let you manipulate their **save** commands via AppleScript, just as you did with TextEdit in Chapter 3. But with some other applications, you may need to save a document in different ways. For these cases, AppleScript provides the **choose file name** command, which you'll learn to use in this section.

The **choose file name** command does what it says on the tin: It lets the user choose the name for a file, but it doesn't actually save the file. So you normally use the **choose file name** command to create a file reference that you pass to a variable, and then use the contents of the variable when you need to save the file.

```
set myDocName to choose file name
```

### NOTE
The file reference isn't a string, but you can coerce it to a string if you need to display it in a dialog box or alert.

## Adding a Custom Prompt to the Choose File Name Dialog Box

The **choose file name** dialog box always shows Choose File Name in the title bar. By default, the dialog box shows the prompt *Choose new file name and location,* but you can customize this by adding the **with prompt** parameter and a suitable text string. Here's an example:

```
choose file name with prompt ¬
    "Choose the folder and name for the document the script will
create:"
```

## Setting a Default Location and Filename

To encourage the user to create a file reference in a suitable location, you can set the default location by setting the **default location** parameter. This makes the **choose file name** dialog box show that folder first. The user can choose another folder if they wish.

Often, it's a good idea to provide a default filename for the file reference so that the files have a good chance of getting standard names. To do so, add the **default name** parameter to the **choose file name** command and supply a text string for the name.

Here's an example of setting a default location and name (see Figure 8-15):

```
choose file name with prompt ¬
    "Choose the folder and name for the document the script will
create:" ¬
    default location (path to documents folder) ¬
    default name "Head Office Report.doc"
```

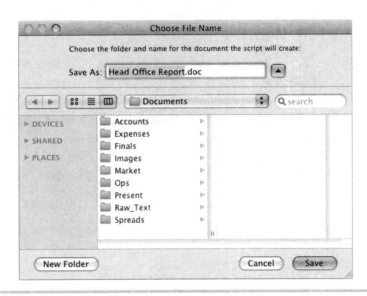

**Figure 8-15**   You can customize the Choose File Name dialog box by adding a prompt and specifying the default location and filename.

# Letting the User Choose from a List of Items

AppleScript's dialog boxes are great for making choices from among two or three courses of action, but often, you'll need to present the user with a list of choices so that they can choose one or more items. To do so, you use the **choose from list** command.

## Creating the List of Items

The only essential part of the **choose from list** command is the list of items. To create the list, you type an opening brace, each item within double quotation marks and separated by commas, and then the closing brace. For example, the following **choose from list** command displays a list containing the cities Madrid, Paris, and San Francisco:

```
choose from list {"Madrid", "Paris", "San Francisco"}
```

When you run this command, the basic form of the **choose from list** dialog box appears. As you can see in Figure 8-16, the dialog box has no title bar, a bland "Please make your selection" prompt, and an OK button and a Cancel button. You can change the prompt and the buttons, and add a title bar, as you'll see shortly.

## Seeing Which Item the User Chose

After the user picks an item in the list, the **choose from list** command returns a list of the items they chose. Returning a list of items seems weird, but the command does this because you can set up the list so that the user can select multiple items. Unless you specifically allow multiple selections, AppleScript gives you a single-selection list, which means that the command returns a "list" containing a single item.

So if the user chooses the Paris item and clicks the OK button in the example dialog box, the command returns a list containing the item "Paris", like this:

```
{"Paris"}
```

To get an item from the list, you can specify it by its item position—for example:

```
item 1 of result
```

**Figure 8-16** The Choose From List dialog box enables you to let the user choose from among several predefined options.

But when you're dealing with a single-item list, you can simply coerce the list into a string by putting the **choose from list** command and list into parentheses and adding **as string** after the list, like this:

```
(choose from list {"Madrid", "Paris", "San Francisco"}) as string
```

Coercing the list into a string makes the command return a string that you can manipulate without further ado.

If the user clicks the Cancel button in the **choose from list** dialog box, the dialog box returns the value **false** rather than returning the standard AppleScript cancel error (error number –128). Because clicking the Cancel button means that the user didn't make a choice in the **choose from list** dialog box, it's best to check for a **false** return before seeing which item (or items) the user chose. The following example displays a dialog box containing the first item in the **result** list, as long as the result is not **false**:

```
choose from list {"Madrid", "Paris", "San Francisco"}
if result is not false then
    display dialog item 1 of result
end if
```

## Adding a Title and Custom Prompt to the Choose From List Dialog Box

To make a **choose from list** dialog box easier to grasp immediately, you can add a title and customize the prompt. It's usually a good idea to do both of these.

To add a title, use the **with title** parameter and provide the text string for the title. Similarly, to customize the prompt from the default ("Please make your selection"), use the **with prompt** parameter and a text string.

For example, the following **choose from list** statement produces the dialog box shown in Figure 8-17:

```
choose from list {"Madrid", "Paris", "San Francisco"} ¬
    with title "Choose Your Destination" ¬
    with prompt "Click the office you will visit:"
```

**Figure 8-17**   Adding a title and customizing the prompt makes the Choose From List dialog box clearer to users.

## Changing the Buttons on the Choose From List Dialog Box

The **choose from list** dialog box comes with a Cancel button on the left and an OK button on the right. You can't change the behavior or position of these buttons, but you can change their names to make their function more obvious (though OK and Cancel are pretty clear) or to make the dialog box conform to your company's or organization's house style.

To change the button names, use the **OK button name** parameter and the **Cancel button name** parameter, as in this example and Figure 8-18:

```
choose from list ¬
    {"FREE! Deluxe airline bag", ¬
    "FREE! Return train ticket", ¬
    "FREE! Manicure and root canal voucher"} ¬
    OK button name "Send Me My Choice" ¬
    cancel button name "No, Thanks"
```

## Choosing One or More Default Items

In many **choose from list** dialog boxes, you'll want to allow the user free rein to select the item that suits him or her. But in others, it will make more sense to select a default item—or, for a **choose from list** dialog box that allows multiple selections, multiple items.

To set a default item in a **choose from list** dialog box, add the **default items** parameter with the list of default items. This parameter has the same name whether the dialog box lets the user select one item or multiple items—there's no singular version such as "default item" without an *s*. As with the result of a single-item **choose from list** dialog box, you simply supply a single-item list if you want to use a single default item.

Here's an example of setting a single default item:

```
choose from list {"Madrid", "Paris", "San Francisco"} ¬
    default items {"Paris"}
```

**Figure 8-18**   You can change the names of the buttons on the Choose From List dialog box.

Here's an example of setting two default items:

```
(choose from list {"Madrid", "Paris", "San Francisco", "Wasilla"} ¬
    default items {"Paris", "Wasilla"} ¬
    with multiple selections allowed
```

### *NOTE*

When you set one or more default items, the user can select one of the other items but can't deselect all items. So there's no point in allowing no selection (as discussed next) if you set one or more default items.

## Letting the User Select Multiple Items or No Items

To allow the user to select multiple items in a **choose from list** dialog box, add the **with multiple selections allowed** parameter. You don't need to set this to **true** or **false**; if you add this parameter to your code, it's **true**, and if you omit the parameter, it's **false**. Here's an example:

```
choose from list {"Madrid", "Paris", "San Francisco"} ¬
    with multiple selections allowed
```

Normally, the OK button in the **choose from list** dialog box is disabled until the user selects an item. This prevents the user from clicking the OK button without making a selection; if they want to dismiss the dialog box without making a selection, they must click the Cancel button (and generate a **false** value).

When you allow multiple selections like this, the **choose from list** command returns a list of items as usual. You can retrieve the items by specifying their position in the list (**item 1 of result**, **item 2 of result**, and so on). Don't coerce them to a string, or AppleScript simply smashes them together (for example, **MadridSan Francisco**).

You may sometimes need to allow the user to select no items and click the OK button anyway, as in the **choose from list** dialog box shown in Figure 8-19. To do so, add the **with empty selection allowed** parameter like this:

```
choose from list {"Fruitarian", "Vegetarian", "Ovo-Vegetarian", ¬
    "Ovo-Lacto Vegetarian", "Pesco-Ovo-Lacto Vegetarian", ¬
    "Pullo-Pesco-Ovo-Lacto-Vegetarian", "Vegan", "Kosher"} ¬
    with prompt "Choose a dietary preference (leave blank for none):" ¬
    with title "Menu Selection" ¬
    with empty selection allowed
```

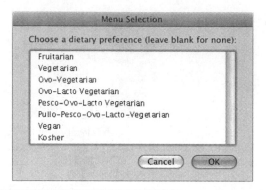

**Figure 8-19**  Sometimes you may need to allow the user to click the OK button in a **choose from list** dialog box without making a selection.

**Try This**  Creating a Choose From List Dialog Box

In this example, you will create the Choose From List dialog box shown in Figure 8-20 and display the user's choice in a dialog box.

**1.** Start a **choose from list** command:

```
choose from list
```

**2.** Add the list of items, as shown in boldface here:

```
choose from list ¬
    {"Mendocino", "Big Sur", "Las Vegas", "Cancun", "Tijuana"}
```

**3.** Set a default item in the list, as shown in boldface here:

```
choose from list ¬
    {"Mendocino", "Big Sur", "Las Vegas", "Cancun", "Tijuana"} ¬
    default items {"Mendocino"}
```

**Figure 8-20**  The Choose From List dialog box you create in this example.

**4.** Add a title and a prompt, as shown in boldface here:

```
choose from list ¬
    {"Mendocino", "Big Sur", "Las Vegas", "Cancun", "Tijuana"} ¬
    default items {"Mendocino"} ¬
    with title "Holiday Destination" ¬
    with prompt "Choose your destination:"
```

**5.** Now put the whole command in parentheses and add **as string** to coerce the result to a string, as shown in boldface here:

```
(choose from list ¬
    {"Mendocino", "Big Sur", "Las Vegas", "Cancun", "Tijuana"} ¬
    default items {"Mendocino"} ¬
    with title "Holiday Destination" ¬
    with prompt "Choose your destination:") as string
```

**6.** Add a **display dialog** command at the beginning with the first part of a prompt, add the result of the **choose from list** command, and then a period at the end, as shown in boldface here:

```
display dialog ("You chose " & (choose from list ¬
    {"Mendocino", "Big Sur", "Las Vegas", "Cancun", "Tijuana"} ¬
    default items {"Mendocino"} ¬
    with title "Holiday Destination" ¬
    with prompt "Choose your destination:") as string) ¬
    & "."
```

**7.** Press ⌘-R or click the Run button on the toolbar to run the script. When the Holiday Destination dialog box appears, click one of the items, and then click the OK button. The script then displays your choice in a dialog box.

**8.** Save the script under a name of your choice.

# Letting the User Choose Files, Folders, Applications, and URLs

AppleScript includes commands for displaying a dialog box so that the user can quickly choose a file, a folder, an application, or a URL. This section shows you how to use these commands in your scripts.

### NOTE

You can use the **choose file** command, **choose folder** command, **choose application** command, and **choose URL** command either inside a **tell** block or outside one. These commands are part of AppleScript's Standard Additions.

## Letting the User Choose a File

Often, you'll need to let the user choose a file—for example, to tell your script exactly which document to slice, dice, or spice. To do so, use the **choose file** command.

On its own, the **choose file** command displays the Choose A File dialog box shown in Figure 8-21. The dialog box opens to the current working directory (which may be helpful or otherwise) and shows every single file in it, including invisible ones. The user can navigate to any other folder in the file system, pick any file they want, and then click the Choose button to tell the script that this is the file he or she wants to open.

### Adding a Prompt to the Choose A File Dialog Box

In most cases, it's a good idea to display a prompt in the Choose A File dialog box to make clear to the user what type of file you're expecting them to choose. This may be blindingly obvious to you as you write the script, and indeed may be clear to the user when he or she runs it, but the Choose A File dialog box can look supremely uninformative if the user comes back to their Mac after a break and finds the dialog box still patiently waiting for their attention.

To display a prompt, add the **with prompt** parameter to the Choose A File dialog box, followed by the string of text. Here's an example:

```
choose file with prompt ¬
    "Choose the source document for the Latest News report."
```

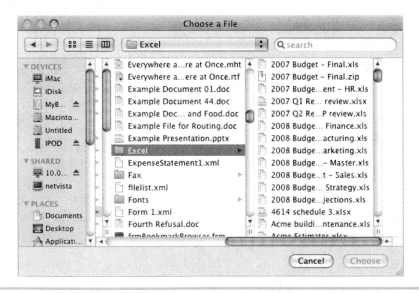

**Figure 8-21** Without any parameters, the Choose A File dialog box shows every file in the current working directory.

## Setting the Default Location for the Choose A File Dialog Box

In many scripts, it's helpful to make the Choose A File dialog box show the folder that contains the files the user will likely need rather than let him flounder through his Mac's plethora of folders. To do so, add the **default location** parameter to the **choose file** command followed by an alias to the folder. Normally, you'll want to use the **path to** command to return a standard path within the Mac OS X file system rather than hard-coding the path to a particular folder, as that folder may be in a different place on other Macs.

Here's an example of using the **choose file** command with the **default location** parameter. The command uses the Documents folder.

```
choose file with prompt ¬
    "Choose the source document for the Latest News report." ¬
    default location (path to the documents folder)
```

## Choosing Whether to Display Invisible Files

By default, the **choose file** command displays every file in the folder to which it opens. This includes any files (and folders) set to be invisible to the user, such as the .DS_Store file that Mac OS X creates in every folder you open to store details such as the position of icons, the size of the Finder window you're using, and other view options.

Only seldom will you need the user to be able to choose an invisible file, so normally, you'll want to keep them invisible. To do so, add the parameter **without invisibles** to the **choose file** command. (To display invisible files, you can either add the parameter **with invisibles** or omit the **invisibles** parameter altogether.)

Here's an example of using the **choose file** command and hiding invisible files:

```
choose file with prompt ¬
    "Choose the source document for the Latest News report." ¬
    default location (path to the documents folder) ¬
    without invisibles
```

## Displaying Only the Right Type of Files

Even if you hide invisible files, it's likely that the folder shown in the Choose A File dialog box will contain files of different types. When you need the user to be able to select only files of a particular type suitable for whatever the script is doing—for example, only rich-text documents for opening in TextEdit, or only Excel workbooks for processing in Microsoft Excel—add the **of type** parameter to specify which kinds of files to display. The files that match the parameter appear listed in black as usual in the Choose A File dialog box, while other files are listed in the dimmed gray that indicates they're not available.

To display only files of a particular type, use Uniform Type Identifiers (UTIs) to identify the file type or types. A Uniform Type Identifier is a Mac OS X means of identifying the file type by its contents rather than just by its file type code (for example, TIFF).

Table 8-2 provides a short list of the UTIs that are normally most useful in scripts. To see a full list of UTIs together with enough detail to numb your brain, steer your web browser to the Apple Developer Connection website (http://developer.apple.com) and search for the document named "Uniform Type Identifiers Overview."

For example, the first of the following two commands displays the Choose A File dialog box showing Keynote presentations without invisibles in the //Server/Presentations/ folder. The second command tells Keynote to open the chosen presentation.

```
set myKey to choose file ¬
    default location (alias "Server:Presentations:") ¬
    of type "com.apple.iwork.keynote.sffkey" ¬
    with prompt "Choose the presentation you want to open:" ¬
    without invisibles
tell the application "Keynote" to open myKey
```

### CAUTION

UTIs work only with Mac OS X 10.4 (Tiger) and later versions. If you need to make sure your scripts work with Panther (10.3) or earlier versions of Mac OS X, use file type codes to identify the file types instead of UTIs.

When you need to display two or more file types, use the **of type** parameter with a list of the types inside braces. The following statement displays Microsoft Word documents (with the .doc file extension) and Microsoft Excel workbooks (with the .xls file extension):

```
choose file ¬
    default location (path to the documents folder) ¬
    of type {"com.microsoft.word.doc", "com.microsoft.excel.xls"} ¬
    without invisibles
```

### NOTE

The **of type** parameter always takes a list. But when you provide a single type, AppleScript automatically coerces it to a list for you, so you don't need to enter it within braces.

### NOTE

The old-style means of choosing which files to display in the Choose A File dialog box is to use their file type codes. This means is no longer recommended for Mac OS X 10.4 or later versions—so if you find this means used in legacy code you're maintaining, update the code to use UTIs instead.

| UTI | UTI Constant | Conforms to Type | Tags | Explanation |
|---|---|---|---|---|
| **Text Files** | | | | |
| public.plain-text | kUTTypePlainText | public.text | .txt, text/plain | Text with no specific encoding (such as UTF-8) and with no markup |
| public.rtf | kUTTypeRTF | public.text | 'RTF ', .rtf, text/rtf, NeXT Rich Text Format 1.0 pasteboard type, NSRTFPBoardType | Rich text (text with formatting) |
| public.html | kUTTypeHTML | public.text | 'HTML', .html, .htm, text/html, Apple HTML pasteboard type | HTML file |
| **Image Files** | | | | |
| public.jpeg | kUTTypeJPEG | public.image | 'JPEG', .jpg, .jpeg, image/jpeg | JPEG image (not JPEG 2000) file |
| public.jpeg-2000 | kUTTypeJPEG2000 | public.image | 'jp2', .jp2, image/jp2 | JPEG 2000 image file |
| public.tiff | kUTTypeTIFF | public.image | 'TIFF', .tif, .tiff, image/tiff, NeXT TIFF v4.0 pasteboard type, NSTIFFPBoardType | TIFF image file |
| public.camera-raw-image | N/A | public.image | N/A | RAW digital camera image (base type) |
| public.png | kUTTypePNG | public.image | 'PNGf', .png, image/png | PNG image file |
| com.apple.quicktime-image | kUTTypeQuickTimeImage | public.image | 'qtif', .quf, qtif, image/x-QuickTime | QuickTime image file |
| com.adobe.pdf | kUTTypePDF | public.data, public.composite-content | 'PDF ', .pdf, application/pdf, Apple PDF pasteboard type | PDF file |
| com.compuserve.gif | kUTTypeGIF | public.image | 'GIFf', .gif, image/gif | GIF image file |
| com.microsoft.bmp | kUTTypeBMP | public.image | 'BMP', 'BMPf', .bmp | Windows bitmap image file |

**Table 8-2** Uniform Type Identifiers (UTIs) for Widely Useful File Types

| UTI | UTI Constant | Conforms to Type | Tags | Explanation |
|---|---|---|---|---|
| **Movie Files** | | | | |
| com.apple.quicktime-movie | kUTTypeQuickTimeMovie | public.movie | 'MooV', .mov, .qt, video/quicktime | QuickTime movie |
| public.avi | N/A | public.movie | .avi, .vfw, 'VfW', video/avi, video/msvideo, video/x-msvideo | AVI file |
| public.mpeg | kUTTypeMPEG | public.movie | 'MPG', 'MPEG', .mpg, .mpeg, .m75, .m15, video/mpg, video/mpeg, video/x-mpg, video/x-mpeg | MPEG-1 or MPEG-2 file |
| public.mpeg4 | kUTTypeMPEG4 | public.movie | 'mpg4', .mp4, video/mp4, video/mp4v | MPEG-4 file |
| **Audio Files** | | | | |
| public.mp3 | kUTTypeMP3 | public.audio | 'MPG3', 'mpg3', 'Mp3', 'MP3', 'mp3!', 'MP3!', .mp3, audio/mpeg, audio/mpeg3, audio/mpg, audio/mp3, audio/x-mpeg, audio/x-mpeg3, audio/x-mpg, audio/x-mp3 | MPEG-3 audio file or MP3 audio file |
| public.mpeg-4-audio | kUTTypeMPEG4Audio | public.audio, public.mpeg4 | 'M4A', .m4a | MPEG-4 audio file |
| public.aiff-audio | N/A | public.audio | .aiff, .aif, 'AIFF', audio/aiff, audio/x-AIFF | AIFF audio file |
| com.microsoft.waveform-audio | N/A | public.audio | .wav, .wave, 'WAV', 'WAVE', audio/wav, audio/wave | WAV audio file |

**Table 8-2** Uniform Type Identifiers (UTIs) for Widely Useful File Types (continued)

| UTI | UTI Constant | Conforms to Type | Tags | Explanation |
|---|---|---|---|---|
| **Microsoft Office Documents** | | | | |
| com.microsoft.word.doc | N/A | public.data | 'W8BN', .doc, application/msword | Microsoft Word document (.doc file extension) |
| com.microsoft.excel.xls | N/A | public.data | 'XLS8', .xls, application/vnd.ms-excel | Microsoft Excel document (.xls file extension) |
| com.microsoft.powerpoint.ppt | N/A | public.data, public.presentation | .ppt, 'SLD8', application/mspowerpoint | Microsoft PowerPoint presentation (.ppt file extension) |
| com.microsoft.word.openxml.document | N/A | public.data | N/A | Microsoft Word document (.docx file extension) |
| com.microsoft.excel.openxml.workbook | N/A | public.data | N/A | Microsoft Excel workbook (.xlsx file extension). |
| com.microsoft.powerpoint.openxml.presentation | N/A | public.data | N/A | Microsoft PowerPoint presentation (.pptx file extension) |
| **iWork Documents** | | | | |
| com.apple.iwork.pages.sffpages | N/A | N/A | .pages | Pages document files |
| com.apple.iwork.numbers.sffnumbers | N/A | N/A | .numbers | Numbers spreadsheet files |
| com.apple.iwork.numbers.sffkey | N/A | N/A | .key | Keynote presentation files |

**Table 8-2** Uniform Type Identifiers (UTIs) for Widely Useful File Types *(continued)*

## Letting the User Choose Two or More Files

In many scripts, you'll need to let the user choose only a single file each time you display the Choose A File dialog box. But in others, you'll need to let the user choose multiple files for the script to work on—for example, when the user is identifying a group of files for batch processing by your script.

To let the user choose multiple files, add the **with multiple selections allowed** parameter to the **choose file** command, like this:

```
choose file with prompt ¬
    "Choose the photos you want to crop to 4 x 3:" ¬
    default location (path to the pictures folder) ¬
    with multiple selections allowed ¬
    without invisibles
```

### NOTE

There's one other parameter for the **choose file** command: the **showing package contents** parameter. Add this parameter when you need the user to be able to poke inside package files and pick out files they contain. The contents of package files are normally hidden, but you can display them in the Finder by CTRL-clicking or right-clicking a package file and choosing Show Package Contents from the shortcut menu.

## Seeing Which File the User Chose

After the user picks a file in the Choose A File dialog box and clicks the Choose button, the **choose file** command returns an alias to the file—for example:

```
alias "Server:Docs:2010 Business Plan - rough.doc"
```

When you're dealing with a single file, often the easiest way of dealing with it is to assign the file to a variable, as in the Keynote example you saw earlier in this chapter:

```
set myKey to choose file ¬
    default location (alias "Server:Presentations:") ¬
    of type "com.apple.iwork.keynote.sffkey" ¬
    with prompt "Choose the presentation you want to duplicate:" ¬
    without invisibles
```

If you use the **with multiple selections allowed** parameter, AppleScript returns a list of the files selected, even if the user chose only a single file. Here's an example of a two-item list:

```
{alias "Server:Excel:2010 Budget - Final.xls", ¬
    alias "Server:Excel:2010 Budget by Department - HR.xls"}
```

To return one of the files, identify it by item—for example:

```
set myFile1 to item 1 of result
```

**Try This**  Letting the User Choose a File

In this example, you display the Choose A File dialog box and prompt the user to choose a text file. This example works with the Try This example in the section "Using the Choose Application Dialog Box to Open a Document in a Particular Application" later in this chapter, in which the user picks an application; the script then opens the text file using the application. Follow these steps:

1. Press ⌘-N or choose File | New to create a new script.

2. Start a **set** statement that assigns the result of the **choose file** command to a variable named **userFile**:

```
set userFile to choose file
```

3. Add the **of type** parameter to specify the file type you want the Choose A File dialog box to display, as shown in boldface here:

```
set userFile to choose file ¬
    of type "public.text"
```

4. Add the **with prompt** parameter and the text of the prompt, as shown in boldface here:

```
set userFile to choose file ¬
    of type "public.text" ¬
    with prompt "Choose the text file you want to open:"
```

5. Add the **default location** parameter and specify the path to the Documents folder, as shown in boldface here:

```
set userFile to choose file ¬
    of type "public.text" ¬
    with prompt "Choose the text file you want to open:" ¬
    default location (path to the Documents folder)
```

6. Add the **without invisibles** parameter to suppress the display of invisible files, as shown in boldface here:

```
set userFile to choose file ¬
    of type "public.text" ¬
    with prompt "Choose the text file you want to open:" ¬
    default location (path to the Documents folder) ¬
    without invisibles
```

7. Press ⌘-R or click the Run button on the toolbar to run the script. The Choose A File dialog box opens, as shown in Figure 8-22.

*(continued)*

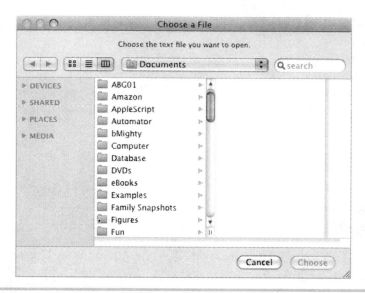

**Figure 8-22**  The Choose A File dialog box appears with your custom prompt and showing the contents of the Documents folder.

8. Navigate to a text file (go on, you must have one lurking somewhere), select it, and then click the Choose button.

9. Verify that the document's name and path appears in the Result pane.

10. Press ⌘-s and save this script under a name of your choice. Keep the script open so that you can add to it in the chapter's final Try This section.

## Letting the User Choose a Folder

To let the user choose a folder, use the **choose folder** command. This works in much the same way as the **choose file** command, so we'll just go over the parameters quickly here.

On its own, the **choose folder** command displays the Choose A Folder dialog box shown in Figure 8-23.

You can use the following parameters with the **choose folder** command:

● **with prompt**   Add this parameter and a text string to make the Choose A Folder dialog box display a prompt at the top. Adding a prompt is usually a good idea for clarity.

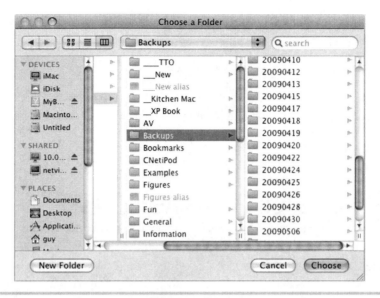

**Figure 8-23**  Without any parameters, the Choose A Folder dialog box displays no prompt and hides invisible folders.

- **default location**   Add this parameter and an alias to control which folder the Choose A Folder dialog box displays at first. In most cases, it's helpful to direct the user to the right place to start choosing a folder.

- **with invisibles/without invisibles**   Add the **with invisibles** parameter to make the Choose A Folder dialog box display invisible folders. Either omit the **invisibles** parameter or add **without invisibles** to make the dialog box hide invisible folders.

- **with multiple selections allowed**   Add this parameter if you want the user to be able to select multiple folders. Omit this parameter to allow the user to select only a single folder.

- **showing package contents**   Add this parameter if you want the Choose A Folder dialog box to show the contents of package files instead of hiding them (as it normally does).

For example, the following command displays the Choose A Folder dialog box with a custom prompt and showing the contents of a folder named Photos on a server:

```
choose folder ¬
    with prompt "Choose the folder to store the processed images in:" ¬
    default location alias "Server:Examples:Photos:"
```

When you use the **choose folder** command without the **with multiple selections allowed** parameter, it returns the alias to the folder chosen—for example:

```
alias "Server:Examples:Photos:Processed:"
```

When you use the **choose folder** command with the **with multiple selections allowed** parameter, it returns a list containing the alias to each folder chosen—for example:

```
{alias "Transfer:Examples:Photos:Processed:", ¬
    alias "Transfer:Examples:Photos:Second Generation:"}
```

## Letting the User Choose an Application

To let the user choose an application, use the **choose application** command.

When you use the command on its own, as in the following example, Mac OS X displays the Choose Application dialog box with the terse prompt "Select an application" (see Figure 8-24).

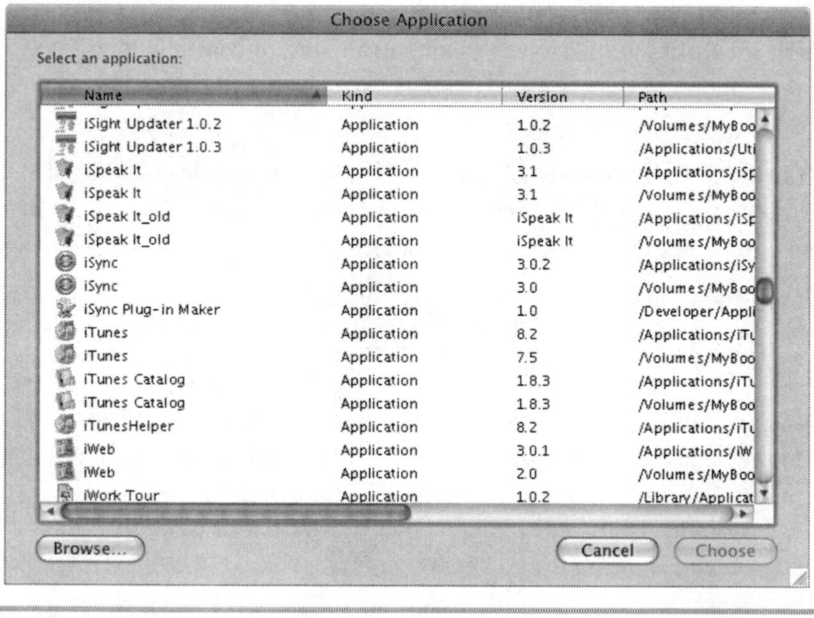

**Figure 8-24**   Display the Choose Application dialog box to let the user pick the application with which to perform a task.

### CAUTION
The first time you issue the **choose application** command, Mac OS X hunts for all the applications on the Mac's startup disk and other connected disks so that it can show them all in the dialog box. This may take a while, so be prepared to watch the "wait" cursor for a minute or two.

## Changing the Title and Prompt of the Choose Application Dialog Box

You can also customize the Choose Application dialog box by giving it your own title and prompt. These are the parameters to use:

- **with title**   Add this optional parameter and a string with the text you want to show in the title bar of the dialog box.

- **with prompt**   Add this optional parameter and a string with the text with which you want to replace the default prompt ("Select an application").

## Letting the User Choose Multiple Applications

AppleScript also lets you decide whether to let the user select multiple applications instead of just one. Usually, you'll want just a single application, and this is the default setting. To let the user choose multiple applications, add the **with multiple selections allowed** parameter:

```
choose application with multiple selections allowed
```

If you omit the **multiple selections allowed** parameter, AppleScript limits the user to a single selection.

## Getting an Alias to the Application Rather Than Launching It

Normally, when the user chooses an application in the Choose Application dialog box, Mac OS X launches the application. Sometimes this is handy, but other times, it may not be what you want.

Instead of letting the application launch, you can set the Choose Application dialog box up to return an alias to the application. You can then use this information as needed— for example, to run the application later rather than now. To return the alias, add the **as alias** parameter to the **choose application** command:

```
choose application as alias
```

## Try This Using the Choose Application Dialog Box to Open a Document in a Particular Application

In this example, you'll add to the script you created in the previous Try This section.

So far, the script displays the Choose A File dialog box, prompts the user to select a text file, and stores the file's details in a variable named userFile. Here, you will display the Choose Application dialog box, give it a custom title bar and prompt to make sure the user understands what to do with it, and then use the application returned to open the text file.

Follow these steps:

1. In AppleScript Editor, activate the script window containing the script you created in the previous Try This section.

2. At the end of the script, type a **set** statement to assign the result of the **choose application** command to the variable named **userApp**:

   ```
   set userApp to choose application
   ```

3. Add the **with title** parameter and a string to the statement, as shown in boldface here:

   ```
   set userApp to choose application ¬
       with title "Select Document Application"
   ```

4. Add the **with prompt** parameter and a suitable string, as shown in boldface here:

   ```
   set userApp to choose application ¬
       with title "Select Document Application" ¬
       with prompt "Select the TextEdit application and click the
   Choose button."
   ```

5. Add the **as alias** parameter:

   ```
   set userApp to choose application ¬
       with title "Select Document Application" ¬
       with prompt "Select the TextEdit application and click the
   Choose button." ¬
       as alias
   ```

6. Add a **tell** statement telling Finder to open **userFile** using **userApp**:

   ```
   tell application "Finder" to open userFile using userApp
   ```

7. Press ⌘-s to save the script.

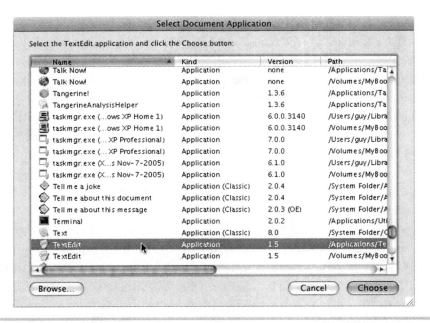

**Figure 8-25**   The Choose An Application dialog box appears with the custom title and prompt you set.

8. Press ⌘-R or click the Run button on the toolbar to run the script. The Choose A File dialog box appears as before. After you choose the text file and click the Choose button, the Select Document Application dialog box appears (see Figure 8-25).

9. Select the TextEdit application (if there's more than one, select the latest one on your Mac's hard disk), and then click the Choose button. AppleScript causes Finder to open the text file in TextEdit.

10. Quit TextEdit (for example, press ⌘-Q or choose TextEdit | Quit TextEdit).

## Letting the User Choose a URL

As you probably know, a URL is a *uniform resource locator*—in other words, the address of a file, website, or other resource on the Internet or another TCP/IP network.

When your script requires the user to choose a URL to which to connect, use the **choose URL** command. This command displays a dialog box that enables the user to either select a URL from a list you present to them or type a URL of his or her choosing. Your script can then use this URL as necessary—Mac OS X doesn't open a browser window to the URL automatically when the user dismisses the Choose URL dialog box.

If you use the **choose URL** command on its own, without any parameters, it displays a dialog box showing available file servers on the network to which your Mac is attached (see Figure 8-26). These are any Macs or other computers configured to offer file services on the network.

In most cases, you'll want to add the **showing** parameter with one of the items explained in Table 8-3.

Normally, the Server Address box at the top of the Choose URL dialog box is enabled so the user can type in a URL that doesn't appear in the list box. (Or, if the user is feeling ornery, he or she user can type in one of the listed URLs.) You can disable the Server Address box by adding the parameter **without editable URL** to the **choose URL** command. The box then appears without a black outline around it—a visual distinction subtle enough to be lost on many users, who will try to click in the box anyway.

The following example displays the Choose URL dialog box showing file servers and then mounts the chosen server using the **open location** command:

```
open location (choose URL showing File servers)
```

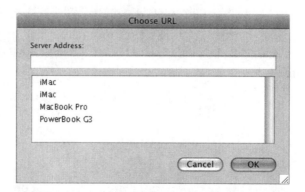

**Figure 8-26** Without any parameters, the **choose URL** command displays available file servers on your network.

| URL Item | Shows a List of |
|---|---|
| Web servers | http (unsecured) and https (secured) services |
| FTP servers | FTP (File Transfer Protocol) servers |
| Telnet hosts | telnet hosts (which are little used these days, largely because telnet has minimal security |
| File servers | File servers offering AFP (Apple File Protocol), NFS (Network File System), and SMB (Server Message Block) services. Each protocol appears as a different server, so if a computer is running both AFP and SMB, for example, it appears as two servers. |
| News servers | NNTP (Network News Transfer Protocol) servers |
| Directory services | LDAP (Lightweight Directory Access Protocol) services |
| Media servers | RTSP (Real Time Streaming Protocol) servers |
| Remote applications | Applications available for running on remote computers |

**Table 8-3**   URL Items for the **showing** Parameter of the **choose URL** command

# Chapter 9

## Repeating Actions in Your Scripts

## Key Skills & Concepts

- Understanding AppleScript's various kinds of loops

- Understanding what hard-coding is and when to use it

- Repeating actions with a **repeat** loop

- Repeating actions a set number of times with a **repeat… times** loop

- Repeating actions using a loop variable

- Repeating actions for each item in a list

- Repeating actions as long as a condition remains **true**

- Repeating actions as long as a condition remains **false**

To work swiftly and efficiently with multiple files, windows, or other objects, you'll often need to repeat one or more actions in your scripts. For example, you may need to process several files in Preview, or take the same action in a Microsoft Word document for every paragraph that's formatted with the Normal style. This chapter shows you how to repeat actions however many times you need using the various mechanisms that AppleScript provides.

## Getting an Overview of the Types of Loops That AppleScript Provides

AppleScript provides six different kinds of **repeat** loops.

- **repeat with a termination condition**   Lets you repeat a set of actions forever. You must set a condition to terminate the loop; otherwise, it won't stop running.

- **repeat a number of times**   Lets you repeat a set of actions the number of times specified by the number.

- **repeat with a counter variable**   Lets you repeat a set of actions using a counter variable. The counter variable starts at a start value, increases or decreases on each repetition, and ends the loop when it reaches the end value.

- **repeat for each item in a list**    Lets you repeat a set of actions for each item in a list. For example, if you create a list of documents, you can repeat the actions for each item in turn.

- **repeat as long as a condition is true**    Lets you run a set of actions if a condition is **true** and keep repeating the actions as long as the condition remains **true**.

- **repeat until a condition becomes true**    Lets you run a set of actions if a condition is **false** and keep repeating the actions until the condition becomes **true**.

# Understanding What Hard-Coding Is and When to Use It

The simplest way to repeat an action in AppleScript is to repeat the command for the action. This is called *hard-coding;* it's considered simplistic by most programmers, but it works well for simple tasks, and there's no reason why you shouldn't use it when it meets your needs.

For example, if you need to create two new documents in TextEdit, you can use a **tell** block such as this:

```
tell the application "TextEdit"
    make new document
    make new document
end tell
```

If your script always needs TextEdit to create two new documents, this code works fine. But if you need to make your code flexible—for example, so that it can tell TextEdit to create different numbers of new documents as necessary, or to work through each of the open documents before creating a new document—you can use loops to repeat actions instead.

### NOTE
A *loop* is a section of code that AppleScript can go around and repeat rather than simply going through. If the conditions are right, AppleScript repeats the loop; if not, it goes on to the code that appears after the end of the loop in the script.

# Repeating Actions Until a Termination Condition Becomes True

In many scripts, you'll need to repeat a set of actions until a condition becomes true. This condition is known as a *termination condition* because it causes the loop to terminate. For example, you could set a termination condition that stopped the loop after it had created a certain number of documents, or a condition that checked the time and stopped the loop from running at a particular moment.

### CAUTION

It's vital to use a termination condition with a plain **repeat** loop; otherwise, the loop will run forever (or until it encounters an error). If you forget to include a termination condition, or if your termination condition doesn't work the way you planned, press ⌘-. (⌘ and the period key) to end execution of the script. You'll then see an AppleScript Error alert telling you that "User canceled out of wait loop for reply or receipt," which is pretty good gobbledygook for your having sandbagged the script.

To repeat actions until a condition becomes true, you use a **repeat** loop. The loop's structure looks like this:

```
repeat
    actions
    [check the termination condition] exit repeat
end repeat
```

The **exit repeat** statement ends the execution of the **repeat** loop. The script continues running at the statement after the loop.

### NOTE

The **exit repeat** statement works for all kinds of **repeat** loops.

For example, the following script closes every Finder window except the front one:

```
tell the application "Finder"
    repeat
        if (count of Finder windows) is not greater than 1 then ¬
    exit repeat
        close the back Finder window
    end repeat
end tell
```

Here's how this works:

- The **if (count of Finder windows) is not greater than 1 then exit repeat** statement makes the script end when only one Finder window is left open or if no Finder window is open in the first place.

- If the script is still running, the **close the back Finder window** statement closes the Finder window at the back of the stack.

### NOTE

Instead of using **exit repeat** to exit the **repeat** loop, you can use a **return** statement to exit the **repeat** loop and end execution of the script. This statement is useful when you want to stop the script at the point where it exits the repeat loop rather than continuing with whichever statements follow the loop.

## Try This Using a repeat Loop to Close All Open Finder Windows Except One

In this example, you create a script that closes all open Finder windows except one. This script uses a **repeat** loop to close the windows.

To create the script, follow these steps:

1. In AppleScript Editor, press ⌘-N or choose File | New to create a new script.

2. Create a **tell** block to the Finder:

```
tell the application "Finder"

end tell
```

3. Inside the **tell** block, create a **repeat** block, as shown in boldface here:

```
tell the application "Finder"
    repeat
    end repeat
end tell
```

4. Inside the **repeat** block, add an **if** statement that gives the **exit repeat** command if the count of Finder windows is not greater than 1, as shown in boldface here:

```
tell the application "Finder"
    repeat
        if (count of Finder windows) is not greater than 1 ¬
    then exit repeat
    end repeat
end tell
```

5. Add the command for closing the back Finder window, as shown in boldface here:

```
tell the application "Finder"
    repeat
        if (count of Finder windows) is not greater than 1 ¬
    then exit repeat
        close the back Finder window
    end repeat
end tell
```

6. Open plenty of Finder windows for the script to close. The easiest way to do so is to click the Desktop or the Finder icon on the Dock and then keep pressing ⌘-N until doing so ceases to amuse you.

7. Press ⌘-R or click the Run button on the toolbar to run the script. Verify that it closes all but the frontmost Finder window.

8. Press ⌘-S and save the script under a name of your choice.

## Repeating Actions a Set Number of Times

To repeat a group of actions a set number of times, use a **repeat… times** loop.

A **repeat… times** loop looks like this:

```
repeat number times
    actions
end repeat
```

As you can see, this is very straightforward: You specify the number of times you want the loop to repeat, and AppleScript automatically counts that number of times. You don't need to use a counter variable or other means of tracking how many times the loop has run.

For example, the following script uses a **repeat 5 times** command to make TextEdit create five new documents and resize and reposition the window of each:

```
tell the application "TextEdit"
    repeat 5 times
        make new document at the front
        set the bounds of the front window to {1, 22, 400, 422}
    end repeat
end tell
```

How useful this type of hard-coded repetition is depends on the kinds of tasks you need to automate with AppleScript. In general, loops that have greater flexibility are more useful—but you can build some flexibility into a straightforward **repeat… times** loop by using a dialog box, as in the next Try This example.

## Try This   Using a repeat… times Loop Controlled by a Dialog Box

In this example, you create a **repeat… times** loop whose number of repetitions is controlled by a **choose from list** dialog box rather than being hard-coded in. The **choose from list** command (discussed in detail in Chapter 8) displays a list of choices (from which the user can pick only one) in a dialog box with a prompt and standard buttons (an OK button and a Cancel button), as shown in Figure 9-1.

Follow these steps to create the script:

1. In AppleScript Editor, press ⌘-N or choose File | New to create a new script.

2. Create the **choose from list** statement like this:

```
choose from list ¬
    {"1", "2", "3", "4", "5", "6", "7", "8", "9", "10"} ¬
    with prompt "Open this many TextEdit documents:"
```

3. Press ⌘-R or click the Run button on the toolbar to run the script. You'll see the **choose from list** dialog box. Click a number and click the OK button to dismiss the dialog box. Beyond returning your choice, the dialog box doesn't take any action because it's not hooked up to code.

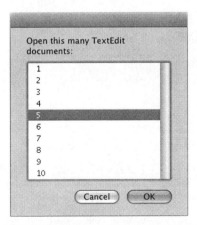

**Figure 9-1**   This choose from list dialog box lets the user pick how many times the repeat… times loop runs.

*(continued)*

4. Assign the result of the **choose from list** dialog box to a variable named **loopTimes**, as shown in boldface here:

```
set loopTimes to choose from list ¬
    {"1", "2", "3", "4", "5", "6", "7", "8", "9", "10"} ¬
    with prompt "Open this many TextEdit documents:"
```

5. Create a **tell** block for TextEdit, as shown in boldface here:

```
set loopTimes to choose from list ¬
    {"1", "2", "3", "4", "5", "6", "7", "8", "9", "10"} ¬
    with prompt "Open this many TextEdit documents:"
tell the application "TextEdit"

end tell
```

6. Add the **repeat... times** loop within the **tell** block, as shown in boldface here:

```
set loopTimes to choose from list ¬
    {"1", "2", "3", "4", "5", "6", "7", "8", "9", "10"} ¬
    with prompt "Open this many TextEdit documents:"
tell the application "TextEdit"
    repeat loopTimes times
        make new document at the front
    end repeat
end tell
```

7. Press ⌘-R or click the Run button on the toolbar to run the script. Choose a number in the **choose from list** dialog box, click the OK button, and verify that TextEdit creates the number of documents you chose.

8. Save the script under a name of your choice.

# Repeating Actions Using a Loop Controlled by a Loop Variable

Another way of controlling the number of times a loop repeats is to use a *loop variable*, a variable that AppleScript automatically changes on each iteration through the loop. You tell AppleScript the start value and end value for the loop variable; AppleScript starts the loop at the start value and runs it until it reaches the end value.

A loop controlled by a loop variable looks like this:

```
repeat with loop_variable from start_value to end_value [by increment]
    actions
end repeat
```

As you can see, this is pretty straightforward. You supply a name for the loop variable, such as **myCounter**, the start value (for example, 1), and the end value (for example, 10). Optionally, you can supply the increment, the number by which to increase or decrease the value of the loop variable. If you don't provide the increment, AppleScript increments the value by 1 on each iteration through the loop. This is nice, logical, and effective for many scripts.

Here's an example of a loop controlled by a loop variable using the default increment of 1. The code sets the **startvalue** variable to 1, prompts the user to choose the value of the **endvalue** variable from a **choose from list** dialog box, and then runs from the value of **startvalue** to the value of **endvalue**. On each iteration, AppleScript automatically increments the **numWindows** counter variable by 1:

```
set startvalue to 1
set endvalue to choose from list {"3", "4", "5", "6", "7"}
repeat with numWindows from startvalue to endvalue
    tell application "Finder" to make new Finder window
end repeat
```

# Ask the Expert

**Q:** **Can I make a loop run backward?**

**A:** Yes, if you need to.

The easiest way to make a loop run backward is to use a negative increment. To do this, just specify an increment with a negative number rather than a positive number.

For example, if you specify an increment of −1, each loop counts down by one: 10, 9, 8, 7, and so on. If you specify −2, each loop counts down by two: 10, 8, 6, and so on.

When you use a negative increment, you must make sure that the end value is lower than the start value. This is easy enough to do when you're paying attention, but it's easy enough to get wrong if you're working under pressure. So if you find your negative increments are sending your scripts into a terminal tailspin, double-check the end value against the start value.

Here's the example loop using the **by** parameter (shown in boldface) to increment the counter variable by 2 instead of the default 1:

```
set startvalue to 1
set endvalue to choose from list {"3", "4", "5", "6", "7"}
repeat with numWindows from startvalue to endvalue by 2
    tell application "Finder" to make new Finder window
end repeat
```

Here's the same loop back for a second encore using the **by** parameter with a negative value to decrement the counter variable by 1 instead of incrementing it. This example sets **startvalue** to 10 to ensure it is larger than **endvalue**. The changes appear in boldface:

```
set startvalue to 10
set endvalue to choose from list {"3", "4", "5", "6", "7"}
repeat with numWindows from startvalue to endvalue by -1
    tell application "Finder" to make new Finder window
end repeat
```

## Try This  Using a Loop Controlled by a Loop Variable

In this example, you create a loop controlled by a loop variable. The loop simply displays a dialog box showing the current value of the loop variable, allowing you to watch as it changes.

To create and run the script, follow these steps:

1. In AppleScript Editor, press ⌘-N or choose File | New to create a new script.

2. Type the following **repeat with** loop:

```
repeat with myCounter from 1 to 5
    display dialog myCounter
end repeat
```

3. Press ⌘-R or click the Run button on the toolbar to run the script. You'll see a dialog box showing the value assigned to the **myCounter** variable—1 on the first iteration.

4. Click the OK button to dismiss the dialog box. Back it comes in a moment, showing the next value of the **myCounter** variable: 2.

5. Continue until **myCounter** reaches 5; the script ends after you close the dialog box.

# Repeating Actions for Each Item in a List

AppleScript also gives you an easy way to repeat an action for each item in a list. This is great when you need to take the same action for each of the items because AppleScript automatically tracks its progress through the list so that you don't have to.

A loop controlled by a list looks like this:

```
repeat with list_item in list_items
    actions
end repeat
```

AppleScript performs one iteration of the **repeat** block for each individual item (*list_item*) in the list (*list_items*). The following example creates a list named **offices** with four entries (Ashland, Cupertino, Mendocino, and Sebastopol). The loop then repeats for each of the **office** items in the **offices** list—first Ashland, then Cupertino, and so on.

```
set offices to {"Ashland", "Cupertino", "Mendocino", "Sebastopol"}
repeat with office in offices
    set officename to contents of office
    tell application "TextEdit"
        make new document
        set the text of the front document to "Report for " ¬
        & officename & " office"
    end tell
end repeat
```

Inside the loop, the script sets the **officename** variable to the contents of the **office** item. This is because the **office** item contains a reference to the item rather than to the item's actual value. The script then tells TextEdit to make a new document and insert text in it ("Report for Ashland office," "Report for Cupertino office," and so on).

**Try This** ## Using a repeat with list Command to Close Some Finder Windows

In this example, you create a script that uses a **repeat with list** loop to close every Finder window that's open to your Documents folder (or any other folder named Documents) but leave all other Finder windows open.

Follow these steps to create the script:

**1.** In AppleScript Editor, press ⌘-N or choose File | New to create a new script.

**2.** Create a **tell** block to the Finder:

```
tell the application "Finder"

end tell
```

(continued)

3. Within the **tell** block, create a list named **windowNames** that gets the name of every open Finder window, as shown in boldface here:

```
tell the application "Finder"
    set windowNames to get the name of every window
end tell
```

4. Add a **repeat with list** loop that works with each **windowName** item in the **windowNames** list, as shown in boldface here:

```
tell the application "Finder"
    set windowNames to get the name of every window
    repeat with windowName in windowNames
    end repeat
end tell
```

5. Inside the **repeat** loop, add an **if** statement that compares the contents of **windowName** to **"Documents"** and closes the window identified by **windowName** if it matches. The **if** statement appears in boldface here:

```
tell the application "Finder"
    set windowNames to get the name of every window
    repeat with windowName in windowNames
        if contents of windowName is "Documents" then
            close window (windowName)
        end if
    end repeat
end tell
```

6. Open some Finder windows to various folders, including your Documents folder.

7. Press ⌘-R or click the Run button on the toolbar to run the script. Verify that the script closes all windows open to the Documents folder or other folders named Documents.

8. Save the script under a name of your choice.

# Repeating Actions as Long as a Condition Remains True

You can also control a loop by tying it to a condition evaluating to **true**. This kind of loop is called **repeat while**, and it stops as soon as the condition becomes **false**.

The **repeat while** loop looks like this:

```
repeat while condition
    actions
end repeat
```

The following example uses a **repeat while** loop to make sure five documents are open in TextEdit. If the **count of documents** is less than 5, the **repeat** loop makes TextEdit create a new document at the front.

```
tell the application "TextEdit"
    repeat while (count of documents) is less than 5
        make new document at the front
    end repeat
end tell
```

If the number of documents is already 5 or more, the condition evaluates as **false** and the code inside the loop doesn't run at all.

**Try This** Using a repeat while Loop

In this example, you create a script that uses a **repeat while** loop to make sure the user enters a code in the dialog box (see Figure 9-2) that prompts him or her for it. This example is simplistic, in that you would normally check the code further (for example, to make sure that it's valid, or at least that it's the right length), but it lets you put the **repeat while** loop into action.

Follow these steps to create the script:

1. In AppleScript Editor, press ⌘-N or choose File | New to create a new script.

2. Type a **set** statement that declares a variable named **employee_code** and sets its value to an empty string (""):

```
set employee_code to ""
```

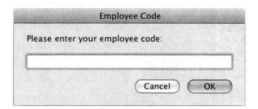

**Figure 9-2**    If the user clicks the OK button in the Employee Code dialog box without entering any text, the repeat while loop makes the dialog box appear again.

*(continued)*

3. Add a **repeat while** loop that runs as long as the value of the **employee_code** variable is an empty string, as shown in boldface here:

```
set employee_code to ""
repeat while employee_code is ""
end repeat
```

4. Inside the **repeat while** loop, add the statement for displaying the dialog box and assigning the **text** property of its **result** to the **employee_code** variable, as shown in boldface here:

```
set employee_code to ""
repeat while employee_code is ""
    display dialog ¬
        "Please enter your employee code:" default answer "" ¬
with title "Employee Code"
    set employee_code to the text returned of the result
end repeat
```

5. Press ⌘-R or click the Run button on the toolbar to run the script. When the Employee Code dialog box appears, click the OK button without entering text. AppleScript immediately displays the dialog box again.

6. This time, type one or more characters in the text-entry box, and then click the OK button. The dialog box closes and doesn't reappear.

7. Save the script under a name of your choice.

# Repeating Actions Until a Condition Becomes True

The last way of controlling loops in AppleScript is by repeating the loop as long as a specified condition is **false** and stopping when the condition becomes **true**. This type of loop is called **repeat until**, and it's similar to the **repeat while** loop; often, you can achieve the same effect with both types of loops by structuring the condition differently.

The **repeat until** loop looks like this:

```
repeat until condition
    actions
end repeat
```

The following example uses a **repeat until** loop to close Finder windows until only one is left open:

```
tell the application "Finder"
    repeat until (count of Finder windows) is not greater than 1
        close the back Finder window
    end repeat
end tell
```

As with the **repeat while** loop, if the condition evaluates as **true** on the first check, the code inside the loop doesn't run at all.

## Try This | Using a repeat until Loop

In this example, you change the **repeat while** loop you created in the previous Try This example into a **repeat until** loop. Follow these steps:

1. Open the script you created in the previous Try This example.

2. Press ⌘-**SHIFT-S** or choose File | Save As to display the Save As dialog box. Save the script under a different name. The script looks like this:

```
set employee_code to ""
repeat while employee_code is ""
    display dialog ¬
        "Please enter your employee code:" default answer "" ¬
with title "Employee Code"
    set employee_code to the text returned of the result
end repeat
```

3. Edit the **repeat while employee_code is ""** statement to make it a **repeat until** statement. The changes appear in boldface here; the rest of the script remains the same.

```
repeat until employee_code is not ""
```

4. Press ⌘-**R** or click the Run button on the toolbar to run the script. You'll find it behaves in the same way as before.

5. Save the changes to the script.

# Chapter 10

## Debugging and Handling Errors

## Key Skills & Concepts

- Understanding AppleScript errors

- Suppressing an error with a **try** block

- Creating an error handler

- Finding out which errors you need

- Making your scripts resistant to errors

In the best of all possible worlds, you'll write perfect code that always runs smoothly under ideal conditions. But in the real world, your code will run into pitfalls and speed bumps as it executes, so it needs to be able to handle errors that occur.

The easiest way to handle an error is to suppress it by using a **try** block, but what you'll usually want to do is add error-handling code to your scripts. An error handler enables a script to handle errors gracefully, no matter whether they're built-in AppleScript errors or custom errors that you cook up yourself.

First, though, you need to know what happens when an error occurs. Let's start there.

# Understanding What Happens When an Error Occurs

When an error occurs, the script crashes. For example, if you tell an application to do something impossible, such as to open a file that doesn't exist, it returns an error.

Figure 10-1 shows an example of a typical error message. The message—*TextEdit got an error: Can't get document 1. Invalid index*—is intelligible enough if you know what the script is trying to do, which is to perform an action on the front document. TextEdit can't get (return) document 1 because the index number is invalid—in other words, there's no front document in TextEdit at the moment. But when a user of the script runs into the error, the message will probably mean little to him or her ("an index of invalids?"), and will be about as welcome as a fly in the soup.

AppleScript makes an exception to a script crashing when an error occurs. When the user clicks the Cancel button in a dialog box, AppleScript returns a special error, error –128, which doesn't raise an error dialog box. Instead, when error –128 occurs, AppleScript quietly stops running the script.

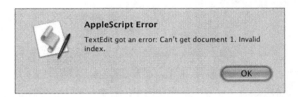

**Figure 10-1**    When a script runs into an error, it displays an error message.

You've seen this behavior already in this book, where you used an OK/Cancel dialog box to let the user choose whether to run a script or cancel out of it. As you'll see later in this chapter, you can check for this special error and take advantage of it in your scripts.

## Try This Causing Errors Deliberately

In this example, you cause two errors deliberately in a script and watch how AppleScript handles them. Follow these steps:

1. In AppleScript Editor, press ⌘-N or choose File | New to create a new script.

2. Type the following short script, which tells the Finder to close every Finder window and then return the position of the front window. This is guaranteed to cause an error every time.

```
tell application "Finder"
    close every Finder window
    get the position of the front Finder window
end tell
```

3. Press ⌘-R or click the Run button on the toolbar to run the script. You'll get an AppleScript Error message, as shown in Figure 10-2.

4. Click the OK button to dismiss the error message.

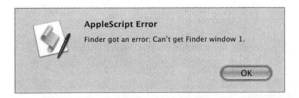

**Figure 10-2**    The sample script produces an error message because it tries to return the position of the front Finder window when no Finder window is open.

*(continued)*

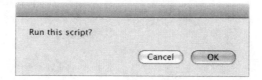

**Figure 10-3**   Click the Cancel button in the dialog box to produce an error that stops the script from running.

5. At the beginning of the script, add a **display dialog** statement that prompts the user to run this script, as shown in boldface here:

```
display dialog "Run this script?"
tell application "Finder"
    close every Finder window
    get the position of the front Finder window
end tell
```

6. Run the script. The dialog box appears, as shown in Figure 10-3.

7. Click the Cancel button. Notice that the script simply stops running and doesn't execute the **tell** block to the Finder.

8. Save the script under a name of your choice.

9. Leave the script open so that you can work with it in the next Try This example.

# Suppressing an Error with a Try Block

The first stage of handling errors in your scripts is to prevent the user from seeing them. To do this, you use a **try** block. When an error occurs in a **try** block, AppleScript ignores the error, goes to the end of the **try** block, and keeps on running the script.

A **try** block starts with the **try** statement and ends with the **end try** statement, like this:

```
try
end try
```

Inside the block goes the statement or statements that may cause the error, like this:

```
try
    tell application "Finder"
        get the position of the front Finder window
    end tell
end try
```

The key thing to remember about **try** blocks is that as soon as an error occurs, AppleScript stops executing the statements in the **try** block and continues with the statement after the **end try** statement. This means that you need to arrange your **try** blocks carefully to make sure that an error doesn't cause AppleScript to skip any vital statements: Simply placing the whole of a script inside a **try** block doesn't usually do much good unless the script contains only a single command that you care about.

You can put **try** blocks in sequence, as you'll see in the next example. You can also nest one **try** block inside another **try** block, as shown in boldface here:

```
try
    tell application "Finder"
        get the position of the front Finder window
        try
            set the target of the front Finder window ¬
                to folder "Sludge" of folder "Documents" of home
        end try
        set the bounds of the front Finder window to {0, 44, 800, 844}
    end tell
end try
```

If the current user's Documents folder doesn't contain a folder named Sludge (and no, mine doesn't either), the inner **try** block captures the error, so the **set the bounds of the front Finder window** statement still runs.

## Try This Adding a Try Block to a Script

In this example, you add a **try** block to the script you created in the previous example. Follow these steps:

**1.** Activate the window that contains the script you created in the previous example.

**2.** Type two hyphens to comment out the **display dialog** statement at the beginning, as shown in boldface here:

```
-- display dialog "Run this script?"
tell application "Finder"
    close every Finder window
    get the position of the front Finder window
end tell
```

**3.** Place a **try** block around the **tell** block, as shown in boldface here:

```
-- display dialog "Run this script?"
try
tell application "Finder"
```

*(continued)*

```
      close every Finder window
      get the position of the front Finder window
   end tell
end try
```

4. Click the Compile button on the toolbar or press ⌘-K to compile the script. AppleScript Editor indents the **tell** block to make the script's hierarchy clear:

```
-- display dialog "Run this script?"
try
    tell application "Finder"
        close every Finder window
        get the position of the front Finder window
    end tell
end try
```

5. Press ⌘-R or click the Run button on the toolbar to run the script. Notice that AppleScript displays no error message, even though the script tries to return the position of a Finder window that isn't open.

6. Open a few Finder windows. For example, click the Finder button on the Dock, and then press ⌘-N a few times.

7. Delete the two hyphens to uncomment the **display dialog** statement, and then put it in its own **try** block. The changes appear in boldface here:

```
try
    display dialog "Run this script?"
end try
try
    tell application "Finder"
        close every Finder window
        get the position of the front Finder window
    end tell
end try
```

8. Press ⌘-R or click the Run button on the toolbar to run the script. When the dialog box appears, click the Cancel button.

9. Notice that even though you canceled the dialog box, the script continues to run and closes all the Finder windows you opened. This is because the **try** block around the **display dialog** statement captures the error from the Cancel button.

10. Press ⌘-S to save the changes you've made to the script.

# Creating an Error Handler

As you've seen earlier in this chapter, a **try** block is a handy tool for trapping an error that occurs in a script and preventing it from troubling the user. But what you'll often want to do is create an error handler that lets you deal with the error in a smart way. The error handler grabs the details of the error; you can then check which number the error has, which tells you what has gone wrong and enables you to decide what to do about it.

## Understanding the Basics of Error Handlers

To create an error handler, you add an **on error** statement within a **try** block. Normally, you want to put the **on error** statement and the commands it executes directly before the **end try** statement for the **try** block, without any other commands that aren't related to the error handler after them. Here's the basic layout for an error handler:

```
try
    -- commands that may produce errors
on error
    -- commands for dealing with the errors
end try
```

### NOTE
You can use the **on error** statement only within a **try** block.

## Returning the Error Number and Error Message

The form of the **on error** statement shown in the previous section is stripped down to its essentials—only the keywords **on error**. What you'll usually want to do is return the number of the error that has occurred and the message that explains what the error is.

To return the error number, add the **number** parameter and the name of the variable in which you want to store the error. The following example uses the variable name **myErrorNumber**:

```
on error number myErrorNumber
```

To return the error message as well, you add not another parameter called something like "message" (as you might expect), but just another variable to contain the message—and you put it *before* the **number** parameter rather than after it. The following example uses the variable name **myErrorMessage**:

```
on error myErrorMessage number myErrorNumber
```

This looks odd, but it works just fine. This type of parameter without a name is called the *direct parameter.*

## Dealing with the Error

When you know which errors your error handler needs to trap, you can write statements that deal with them.

Depending on what the script is doing, you may need to deal with only a single error or with handfuls of different errors. If you've established that the script can easily produce a wide variety of errors, you may choose to handle only those that are most likely to occur and alert the user to a problem if they contrive to produce one of the unusual errors.

The following example is for a script that tries to delete a specific file. Various errors can occur when you try to delete a file, but here are the two errors with which the script is designed to deal:

- **Error –1728**   This error has the message "Finder got an error. Can't get file" followed by the name of the file that's presumably cavorting around somewhere else. The error occurs when Finder can't find the file you've told it to manipulate. This can mean that the file isn't in the folder, or that the folder name is wrong.

- **Error –45**   This error has the message "The operation could not be completed because the file *filename* is locked." The error occurs when the script tries to perform an action that doesn't work with a locked file, such as deleting it or moving it.

Once you've grabbed the error number (and the error message, if you care to get that too), you can check the error number and take action accordingly. Here's what happens in the following script:

- The **try** block starts at the beginning and ends at the end.

- The **tell** block tells the Finder to delete a file—the file named **Picture 5** and stored on the Desktop. If the Finder finds the file and deletes it, all is well. Otherwise, the error handler runs.

- The **on error myErrorMessage number myErrorNumber** statement begins the error handler. This statement assigns the error message to the variable **myErrorMessage** and the error number to the variable **myErrorNumber**.

- The **if** statement checks to see whether **myErrorNumber** is equal to 1728, the error that means the Finder couldn't find the file. If so, the script displays an alert (see Figure 10-4) explaining the problem and asking the user to check the filename, and then the error handler ends.

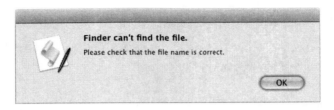

**Figure 10-4**   The script displays this alert if the Finder can't find the file it's supposed to delete.

- If the **if** statement isn't **true**, the **else if** statement runs. This statement checks to see whether **myErrorNumber** is equal to –45, the error that means the Finder couldn't delete the file because it was locked. If this is the error number, the script displays an alert (see Figure 10-5) telling the user what is amiss and asking them to unlock the file.

- If the **else if** statement isn't **true** either, the **else** statement displays an alert saying that the script cannot delete the file and showing the error message for the error that has occurred.

```
try
    tell the application "Finder"
        delete file "Picture 5" of desktop
    end tell
on error myErrorMessage number myErrorNumber
    if myErrorNumber is equal to -1728 then
        display alert "Finder can't find the file." ¬
            message "Please check that the file name is correct."
    else if myErrorNumber is equal to -45 then
        display alert "The file is locked" message ¬
            "Please unlock the file and run this script again."
    else
        display alert "Cannot delete the file" ¬
            message "The following error occurred:" ¬
            & return & return & myErrorMessage
    end if
end try
```

**Figure 10-5**   The script displays this alert if the file is locked.

**Try This** Building an Error Handler

In this example, you create the error handler shown in the previous section but adapt it to work with a file on your Mac. Follow these steps:

1. In AppleScript Editor, press ⌘-N or choose File | New to create a new script.

2. Type the code shown in the previous section.

3. Edit the **delete file** statement near the beginning so that it works with a file in your file system that you're prepared to delete.

   ● Unless you've recently emptied the Trash, the easiest way to pick a victim is to open the Trash and then drag a file from it to your Desktop.

   ● If the Trash is empty, open a Finder window to a folder that contains a blameless file. Press ⌘-D to duplicate the file, and then drag the duplicate to your Desktop so that you'll remember to get rid of it later if the script doesn't trash it for you.

4. Lock the file on your Desktop. Click the file, press ⌘-I to display the Info window, and then select the Locked check box. Leave the Info window open for the time being.

5. Press ⌘-R or click the Run button on the toolbar to run the script. Because the file is locked, AppleScript cannot delete it, so error –45 occurs, and the alert warning that the file is locked appears.

6. In the Info window, clear the Locked check box to unlock the file, and then close the Info window.

7. Press ⌘-R or click the Run button on the toolbar to run the script again. This time, the script deletes the file, and you will see it disappear from your Desktop.

8. Press ⌘-R or click the Run button on the toolbar to run the script a third time. Because the file is no longer there, error –1728 occurs, and AppleScript displays the alert warning you that Finder cannot find the file.

9. Save the script under a name of your choice.

# Finding Out Which Errors You Need

To deal effectively with errors in your scripts, you need to find out which errors are likely to occur, and then build handlers for them.

## Handling a Cancel Button in a Dialog Box

The error that's most likely to occur in any script that uses a dialog box is error –128. As you saw earlier in this chapter, this is the error that occurs when the user clicks the Cancel button, and it has special status: AppleScript doesn't display an error dialog box, the way it does for other errors, but simply stops running the code. So the user gets to see neither the error number nor its message, *User canceled,* which is laconic but mostly unambiguous.

To prevent the click of a Cancel button from stopping a script in its tracks, put the command for the dialog box (the **display dialog** command, the **display alert** command, the **choose from list** command, or whatever) inside a **try** block. Include an **on error number –128** statement to test whether the user has clicked the Cancel button, and then take action accordingly.

The following example shows a **try** block set up this way. The **display dialog** statement craftily includes only a Cancel button, so that's all the user has to click. When error –128 occurs, the **on error number –128** error handler catches it. You can then take whatever action is necessary; in the example, the script simply displays a dialog box with the information that the user clicked the Cancel button.

```
try
    display dialog "Cancel me!" buttons {"Cancel"}
on error number -128
    -- take other actions here instead of display dialog
    display dialog "User clicked the Cancel button." buttons {"OK"}
end try
```

## Identifying Errors by Running a Script

Often, the best way to find out which errors are likely to occur is to run a script under the wrong conditions and see what happens. For example, in a script that creates a document and saves it to a folder, you may need to trap errors such as these:

- The folder doesn't exist in the file system.

- A document of the same name is already lurking in the folder.

Besides producing as many errors as you can while developing and testing your script, you may also need to update your scripts when users produce new errors. Many hands make light work, but many users whaling on your scripts in creative ways will likely produce errors you had never considered.

## Looking Up Errors in the Application's Documentation

Another approach is to look up the errors in the application's documentation. This should give you a clear picture of the hundreds of different errors that can (but usually don't) occur, but it may make it harder to zero in on those errors that users are actually likely to produce when they run your scripts.

## Creating Your Own Errors

When you're starting to build scripts in AppleScript, chances are you'll cause plenty of errors—some by accident, as you figure out what works and what doesn't, and others deliberately, as you explore the errors that can crop up as a particular script runs.

These errors you run into will be ones built into AppleScript and the applications you're using. But you can also define your own errors using AppleScript's **error** command. This lets you produce a custom error suited to your script. (You can also produce custom errors to confuse users of your scripts, but the entertainment will probably pall when they come to you for help.)

### NOTE

Generating an error is sometimes called *throwing* an error.

The **error** command works in much the same way as the **on error** command.

- Start the **error** statement with the **error** keyword.

  ```
  error
  ```

- Add a string containing the message for the error. As with the **error** command, the message is a direct parameter and doesn't have a parameter keyword, such as "message," as parameters usually do.

  ```
  error "Your Mac does not have an Intel processor."
  ```

- Add the **number** parameter and the number you want to give the error. You can choose your own error number freely—you don't have to apply in triplicate to a bureaucracy for it—but it's best to stay out of the ranges that most applications use: negative numbers, and 0 to 500 on the positive side.

  ```
  error "Your Mac does not have an Intel processor." number 501
  ```

***NOTE***

AppleScript gives your error the generic error number, –2700, if you don't assign an error number—so you should always assign one. Likewise, you should always assign an error message; if you don't, AppleScript gives your error a blank string, which is no help to man, beast, or Mac.

Here's a code snippet that checks two properties of the **system info** command and throws an error if the system isn't deemed rugged, windswept, and handsome enough to run a putative demanding application. These are the two **system info** properties used:

- **CPU type**   This property returns a string describing the CPU type—for example, **Intel 80486** for a Core 2 Duo CPU (*not* one of the 486-numbered chips that preceded the first Pentiums) or **PowerPC 7450** for an ageing PowerBook's overwhelmed G4 processor.

- **CPU speed**   This property returns an integer giving the CPU speed in megahertz— for example, **2000** for a 2GHz chip, or **999** for a 1GHz chip.

Here's what the code does:

- First, it assigns the **CPU type** to the variable **thisCPU** and the **CPU speed** to the variable **thisMHz**.

- The outer **if** statement then checks to see if **thisCPU** starts with **PowerPC**; if so, the first **error** statement runs, throwing an error with a message about this not being an Intel processor (see Figure 10-6).

- If the processor passes the PowerPC test, the nested **if** statement checks to see whether **thisMHz** is less than **2000**. If the CPU is slower than 2GHz, the second **error**

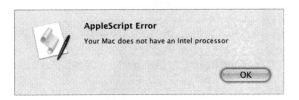

**Figure 10-6**   You can assign any string to a custom error message.

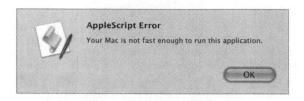

**Figure 10-7**   A custom error message appears as a genuine AppleScript error, just like built-in errors your scripts encounter.

statement runs, causing an error with a message about the Mac not being fast enough (see Figure 10-7).

```
set thisCPU to the CPU type of (system info)
set thisMHz to the CPU speed of (system info)
if thisCPU starts with "PowerPC" then
    error "Your Mac does not have an Intel processor" number 501
else
    if thisMHz < 2000 then
        error "Your Mac is not fast enough to run this
application." number 555
    end if
end if
```

Errors you produce may be custom, but they're not fake: AppleScript treats a custom error in exactly the same way as a built-in error, bringing the script to a screeching halt and putting up a dialog box on screen to warn the user what has happened. This means you need to handle your custom errors in the same way as built-in errors—by putting them inside **try** blocks, and by building error handlers to catch and process them.

Here is an example of trapping the two custom errors and displaying an alert (see Figure 10-8) that covers them both. The lines in boldface are the ones added to the previous code snippet to create the error handler:

```
try
    set thisCPU to the CPU type of (system info)
    set thisMHz to the CPU speed of (system info)
    if thisCPU starts with "PowerPC" then
        error "Your Mac does not have an Intel processor" number 501
    else
        if thisMHz < 2000 then
            error "Your Mac is not fast enough to run this
application." number 555
        end if
    end if
on error myErrorMessage number myErrorNumber
```

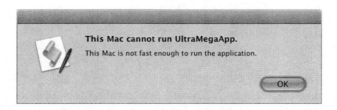

**Figure 10-8** With an error handler added, the script displays an alert that encompasses both custom error messages.

```
    if myErrorNumber is equal to 501 or ¬
        myErrorNumber is equal to 555 then
        display alert "This Mac cannot run UltraMegaApp." ¬
            message "This Mac is not fast enough to run the
application."
    end if
end try
```

# Making Your Scripts Resistant to Errors

Just as it's a good idea to boost your immune system with sleep, sunlight, and vitamins and to vaccinate yourself (or preferably your children) against standard diseases, so should you try to make your scripts resistant to errors. This section shows you three ways of doing so:

● Making sure an item exists before you try to use it.

● Referring to an application by its formal name rather than its common name.

● Breaking up a script into subroutines.

These methods of resisting errors are a solid start, not a panacea. Even if you use them religiously, you may run into unexpected errors, just as swine flu or avian flu may turn up and brush aside all your health precautions.

## Verifying That an Item Exists Before You Use It

Because your scripts will often run under conditions you don't control, you can save yourself a great deal of grief by verifying that an item exists before you try to use it. For example, instead of producing an error by trying to close a window that isn't open, you can check to see if the window is open, and then close it only if it is.

To see whether an item exists, use the **exists** command. This returns **true** if the item exists and **false** if it doesn't. For example, the following **tell** block uses **exists** to find out whether the current user's ~/Documents/ folder contains a folder named Temp. If the folder doesn't exist, AppleScript creates it:

```
tell the application "Finder"
    if not (exists folder "Temp" of folder "Documents" of home) then
        make new folder of folder "Documents" of home ¬
        with properties {name:"Temp"}
    end if
end tell
```

Similarly, the following **tell** block makes TextEdit check whether there's a **front document** before attempting to assign text to it:

```
tell the application "TextEdit"
    if exists front document then
        set the text of the front document to ¬
        "Bankers' Remuneration Policy"
    end if
end tell
```

The **exists** command works widely in AppleScript, and you can spare yourself plenty of errors by using it to look before you leap.

## Referring to an Application by Its Formal Name

So far in this book, we've used the names of applications to refer to them. For example, to make the application TextEdit take an action, we've used a **tell** block to the **application "TextEdit"**:

```
tell the application "TextEdit"
    -- do something or other here
end tell
```

This means of referring to an application is straightforward and works fine as long as there's an application with the name you use. If there's no application with that name, AppleScript displays the Choose Application dialog box to let you pick the application, which is much neater than displaying an error dialog box that merely chastises you for using the wrong name. (If you cancel the Choose Application dialog box, AppleScript does give you that error.)

To make sure you get the application you intend, you can use the application's **id** property. This property returns what's known as its *bundle identifier* for recent applications; if the application doesn't have a bundle identifier, the **id** property returns the *creator code* instead, an older means of identifying an application. A bundle identifier takes the form **com.apple.iTunes** (for iTunes), while a creator code is a four-letter string—for example, **XCEL** for Microsoft Office Excel 2004 for Mac.

To communicate with the application, use a **tell** statement with **application id** and the application's bundle identifier or creator code as a string. For example, to tell iTunes to do something:

```
tell the application id "com.apple.iTunes"
end tell
```

Here's an example using the creator code, which works in just the same way:

```
tell the application id "XCEL"
end tell
```

To find out the bundle identifier or creator code for an application, return its **id** property. For example, the following statement returns the bundle identifier of iTunes:

```
get id of application "iTunes"
```

For quick reference, Table 10-1 lists the bundle identifier or creator code that the **id** property returns for a slew of the most widely used applications.

| Application Name | Bundle Identifier | Creator Code |
| --- | --- | --- |
| Activity Monitor | com.apple.ActivityMonitor | — |
| Address Book | com.apple.AddressBook | — |
| AppleScript Editor | com.apple.ScriptEditor2 | — |
| Automator | com.apple.Automator | — |
| Backup | com.apple.Backup | — |
| Calculator | com.apple.calculator | — |
| Camino | org.mozilla.camino | — |
| Dashboard | com.apple.dashboardlauncher | — |
| Dictionary | com.apple.Dictionary | — |
| Exposé | com.apple.exposelauncher | — |
| Firefox | org.mozilla.firefox | — |
| Front Row | com.apple.frontrow | — |
| GarageBand | com.apple.garageband | — |
| iCal | com.apple.ical | — |
| iChat | com.apple.ichat | — |
| iDVD | com.apple.iDVD | — |
| Image Capture | com.apple.ImageCaptureApp | — |
| iMovie '09 | com.apple.iMovie8 | — |

**Table 10-1**  Bundle Identifiers and Creator Codes for Widely Used Applications

| Application Name | Bundle Identifier | Creator Code |
|---|---|---|
| iPhoto | com.apple.iPhoto | — |
| iTunes | com.apple.iTunes | — |
| iWeb | com.apple.iWeb | — |
| Keynote | com.apple.iWork.Keynote | — |
| Mail | com.apple.mail | — |
| Microsoft Entourage 2004 | — | OPIM |
| Microsoft Entourage 2008 | com.microsoft.Entourage | — |
| Microsoft Excel 2004 | — | XCEL |
| Microsoft Excel 2008 | com.microsoft.Excel | — |
| Microsoft PowerPoint 2004 | — | PPT3 |
| Microsoft PowerPoint 2008 | com.microsoft.PowerPoint | — |
| Microsoft Word 2004 | — | MSWD |
| Microsoft Word 2008 | com.microsoft.Word | — |
| Numbers | com.apple.iWork.Numbers | — |
| OpenOffice.org | org.openoffice.script | — |
| Pages | com.apple.iWork.Pages | — |
| Preview | com.apple.Preview | — |
| QuickTime Player | com.apple.quicktimeplayer | — |
| Remote Desktop Connection | com.microsoft.rdc | — |
| Safari | com.apple.safari | — |
| Screen Sharing | com.apple.ScreenSharing | — |
| Spaces | com.apple.spaceslauncher | — |
| System Preferences | com.apple.systempreferences | — |
| Terminal | com.apple.Terminal | — |
| TextEdit | com.apple.TextEdit | — |
| Time Machine | com.apple.backup.launcher | — |

**Table 10-1** Bundle Identifiers and Creator Codes for Widely Used Applications *(continued)*

### CAUTION

Even the bundle identifiers and creator codes don't work entirely as they should. For example, Microsoft Office Excel 2004 has the creator code XCEL, while Microsoft Office Excel 2008 has the bundle identifier **com.microsoft.Excel**. If you have both of these versions of Office on the same Mac, telling the application with the **id "com.microsoft.Excel"** to activate normally launches Excel 2008—but so does telling the application with the **id "XCEL"** to activate.

# Breaking Up a Script into Subroutines

The third technique for making your code more resilient is to make it *modular,* dividing it up into separate parts that perform different tasks. Each part is called a *subroutine,* performs a specific function when you call it, and returns a result. After breaking up your code, you run whichever of the subroutines you need in order to get a single larger task done.

Making your code modular makes each section easier to debug—because there's less in any part of it to go wrong, you should be able to iron out any problems more quickly. And it enables you to repeat actions wherever needed by simply calling the relevant subroutine rather than having to add the same code to your script again.

To create a subroutine, you make the relevant code into its own block, starting with an **on** keyword, the name you want to give the subroutine, and a pair of parentheses. The subroutine ends with the **end** keyword and the subroutine's name again to make clear what's ending. For example, here's the shell of a subroutine named **get_user_name**, which returns the short user name from the System Info:

```
on get_user_name()

end get_user_name
```

## NOTE

You can use the **to** keyword instead of the **on** keyword to start a subroutine. In general, the **on** keyword is more widely used, and this book follows that practice.

Within the shell, you enter the statements that the subroutine executes. For example, if you just want the **get_user_name** subroutine to display a dialog box showing the "short user name" of the current user (this is the name used for the user account, not the full name, which is usually longer), you can create a subroutine like this:

```
on get_user_name()
    display dialog short user name of (system info)
end get_user_name
```

If you just create a subroutine like this in AppleScript Editor and click the Run button, the code won't run. To make the subroutine run, you need to *call* the subroutine from the main part of the script. To call the subroutine, you just enter its name in the main part of the script, followed by parentheses, as shown in boldface here:

```
get_user_name()

on get_user_name()
    display dialog short user name of (system info)
end get_user_name
```

When the script reaches the call to the subroutine, it hops to the **on** statement, then runs the statements inside the subroutine. When it hits the **end** statement for the subroutine, it picks up at the next command after the one that called the subroutine. (There's no next command here, but you get the idea.)

The parentheses after the subroutine's name have a certain grotesque elegance, but aren't merely decorative: You use them to pass any parameters to the subroutine. For example, the following code creates a variable named **mySpeed** and sets its value to 99, then passes **mySpeed** to the **howfast()** subroutine, which expects a **Speed** parameter. The subroutine evaluates the value passed to it and then returns the result (in this case, **"Medium"**).

```
set mySpeed to 99
howfast(mySpeed)

on howfast(Speed)
    if Speed < 50 then
        return "Slow"
    else if Speed < 100 then
        return "Medium"
    else
        return "Dangerous"
    end if
end howfast
```

When you pass parameters like this, you must pass the same number of parameters and pass them in the same order as the subroutine is expecting them. Separate the parameters with commas.

## Try This Creating a Subroutine

In this example, you create a subroutine for trimming any leading spaces or trailing spaces off a string of text. As mentioned in Chapter 5, trimming off spaces is useful when you need to make sure that a string of text you use doesn't start or end with a space—for example, to avoid layout problems in documents or errors in sorting.

To create the subroutine, follow these steps:

1. In AppleScript Editor, press ⌘-N or choose File | New to create a new script.

2. Create the variable **myString** and assign to it the word *agriculture* with several leading spaces and several trailing spaces.

   ```
   set myString to "      agriculture      "
   ```

**3.** Add a **display dialog** statement to a dialog box that contains the trimmed version of the **myString** variable between two pairs of asterisks, as shown in boldface here. The dialog box shows you the effect of the trimming, with the asterisks making it easier to see that there are no spaces. To call the subroutine, this statement uses the subroutine's name (**trim**) and passes the variable to it as the string to trim.

```
set myString to "    agriculture    "
display dialog "**" & trim(myString) & "**"
```

**4.** Type the **on trim(myString)** statement to begin the subroutine and the **end** statement to end it, as shown in boldface here:

```
set myString to "    agriculture    "
display dialog "**" & trim(myString) & "**"

on trim(myString)
end
```

**5.** Press ⌘-K or click the Compile button on the toolbar to compile the script. AppleScript Editor automatically adds **trim** to the **end** statement to make clear what's ending, as shown in boldface here:

```
set myString to "    agriculture    "
display dialog "**" & trim(myString) & "**"

on trim(myString)
end trim
```

**6.** Inside the **trim** subroutine, type a **repeat** loop that runs until **myString** doesn't end with a space. As long as this condition isn't met, the statement inside the loop sets **myString** to **text 1 through −2 of myString**, thus shortening it by one character each time. The **repeat** loop appears in boldface here:

```
set myString to "    agriculture    "
display dialog "**" & trim(myString) & "**"

on trim(myString)
    repeat until myString does not end with " "
        set myString to text 1 through -2 of myString
    end repeat
end trim
```

**7.** Below the first **repeat** loop, type a second **repeat** loop. This one works in a similar way, but with the beginning of the string: Until the **first character of myString is not** **" "** (a space), the **set myString to text 2 through −1 of myString** lops off the first character of the string. The second **repeat** loop appears in boldface here:

```
set myString to "    agriculture    "
display dialog "**" & trim(myString) & "**"
```

*(continued)*

```
on trim(myString)
    repeat until myString does not end with " "
        set myString to text 1 through -2 of myString
    end repeat
    repeat until first character of myString is not " "
        set myString to text 2 through -1 of myString
    end repeat
end trim
```

8. Finally, add a **return** statement (as shown in boldface here) telling the subroutine to return the contents of **myString**:

```
set myString to "      agriculture       "
display dialog "**" & trim(myString) & "**"

on trim(myString)
    repeat until myString does not end with " "
        set myString to text 1 through -2 of myString
    end repeat
    repeat until first character of myString is not " "
        set myString to text 2 through -1 of myString
    end repeat
    return myString
end trim
```

9. Press ⌘-R or click the Run button on the toolbar to run the script. You'll see a dialog box containing the string with all spaces trimmed off (see Figure 10-9).

10. Click the OK button to close the dialog box.

11. Save the script under a name of your choice.

12. Now try using the subroutine from a **tell** block. Make the changes shown in boldface here to tell TextEdit to do the trimming:

```
tell the application "TextEdit"
    set myString to "      agriculture       "
    display dialog "**" &  trim(myString) & "**"
```

**Figure 10-9** The example code displays the string with the leading and trailing spaces trimmed off.

```
end tell

on trim(myString)
    repeat until myString does not end with " "
        set myString to text 1 through -2 of myString
    end repeat
    repeat until first character of myString is not " "
        set myString to text 2 through -1 of myString
    end repeat
    return myString
end trim
```

**13.** Press ⌘-R or click the Run button on the toolbar to run the script. This time, you'll get an error message (see Figure 10-10): "TextEdit got an error: Can't continue trim." This error occurs because TextEdit assumes you're trying to use a TextEdit command.

**14.** To fix this error, add the **my** keyword before the call to the **trim** subroutine to tell TextEdit that the subroutine is in the script, as shown in boldface here:

```
tell the application "TextEdit"
    set myString to "      agriculture      "
    display dialog "**" & my trim(myString) & "**"
end tell

on trim(myString)
    repeat until myString does not end with " "
        set myString to text 1 through -2 of myString
    end repeat
    repeat until first character of myString is not " "
        set myString to text 2 through -1 of myString
    end repeat
    return myString
end trim
```

**15.** Press ⌘-R or click the Run button on the toolbar to run the script. This time, it works as it should.

**16.** Close the script without saving the changes.

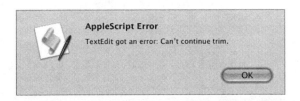

**Figure 10-10**   Trying to run your subroutine from a tell block to TextEdit results in this error unless you use the my keyword.

*(continued)*

**TIP**

You may also want to create a trimming subroutine that removes tabs, linefeed characters, and carriage-return characters from strings. To do so, create a list of the characters that you need to remove from the strings—for example, {" ", **tab, return, linefeed**} and then check that the beginning and ending characters do not appear in the list.

# Chapter 11

# Running Scripts
# Automatically

## Key Skills & Concepts

- Running a script automatically using a droplet
- Running a script automatically with a folder action
- Running a script automatically at login
- Running a script repeatedly at intervals
- Running a script automatically at a specific time

As you've seen earlier in this book, you can run scripts in several ways—directly from AppleScript Editor, from the Script menu, or by turning a script into an application and running it as you would any other Mac OS X application. But what's often handy is to set up scripts that run themselves automatically.

This chapter shows you the five main ways of running scripts automatically. You'll learn to:

- Create a "droplet" application that runs when you drop one or more files or folders on it.
- Assign a script to a folder action so that it monitors the contents of a folder and runs when they change—for example, when someone adds a file to the folder.
- Set a script to run automatically when you log in.
- Run a script repeatedly at intervals by using an idle handler.
- Schedule a script to run automatically at a specific time.

# Running a Script Automatically Using a Droplet

A *droplet* is an AppleScript application that runs automatically when you drag items from a Finder window (or the Desktop) and drop them on the droplet's icon. To recognize this drop action, the droplet has an *open handler* that accepts the input and runs the script.

### NOTE
The open handler is what distinguishes a droplet from a regular script application.

# Turning a Script into a Droplet

To turn a script into a droplet, you add an open handler to it. Start the open handler with the **on open** command followed by the name of the parameter to which the droplet passes the list of files dropped on it. You can call this parameter by any name you choose. This example uses the name **myFiles**:

```
on open myFiles
```

End the open handler with the **end open** statement. You can simply type the **end** keyword and have AppleScript Editor automatically add **open** when you compile the script.

```
on open myFiles
end open
```

Between the **on open** command and the **end open** command, place the statements you want the open handler to run. Here's an example of a droplet for sorting incoming files automatically into the right folders:

```
property ImageTypes : {"public.jpeg", "public.tiff", "public.png", ¬
    "com.adobe.pdf", "com.compuserve.gif"}
property DocTypes : {"com.apple.iwork.pages.sffpages", ¬
    "com.microsoft.word.doc"}
property SpreadTypes : {"com.apple.iwork.numbers.sffnumbers", ¬
    "com.microsoft.excel.xls"}
property PresTypes : {"com.apple.iwork.keynote.sffkey", ¬
    "com.microsoft.powerpoint.ppt"}
property TextTypes : {"public.plain-text", "public.rtf", "public.html"}

on open myFiles
    repeat with myCounter from 1 to count of myFiles
        set myFile to item myCounter of myFiles
        set myFileInfo to info for myFile
        if (folder of myFileInfo is false) then
            tell the application "Finder"
                if (type identifier of myFileInfo is in ImageTypes) then
                    move myFile to path to pictures folder
                else if (type identifier of myFileInfo is in DocTypes) ¬
    then
                    move myFile to folder "Documents" of home
                else if (type identifier of myFileInfo is in ¬
                    SpreadTypes) then
                    move myFile to folder "Spreads" of folder ¬
```

```
                              "Documents" of home
                else if (type identifier of myFileInfo is in PresTypes)
                    then
                    move myFile to folder "Present" of folder
                        "Documents" of home
                else if (type identifier of myFileInfo is in TextTypes)
                    then
                    move myFile to folder "Raw_Text" of folder
                       "Documents" of home
                else
                    move myFile to ¬
                        choose folder with prompt "Choose where to ¬
                        store the file "
                            & name of myFileInfo
                end if
            end tell
        end if
    end repeat
end open
```

Here's how this script works:

- The first **property** statement at the beginning defines the script property **ImageTypes** and assigns to it the Uniform Type Identifiers (UTIs) for five types of image files: JPEG files, TIFF files, PNG files, PDF files, and GIF files. (See Chapter 8 for a list of the UTIs for widely useful file types.)

- Similarly, the next four **property** statements define four further script properties: **DocTypes** (Pages documents and Microsoft Word documents with the .doc file extension), **SpreadTypes** (Numbers documents and Microsoft Excel workbooks with the .xls file extension), **PresTypes** (Keynote documents and Microsoft PowerPoint presentations with the .ppt file extension), and **TextTypes** (plain-text files, RTF files, and HTML files).

- The **on open myFiles** command starts the **open** event handler, assigning to **myFiles** the list of items dropped on the droplet. (If you drop only one item, you get a one-item list.)

- The **repeat** loop uses a counter variable named **myCounter** to run from 1 to **count of myFiles**—in other words, once for each item dropped.

- The first **set** statement assigns to the variable **myFile** the item in the **myFiles** list identified by the value of the **myCounter** counter. So **myFile** refers to the first item on the first iteration through the loop, the second item on the second iteration, and so on.

●   The second **set** statement assigns to the variable **myFileInfo** the **info** for **myFile**. This variable gives us a handy way to access the information for the item currently identified by the **myFile** variable.

●   The outer **if** statement verifies that the item is not a folder by checking that **folder of myFileInfo is false**. This script is designed to handle only files, so if the item is a folder, the script ignores it. (You could improve on this behavior—for example, by displaying the Choose A Folder dialog box so that the user can select the destination folder.)

●   As long as the item isn't a folder, the **tell** block inside the outer **if** statement tells the Finder what to do with the file. The nested **if** statement checks whether the **type identifier** of **myFileInfo** is in **ImageTypes**; if it is, the **move** command moves **myFile** to the Pictures folder.

●   If the file isn't a picture, the first **else if** statement see if it's one of the file types in **DocTypes**. If so, the **move** command moves **myFile** to the Documents folder.

●   Similarly, the next three **else if** statements check to see if **myFile** is one of the file types in **SpreadTypes**, **PresTypes**, or **TextTypes**. If there's a match, the **move** command moves the file to the appropriate folder.

●   If the file isn't any of those types, the **else** statement displays the Choose Folder dialog box and moves the file to the folder the user selects.

## Saving the Droplet as an Application

When you've created the script for your droplet, save the script as an application—it won't work as a script.

Open the Save As dialog box by pressing ⌘-s, if you haven't already saved the script, or ⌘-SHIFT-S, if you have already saved it. Choose Application in the File Format pop-up menu, and then choose suitable options in the Options area.

●   **Clear the Startup Screen check box**   If you want the droplet to run smoothly, clear the Startup Screen check box. Otherwise, the user will have to click through the startup information each time he or she launches the droplet.

●   **Select the Stay Open check box**   If you expect the user to use the droplet more than once, select the Stay Open check box to make the droplet stay open after it has finished running. Keeping the droplet open makes it run faster the next time the user drops a file on it.

This document's file has been changed by another application since you opened or saved it.

The changes made by the other application will be lost if you save. Save anyway?

Save    Don't Save

**Figure 11-1**   You may see this dialog box when you edit a droplet that you have already run. Normally, you will want to click the Save button to save the changes you've just made in AppleScript Editor.

If you want to be able to reach the droplet at a moment's notice (which is often half the point), drag the droplet to the Dock after saving it. You can then drag files to the droplet easily. Or, if you prefer, put the droplet on a part of your Desktop that you keep uncovered.

One other thing—you may well need to edit the droplet after you've saved and run it. When you save the droplet from AppleScript Editor, you may see the dialog box shown in Figure 11-1 warning you that "This document's file has been changed by another application since you opened or saved it. The changes made by the other application will be lost if you save." This is confusing because no application has actually changed the droplet—rather, you've made changes to the droplet's code. So what you'll normally want to do is click the Save button to save those changes. (Don't press RETURN—the default button on the dialog box is the Don't Save button.)

## Try This   Creating and Running a Droplet

In this example, you create the droplet shown in the previous section and adapt the folders it uses so that it will run on your Mac. Follow these steps:

1. In AppleScript Editor, press ⌘-N or choose File | New to create a new script.

2. Type the five **property** statements that define the different file types the script works with. Add extra **property** statements if you want the script to deal with other files as well. For example, create a property named **MusicTypes** and give it file types such as **public.mp3** and **public-mpeg-4-audio**.

3. Type the **on open** event handler as shown in the previous section.

4. If you added another **property** statement, add an **else if** statement to handle it. For example, if you added a **MusicTypes** property, add a statement such as this:

```
else if (type identifier of myFileInfo is in MusicTypes) then
    move myFile to path to music folder
```

5. Edit the folders involved so that they match your file system. For example, if your Mac doesn't have the folder ~/Documents/Spreads/ (as most Macs don't), change the **move myFile to folder "Spreads" of folder "Documents" of home** to a folder you do have. (The alternative is to create the missing folders.)

6. Press ⌘-s or choose File | Save, and then save the script as an application under a name such as File Sorter. Clear the Startup Screen check box, and select the Stay Open check box.

7. Open a Finder window to the folder in which you saved the droplet, and then drag the droplet to the Dock. You'll need to place it on the left side of the Dock divider bar (or in the upper part of the Dock if you've placed the Dock at the side of the screen).

8. Drag one or more files to the droplet's icon on the Dock. The script works through each file in turn. If the file matches one of the types, the script puts it in the appropriate folder; if not, the script displays the Choose Folder dialog box to let you pick the folder in which to put it.

9. Drag one or more files to the droplet's icon on the Dock again. Because the droplet has stayed open, it will execute faster this time.

# Running a Script Automatically with a Folder Action

Droplets are great when you're handling files automatically, but you'll probably want to make the most of Mac OS X's features for monitoring folders automatically for you. To do so, you use folder actions.

A *folder action* is a means of running a script automatically when the contents of a folder change. You set up a folder action like this:

● **Turn on folder actions**  Mac OS X has a master switch for turning on folder actions. You need to turn them on only once, but if they're turned off, you can't get a folder action script to run at all.

- **Write a folder action script** As you'd imagine, you need to create a suitable script for the folder. A folder action script includes an event handler that runs when there's a change in the folder. For example, you can write an event handler that makes your script run when someone adds a file to the folder. You store your folder action scripts in a special folder named Folder Action Scripts so that Mac OS X can distinguish them from your other scripts.

### NOTE

Folder Actions Setup actually checks two Folder Action Scripts folders—the /Library/Scripts/Folder Action Scripts/ folder (which contains the Mac's scripts) and the ~/Library/Scripts/Folder Action Scripts/ folder, which contains the user's own scripts. Mac OS X creates the /Library/Scripts/Folder Action Scripts/ folder automatically; you may need to create the ~/Library/Scripts/Folder Action Scripts/ folder manually if you want to store scripts in your own user account, where other users can't access them.

- **Attach the folder action script to the folder** Once you've made a suitable script, you attach the script to the folder on which you want it to work.

Those are the broad strokes of folder actions. Let's look at the details.

## Turning On Folder Actions

Your first move is to turn on folder actions within Mac OS X so that you can use folder actions. You can do this either manually or by using AppleScript.

### Turning On Folder Actions Manually

To turn on folder actions manually, follow these steps:

1. Click the Desktop or the Finder button on the Dock.

2. Press ⌘-SHIFT-A to open a Finder window showing your Applications folder.

3. Expand the AppleScript folder to display its contents. For example, click the AppleScript folder in Column view, or double-click it in Icon view, List view, or Cover Flow view.

4. Double-click the Folder Actions Setup icon to run the application. Mac OS X displays the Folder Actions Setup window (see Figure 11-2).

5. Select the Enable Folder Actions check box.

6. Either quit the Folder Actions Setup application (press ⌘-Q or choose Folder Actions Setup | Quit Folder Actions Setup as usual) or leave the application open so that you can attach a folder action script to a folder, as discussed later in this chapter.

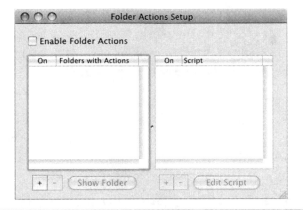

**Figure 11-2**  To turn on folder actions, select the Enable Folder Actions check box in the Folder Actions Setup window.

### Turning On Folder Actions via AppleScript

You can also turn on folder actions using AppleScript by telling the Folder Actions Setup application to set the **folder actions enabled** property to **true**, like this:

```
tell the application "Folder Actions Setup"
    set folder actions enabled to true
end tell
```

To turn off folder actions via AppleScript, set the **folder actions enabled** property to **false**.

## Writing a Folder Action Script

To write a folder action script, you create a script in AppleScript Editor as usual—but you also include one or more folder action event handlers to tell the script what you want it to do. What's often most useful is to take actions when a new file arrives in a folder, so we'll start there.

### Taking Actions When an Item Is Added to the Folder

To take actions when an item is added to the folder, use the **adding folder items** event handler. To create an event handler for this event, set it up like this:

- Start with an **on adding folder items** statement:

  ```
  on adding folder items
  ```

- Assign a variable name to the folder with which the script will work. This folder is the direct parameter for the event handler. The variable name is the name you use to refer to the folder in the script, so it can be pretty much anything you want. The following example uses the uninspired but serviceable name **myFolder**:

```
on adding folder items to myFolder
```

- Add the **after receiving** parameter and assign a variable name to the list of items that have been added. Again, this name is for your use—to enable you to reach the files or folders that were added—so you can call it what you want. The following example uses the straightforward but unimaginative name **new_files**:

```
on adding folder items to myFolder after receiving new_files
```

- Add the **end** statement for the **on** block. When you compile the script, AppleScript Editor automatically adds **adding folder items to** after **end**, but you can also add it manually:

```
on adding folder items to myFolder after receiving new_files
end adding folder items to
```

- Between the **on** statement and the **end** statement, add the commands you want the script to execute.

Here is an example of a folder action script that checks to see whether each new file has the file extension ".doc" or ".docx"; if the file has either of these extensions, the script displays a dialog box (see Figure 11-3) prompting the user to open the file in Microsoft Word. If the user chooses to open one or more documents in Word, the script stores this fact by setting a Boolean variable named **activateWord** to **true**. If **activateWord** is **true**

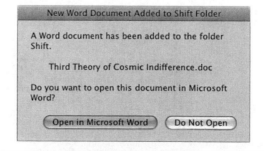

**Figure 11-3** A script that uses the adding folder items folder action to prompt the user to open a file that has arrived in the target folder.

after looping through all the new files, the script activates Word so that the user can see the open document or documents.

```
on adding folder items to myFolder after receiving new_files
    tell the application "Finder" to set myFolderName to name of myFolder
    try
        repeat with myCounter from 1 to number of items in new_files
            set myNewFile to item myCounter of new_files
            set myNewFileInfo to the info for myNewFile
            if the name extension of myNewFileInfo is "doc" or ¬
                the name extension of myNewFileInfo is "docx" then
                    display dialog "A Word document has been added to the
folder " ¬
                        & myFolderName & "." ¬
                        & return & return & tab & name of myNewFileInfo ¬
                        & return & return & ¬
                        "Do you want to open this document in Microsoft
Word?" ¬
                        with title "New Word Document Added to "
& myFolderName & ¬
                        " Folder" buttons {"Open in Microsoft Word",
"Do Not Open"} ¬
                        default button 1
                if the button returned of the result is "Open in
Microsoft Word" then
                    tell application "Microsoft Word"
                        open myNewFile
                        set activateWord to true
                    end tell
                end if
            end if
        end repeat
        if activateWord is true then
            tell application "Microsoft Word" to activate
        end if
    end try
end adding folder items to
```

## Taking Actions When an Item Is Removed from the Folder

To take actions when an item is removed from the folder, use the **removing folder items** event handler. This works in a similar way to the **adding folder items** event handler described in the previous section.

● Start with an **on removing folder items** statement:

```
on removing folder items
```

● Assign a variable name to the folder with which the script will work. This is the direct parameter for the event handler. You can use any name that suits you—for example, **ScriptFolder**:

```
on removing folder items from ScriptFolder
```

● Add the **after losing** parameter and assign a variable name to the items that were removed. For example, the following statement uses the name **Removed_Files**:

```
on removing folder items from ScriptFolder after losing Removed_Files
```

● Add the **end** statement for the **on** block. When you compile the script, AppleScript Editor automatically adds **removing folder items from** after **end**, but you can also add it manually:

```
on removing folder items from ScriptFolder after losing Removed_files
end removing folder items from
```

● Between the **on** statement and the **end** statement, add the commands you want the script to execute.

The following example monitors a folder named Protected Files and warns the user when items are removed from the folder. Figure 11-4 shows an example of the warning.

```
on removing folder items from ScriptFolder after losing Removed_files
    tell application "Finder"
        set myFolderName to name of ScriptFolder
    end tell
    set GoneFiles to ""
    repeat with myCounter from 1 to number of items in Removed_files
        set RemovedFile to item myCounter of Removed_files
        set RemovedFileInfo to the info for RemovedFile
        set GoneFiles to GoneFiles & name of RemovedFileInfo & return
    end repeat
    display alert "Files removed from " & ScriptFolder as warning ¬
        message GoneFiles
end removing folder items from
```

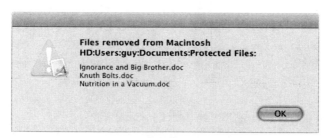

**Figure 11-4** Using a removing folder items folder action to warn the user when files or folders are removed from a key folder.

## Taking Actions When the User Moves or Resizes the Folder's Window

To take actions when the user moves or resizes the folder's window, use the **moving folder window for** event handler.

### *CAUTION*

The **moving folder window for** event handler does not work consistently; because of this, you'll do best to avoid it. First, the event handler tends to run only when the toolbar on the target window is hidden, even though this should make no difference. Second, if you use the folder action script to resize or reposition the window, the script runs again, repositions the window, and runs again—and so on until you crash it.

To create an event handler for this event, set it up like this:

- Start with an **on moving folder window** statement:

  ```
  on moving folder window
  ```

- Assign a variable name to the folder with which the script will work. For example, the following statement refers to the window as **myFolder**:

  ```
  on moving folder window for myFolder
  ```

- Assign a variable name to the **from** parameter to store the coordinates of the window's starting position. Again, you can use any name of your choice; this example uses **starting_position**:

  ```
  on moving folder window for myFolder from starting_position
  ```

- Add the **end** statement for the **on** block. When you compile the script, AppleScript Editor automatically adds **moving folder window for** after **end**, but you can also add it manually if you prefer:

  ```
  on moving folder window for myFolder from starting_position
  end moving folder window for
  ```

- Between the **on** statement and the **end** statement, add the commands you want the script to run.

The following example closes the **myFolder** window if it is resized or moved. This behavior is seldom helpful, but it avoids having the script resize or move the window because this will make the folder action run again:

```
on moving folder window for myFolder from starting_position
    tell the application "Finder"
        close the window of myFolder
    end tell
end moving folder window for
```

## Taking Actions When the User Opens a Finder Window to the Folder

To take actions when the user opens a Finder window to the folder, use the **opening folder** event handler. This event handler takes a single direct parameter that refers to the folder on which the script is operating. As usual, you can give the variable for this parameter any name you like—for example, **myFolder**:

```
on opening folder myFolder
end opening folder
```

The following example displays a dialog box that requests the user not to create any subfolders within the current folder:

```
on opening folder myFolder
    display dialog ¬
    "Please do not create any subfolders within this folder." ¬
        with title "Folder Alert" with icon caution
end opening folder
```

## Taking Actions When the User Closes the Folder's Finder Window

To take actions when the user closes a Finder window that was open showing the folder, use the **closing folder window** event handler. This event handler works in the same way as the **opening folder** event handler discussed in the previous section. It takes a single direct parameter that refers to the folder on which the script is operating:

```
on closing folder window for myClosingFolder
end closing folder window for
```

The following example checks whether the Finder window you're closing is the last one open. If it is, the script opens a new Finder window to the home folder, resizes the window, and positions it in the upper-left corner of the primary monitor.

```
on closing folder window for myFolder
    tell the application "Finder"
        if (count of (Finder windows)) = 0 then
            open home
            set the bounds of the front Finder window to ¬
                {0, 44, 600, 644}
        end if
    end tell
end closing folder window for
```

# Attaching a Folder Action Script to a Folder

You can attach a folder action script to a folder in four different ways:

● Manually, by using the Folder Actions Setup application

● Manually, by working directly from the Finder

● Manually, by using the Script menu

● Automatically, by using AppleScript

Let's look at each of these methods in turn.

## Attaching a Folder Action Script to a Folder Using Folder Actions Setup

The more formal way of attaching a folder action script to a folder is to use the Folder Actions Setup application, which you met earlier in this chapter. Folder Actions Setup is good when you're attaching one or more scripts or you want to get an overview of all the folder actions set up on your Mac.

Here's how to attach a folder action script to a folder using Folder Actions Setup:

**1.** Open the Folder Actions Setup application in one of these ways:

● Press ⌘-SPACEBAR to open Spotlight, start typing **folder actions**, and then open Folder Actions Setup from the hit list. It's usually the top hit, so this is normally a quick way of opening the application.

● Open your Applications folder, expand the AppleScript folder, and then double-click the Folder Actions Setup icon.

**2.** Click the + button under the left pane in the Folder Actions Setup window to open the dialog box for choosing a folder.

**3.** Click the folder, and then click the Open button. Folder Actions Setup adds the folder to the list, and then opens the Choose A Script To Attach dialog box (see Figure 11-5).

**4.** Click the script, and then click the Attach button. The script then appears in the right pane in the Folder Actions Setup window, as shown in Figure 11-6. From here, you can quickly open the script by clicking it and then clicking the Edit Script button, which is handy when you need to change the script (or simply check what it does).

**5.** Add more scripts to folders as needed.

**6.** Press ⌘-Q or choose Folder Actions Setup | Quit Folder Actions Setup to quit Folder Actions Setup.

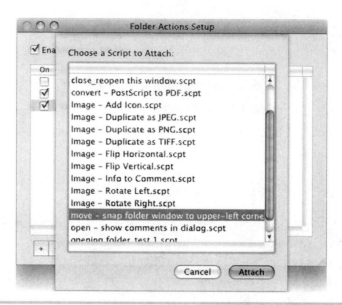

**Figure 11-5** Select the script you want to attach to the folder.

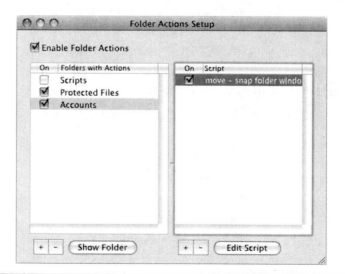

**Figure 11-6** The script appears in the right pane of the Folder Actions Setup window.

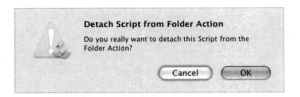

**Figure 11-7**   Folder Actions Setup asks you to confirm the removal of a script from a folder.

When you no longer need a folder action to run on a folder, you can stop it in any of these ways in Folder Actions Setup:

- **Turn the action off**   Clear the check box for the script in the right pane of the Folder Actions Setup window.

- **Remove the action from the folder**   Click the script's entry in the right pane of the Folder Actions Setup window, and then click the – button below the pane. Click the OK button in the Detach Script From Folder Action dialog box that appears (see Figure 11-7).

- **Turn off all actions for the folder**   Clear the check box for the folder in the left pane of the Folder Actions Setup window.

- **Remove all actions from the folder**   Click the folder's entry in the left pane of the Folder Actions Setup window, and then click the – button below the pane. Click the OK button in the Delete Folder Action dialog box that appears (see Figure 11-8).

**Figure 11-8**   Folder Actions Setup also makes you confirm the removal of all scripts from a folder.

## Attaching a Folder Action Script to a Folder Using the Finder

The second way of attaching a folder action script to a folder is by using the Finder like this in Leopard:

1. Open a Finder window to the folder that contains your victim folder.

2. CTRL-click or right-click the victim folder, click or highlight More on the shortcut menu, and then choose Attach A Folder Action, as shown in Figure 11-9. Mac OS X displays the Choose A File dialog box.

### TIP

In Leopard, you can use the shortcut menu's Enable Folder Actions command, and its Disable Folder Actions counterpart that appears when folder actions are turned on, to quickly turn folder actions on and off for your Mac.

3. Navigate to the Folder Action Scripts folder that contains the script, select the script, and then click the Choose button.

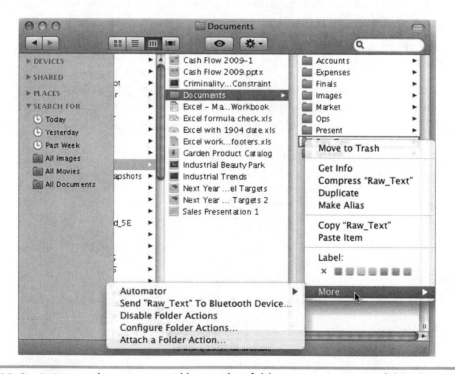

**Figure 11-9**   In Leopard, you can quickly attach a folder action script to a folder by using the shortcut menu in the Finder.

### CAUTION
You can use the Choose A File dialog box to select a script stored in a folder other than one of the Folder Action Scripts folders, but it won't run. Because of this restriction, it's usually best to use the shortcut menu's Configure Folder Actions command as a handy way to open Folder Actions Setup, and then set up your folder action scripts from there, as discussed in the previous section.

You can remove a folder action script by opening a Finder window, CTRL-clicking or right-clicking the appropriate folder, highlighting More on the shortcut menu, highlighting Remove A Folder Action on the submenu, and then clicking the script you want to remove. You can also use the Edit A Folder Action command on the submenu to open one of the attached scripts in AppleScript Editor.

## Attaching a Folder Action Script to a Folder Using the Script Menu
The third way of attaching a folder action script to a folder is by using the Script menu. The Folder Actions submenu on the Script menu provides the following commands:

- **Attach Script To Folder**   Click this item to display the snappily named Select Compiled Script File(s) Containing Folder Actions dialog box (see Figure 11-10). Select the script and click the OK button; then choose the folder in the Choose A Folder dialog box, and click the Choose button.

**Figure 11-10**   The Attach Script To Folder command on the Script menu displays this dialog box for picking a script to attach to a folder.

- **Configure Folder Actions** Click this item to open the Folder Actions Setup application.

- **Disable Folder Actions** Click this item to turn folder actions off.

- **Enable Folder Actions** Click this item to turn folder actions on.

- **Remove Folder Actions** Click this item to remove a folder action script using the two dialog boxes shown in Figure 11-11. First, you select the folder from a dialog box that lists each folder that has folder actions applied; then you select the folder action script from a dialog box that lists the scripts applied to that folder.

## Attaching a Folder Action Script to a Folder via AppleScript

The three manual methods of attaching a folder action script to a folder all work fine, but often it's much more convenient to have AppleScript do the grunt work for you.

To attach a folder action script to a folder, use the **attach action to** command with the System Events application. Use **to folder** and the folder name to specify the folder, followed by **using** and the name of the script you want. Here's an example:

```
tell application "System Events"
    attach action to folder "Macintosh HD:Users:kim:Documents" ¬
        using "add - new item alert.scpt"
end tell
```

**Figure 11-11** The Remove Folder Actions command on the Script menu lets you remove folder actions from a script by using these two dialog boxes.

# Ask the Expert

**Q:** I've got a problem—the Folder Actions submenu doesn't appear on the Script menu.

**A:** You can take care of this problem easily.

If the Folder Actions submenu doesn't appear on the Script menu:

- **Snow Leopard** In AppleScript Editor, press ⌘-, to display the Preferences window. Click the General button, then select the Show Script Menu In Menu Bar text box.

- **Leopard or earlier** Run AppleScript Utility (in the /Applications/AppleScript/ folder), select the Show Computer Scripts check box, and then quit AppleScript Utility. The easiest way to run AppleScript Utility is to open the Script menu and choose Open AppleScript Utility from it.

You may also run into this problem one degree worse—if you like expressing your suffering in mathematical terms: The Script menu doesn't appear on the menu bar either.

You can fix this quickly, too. Wherever you found the Show Computer Scripts check box, select the Show Script Menu In Menu Bar check box too.

To remove a folder action script from a folder, use the **remove action** command. Use **from folder** and the folder name to tell System Events which folder has the action, followed by **using action name** and the name of the folder action you want to remove. Here's an example:

```
tell application "System Events"
    remove action from folder "Macintosh HD:Users:kim:Documents" ¬
        using action name "add - new item alert.scpt"
end tell
```

To enable folder actions via AppleScript, tell the application Folder Actions Setup to set the **folder actions enabled** property to **true**:

```
tell the application "Folder Actions Setup"
    set folder actions enabled to true
end tell
```

To disable folder actions via AppleScript, set **folder actions enabled** to **false**:

```
tell the application "Folder Actions Setup" ¬
    to set folder action enabled to false
```

**Try This** Creating and Using a Folder Action Script

In this example, you create a short folder action script using the **adding folder items** event handler, attach the script to a folder, and make sure folder actions are turned on so that you can run the script. Follow these steps:

1. In AppleScript Editor, press ⌘-N or choose File | New to create a new script.

2. Press ⌘-S or choose File | Save to display the Save As dialog box. Navigate to the /Library/Scripts/Folder Action Scripts/ folder, and then save the script under a name of your choice.

3. Start an **on adding folder items to** event handler, identifying the folder as **myFolder** and using the variable name **added_items** with the **after receiving** parameter:

```
on adding folder items to myFolder after receiving added_items
```

4. Add the **end** statement to end the event handler, as shown in boldface here:

```
on adding folder items to myFolder after receiving added_items
end
```

5. Press ⌘-K or click the Compile button on the toolbar to compile the script. AppleScript Editor automatically adds **adding folder items to** after the **end** statement, as shown in boldface here:

```
on adding folder items to myFolder after receiving added_items
end adding folder items to
```

6. Inside the event handler, add a **tell** statement to tell the Finder to assign the **name** property of the **myFolder** item to the variable **fName**. The changes appear in boldface here:

```
on adding folder items to myFolder after receiving added_items
    tell application "Finder" to set fName to name of myFolder
end adding folder items to
```

7. Add a **try** block after the **tell** statement, as shown in boldface here:

```
on adding folder items to myFolder after receiving added_items
    tell application "Finder" to set fName to name of myFolder
    try
    end try
end adding folder items to
```

8. Within the **try** block, create a blank string variable named **myMessage**, as shown in boldface here:

```
on adding folder items to myFolder after receiving added_items
    tell application "Finder" to set fName to name of myFolder
```

```
    try
        set myMessage to ""
    end try
end adding folder items to
```

9. After the **set myMessage** statement, add a **repeat** block that uses a variable named **myCounter** to run from 1 to the **number of items in added_items**. The new statements appear in boldface here:

```
on adding folder items to myFolder after receiving added_items
    tell application "Finder" to set fName to name of myFolder
    try
        set myMessage to ""
        repeat with myCounter from 1 to ¬
            number of items in added_items
        end repeat
    end try
end adding folder items to
```

10. Within the **repeat** block, set the variable **myNewFile** to the item in **added_items** represented by **myCounter**, and set **myNewFileInfo** to the **info** property for **myNewFile**. Then set **myMessage** to its existing contents, the **name** property of **myNewFileInfo**, and a return, so as to build a list of the files dropped on the droplet. The added statements appear in boldface here:

```
on adding folder items to myFolder after receiving added_items
    tell application "Finder" to set fName to name of myFolder
    try
        set myMessage to ""
        repeat with myCounter from 1 to ¬
            number of items in added_items
            set myNewFile to item myCounter of added_items
            set myNewFileInfo to the info for myNewFile
            set myMessage to myMessage & ¬
                name of myNewFileInfo & return
        end repeat
    end try
end adding folder items to
```

11. Finally, add a **display dialog** statement that displays the **myMessage** string (showing the list of files dropped on the droplet), together with an explanatory title bar and a solitary OK button. The new statement appears in boldface here:

```
on adding folder items to myFolder after receiving added_items
    tell application "Finder" to set fName to name of myFolder
    try
        set myMessage to ""
        repeat with myCounter from 1 to number of items in added_items
```

*(continued)*

```
                set myNewFile to item myCounter of added_items
                set myNewFileInfo to the info for myNewFile
                set myMessage to myMessage ¬
                    & name of myNewFileInfo & return
            end repeat
            display dialog myMessage with title "Files Added to " ¬
                & fName buttons {"OK"}
        end try
    end adding folder items to
```

**12.** Save the changes you've made to the script.

**13.** Press ⌘-SPACEBAR to open Spotlight, start typing **folder actions**, and then open Folder Actions Setup from the hit list.

**14.** Select the Enable Folder Actions check box if it's not already selected.

**15.** Click the + button under the left pane in the Folder Actions Setup window to open the dialog box for choosing a folder.

**16.** Click the folder you want to use, and then click the Open button. Folder Actions Setup adds the folder to the list and then opens the Choose A Script To Attach dialog box (shown in Figure 11-5, earlier in this chapter).

**17.** Click the script you've just created, and then click the Attach button.

**18.** Press ⌘-Q or choose Folder Actions Setup | Quit Folder Actions Setup to quit Folder Actions Setup.

**19.** Open a Finder window to the folder you chose.

**20.** Add several files to the folder—for example, by copying them from another folder and then pasting them in—and verify that the resulting dialog box lists the files. Figure 11-12 shows an example of the dialog box.

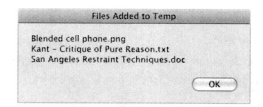

**Figure 11-12**   The folder action script's dialog box lists the files you added to the folder.

# Running a Script at Login

Another time it's often useful to run a script application is when you log in to your Mac. You can run a script that sets up the Mac the way you want it—for example, opening and arranging the applications you find essential.

Create the script, save it as an application, and then follow these steps to set it to run at login:

1. Choose Apple I System Preferences to open System Preferences.

2. In the System category, click the Accounts item to display Accounts preferences.

3. If necessary, click the lock icon and authenticate yourself so that you can make changes.

4. In the list of user accounts, click the account you want to change.

5. Click the Login Items button to display the list of login items.

6. Click the + button, select the script in the dialog box that appears, and then click the Add button.

7. Lock System Preferences again if necessary, and then quit System Preferences.

Now the script application will run automatically each time you log in.

# Running a Script Repeatedly at Intervals

Sometimes you may need to have a script perform the same actions at regular intervals—for example, to empty the Trash or to prompt you to take a break from thrashing your keyboard.

To make a script run repeatedly, use an idle handler and set the script to stay open. When you do this, the script runs and performs its task; it then lurks in the background for however long you've told it to be idle before springing into action again.

To create an idle handler, you use an **on idle** command like this, with a **return** statement specifying how many seconds to wait before performing the actions again (in this example, 3600 seconds, which is one hour):

```
on idle
    --take actions here
    return 3600
end idle
```

Idle handlers don't work in AppleScript Editor, so you need to save the script as an application to make it work. When you save the script, select the Stay Open check box in the Save As dialog box to make the application stay open after you run it rather than closing as normal. You can then run the application, and the idle handler works.

## Try This Creating an Application That Uses an Idle Handler

In this example, you create an AppleScript application that uses an idle handler to run in the background and perform the same action at intervals. The application simply displays a dialog box suggesting you take a break from your computer.

To create the application, follow these steps:

1. In AppleScript Editor, press ⌘-N or choose File | New to create a new script.

2. Enter the code shown here:

```
on idle
    display dialog "Time to take a computer break." ¬
        buttons {"OK"} with title "Break Reminder"
    return 10
end idle
```

3. Press ⌘-s or choose File | Save to display the Save As dialog box.

4. Give the application a name, and choose the folder in which to store it.

5. Choose Application in the File Format pop-up menu.

6. Select the Stay Open check box, and make sure the Run Only check box and Startup Screen check box are cleared.

7. Click the Save button. AppleScript Editor closes the Save As dialog box and saves the application.

8. Run the application from the folder in which you stored it. You'll see the Break Reminder dialog box shown in Figure 11-13.

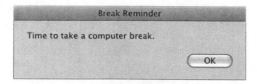

**Figure 11-13** The Break Reminder application uses an idle handler to keep running in the background and display this dialog box at regular intervals.

9. Click the OK button. Ten seconds after you do so, the Break Reminder dialog box appears again.

10. To quit the application, click the OK button in the Break Reminder dialog box, and then press ⌘-Q or choose the Quit command from the application's menu. Alternatively, click the application's icon on the Dock, keep holding down the mouse button until the pop-up menu appears, and then choose Quit.

# Running a Script Automatically at Specific Times

Mac OS X also makes it easy to create scripts that run at specific times. For example, if you decide the still watches of the night are the time for your Mac to perform vital tasks, you can set a script to run at 2 A.M. or whenever you're visiting the Land of Nod.

There are two main ways of running a script at a specific time like this.

First, you can create a script that keeps checking to see whether the time condition you've set has been met. For example, if you want to perform an action on the hour and on the half-hour, you can test whether the current minute of the hour matches 0 or 30.

The problem with this approach is that you need to keep the script running in the background and checking every minute to see if the current minute is one of the action minutes. Mac OS X manages processor time smartly enough that this won't slow your Mac down much, but it's still another task that the Mac needs to run.

As a result, a better approach is to schedule the task as an appointment in iCal. One of the things iCal is great at is checking the time constantly to see if it needs to nag you about something, so you can use this checking to run a script. What's especially handy is that iCal doesn't even have to be running when the event's time rolls around, though your Mac must be running and awake rather than off or dead to the world.

Here's how to set iCal to run a script at a particular time:

1. Write the script and save it. You can make it either a script or an applet—it doesn't matter which. (Make it an applet if you want to be able to run it separately as well.)

2. Open iCal and create a new event by double-clicking the appropriate day. iCal pops up the window for the new event.

3. Type the name you want to give the event in place of New Event.

4. Use the From date and time controls to set the time at which you want the script to run. If you want to run the script repeatedly, use the Repeat controls to set up the repetition.

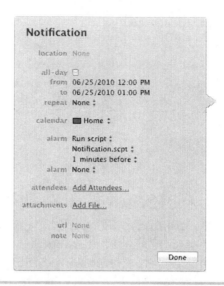

**Figure 11-14** You can use iCal to run a script for you at a particular time—even if iCal itself isn't running at the time.

**5.** Open the Alarm pop-up menu, and choose Run Script.

**6.** Open the pop-up menu that appears below the Alarm pop-up menu (see Figure 11-14), and then click Other. In the iCal: Script To Run As Alarm dialog box, click the script, and then click the Select button.

**7.** In the timing menu below the script's name, set up when you want the script to run—for example, 1 Minutes Before.

**8.** Click the Done button to close the window for the event.

The script will now run at the time you chose, even if iCal is closed.

# Part III

# Automating Major
Applications
with AppleScript

# Chapter 12

## Automating iTunes and iPhoto

## Key Skills & Concepts

- Working with iTunes

- Working with iPhoto

This chapter shows you how to bring AppleScript to bear on iTunes, Apple's widely used audio- and video-management application, and iPhoto, the graphics application in the iLife suite. You'll learn how to work with tracks and playlists in iTunes, and how to work with albums, photos, and keywords in iPhoto.

### NOTE
Both iTunes and iPhoto are powerful applications that perform relatively few tasks but do them well. They have friendly, easy-to-use interfaces that give users most of the functionality they need. As a result, you may not need to perform a wide variety of tasks in iTunes and iPhoto using AppleScript.

# Working with iTunes

As you know, iTunes helps you organize and enjoy your library of songs, videos, podcasts, and other multimedia items. You can add items from a CD, from the iTunes Store, or by dragging in existing media files.

You'll find various objects in iTunes' dictionary, but this chapter focuses on the two objects you'll probably find the most useful:

- **track**   The **track** object represents one of the files in your iTunes library—for example, a song or a TV show.

- **playlist**   The **playlist** object represents a list of songs.

## Working with Tracks

To represent a song, podcast, video file, or other type of file in iTunes, AppleScript uses the **track** object. Table 12-1 explains the properties of the **track** object.

| track Object Property | Explanation |
|---|---|
| album | The name of the album from which the track comes |
| album artist | The album artist assigned for the track |
| album rating | An integer giving the album's overall rating, from 0 (no stars) to 100 (five stars) |
| artist | The artist assigned for the track |
| bit rate | An integer giving the track's bitrate in Kbps. This property is read-only. |
| bookmark | A real number giving the position at which the track is bookmarked for resuming play |
| bookmarkable | **true** if the track's playback position will be remembered for resuming play, **false** if it will not be |
| bpm | An integer giving the track's tempo in beats per minute |
| category | The category assigned to the track |
| comment | Any comments you've added to the track's Comments field |
| compilation | **true** to have iTunes handle this track as being part of a compilation, **false** to handle it as being part of a "normal" album (supposing such a thing exists) |
| composer | The composer credited with the track |
| container | The playlist that contains the track—for example, **user playlist id 28947 of source id 49 of application "iTunes"** |
| database ID | An integer giving the track's unique ID within iTunes. This property is read-only. |
| date added | The date and time the track was added to iTunes. This property is read-only. |
| description | The text from the Description field (on the Video tab of the Item Information dialog box) |
| disc count | An integer giving the number of discs in the album |
| disc number | An integer giving the number of this track's disc within the album (for example, **1** for disc 1 of 2) |
| duration | A real number giving the track's duration in seconds—for example, **146.703002929688**. This property is read-only. |
| enabled | **true** if the track's check box is selected for playback, **false** if the check box is cleared |
| episode ID | The episode ID for the track (for video shows) |
| episode number | The episode number of the track (for video shows) |
| EQ | The name of the equalizer preset to use when playing the track |
| finish | A real number giving the stop time of the track in seconds—for example, **287.476989746094** |

**Table 12-1**   Properties of the track Object

| track Object Property | Explanation |
|---|---|
| gapless | **true** if the track is from a gapless album (one set to play without gaps between songs), **false** if it is from a regular album |
| genre | The music genre of the track |
| grouping | The grouping for the track. Grouping is a text tag you can enter in the Grouping field of the Info tab of the Item Information dialog box to create subgenres. |
| id | An integer giving the track's unique ID within iTunes on your Mac—for example, **30394** |
| index | The track's index number in its current context—for example, **19** when it's the 19th track in a playlist |
| kind | The file type of the track—for example, **AAC Audio File**. This property is read-only. |
| long description | The long description of the track, if any is applied |
| lyrics | The lyrics of the track, if they are in the file |
| modification date | The date and time you last modified the track. This property is read-only. |
| name | The name of the track |
| persistent id | The hexadecimal string that uniquely identifies this track within iTunes—for example, **"6CC5C362D387BB32"** |
| played count | An integer indicating how many times the track has been played from start to end |
| podcast | **true** if this track is a podcast episode, **false** if it is not |
| rating | An integer giving the rating of the track, from 0 (no stars) to 100 (five stars) |
| rating kind | The rating kind used for the track: **user** for a rating you've applied, **computer** for a rating your Mac has applied. This property is read-only. |
| release date | The release date for the track, if available. This property is read-only. |
| sample rate | An integer giving the track's sample rate in hertz (Hz)—for example, **44100** for the CD-standard 44.1 kHz sample rate |
| season number | An integer giving the season number of the track (for TV shows) |
| shufflable | **true** if the track is marked for inclusion in shuffling, **false** if it is not. (In the user interface, select the Skip When Shuffling check box on the Options tab of the Item Information dialog box to exclude a track from shuffling.) |
| skipped count | An integer indicating how many times you've skipped this track |
| skipped date | The date and time you last skipped the track |
| show | The name of the show from which the track comes |

**Table 12-1** Properties of the track Object *(continued)*

| track Object Property | Explanation |
|---|---|
| sort album | The album name to use when sorting the track. If present, this property overrides the **album** property. |
| sort artist | The artist name to use when sorting the track. If present, this property overrides the **artist** property. |
| sort album artist | The album artist name to use when sorting the track. If present, this property overrides the **album artist** property. |
| sort name | The name to use when sorting the track. If present, this property overrides the **name** property. |
| sort composer | The composer name to use when sorting the track. If present, this property overrides the **composer** property. |
| sort show | The show name to use when sorting the track. If present, this property overrides the **show** property. |
| size | An integer giving the track's size on disk in bytes—for example, **3408348** for a 3.3MB file |
| start | A real number giving the start time of the track in seconds—**0.0** until you change it |
| time | The track's time in MM:SS format—for example, **"4:03"** |
| track count | An integer giving the number of tracks on the album this track came from |
| track number | This track's number on the album it came from |
| unplayed | **true** if you've never played this track at all, **false** if you've played even part of it |
| video kind | The kind of video track: **none**, **movie**, **music video**, or **TV show** |
| volume adjustment | An integer giving the volume adjustment you've applied to the track. You can use from −100 to 100. |
| year | The year the track or its album was released |

**Table 12-1**    Properties of the track Object *(continued)*

Most of these properties are pretty straightforward, but these three things aren't immediately obvious:

● **Ratings**    In the user interface, you rate a track by assigning it a number of stars, from one star (irredeemably wretched) to five stars (the best thing since vacuum-packed coffee). Until you assign a rating, the track has no stars. Internally, iTunes uses an integer from 0 to 100 to represent the stars: 0 is no stars, 20 is one star, 40 is two stars, 60 is three stars, 80 is four stars, and 100 is five stars.

- **Overlapping properties**   As you can see from Table 12-1, several properties overlap. For example, the basic way of telling iTunes which artist is responsible for a track is to set the **artist** property. So far, so easy. Normally, that artist is the artist for the album as well. But if the album is by a different artist than the track, you can use the **album artist** property to specify who's guilty. And if you want to sort the track by a different artist than you've assigned it to, you can set the **sort artist** property to tell iTunes how to handle the sorting. Similarly, you can set the **sort album artist** property to override the sorting specified by the **album artist** property (if you've set it) or the **artist** property.

- **The meaning of "unplayed"**   The **unplayed** property tells you whether you've ever played the track at all (**false**) or never played it (**true**). If you play the track all the way to the end (or skip to near the end and then let it finish playing), iTunes adds 1 to the **played count** property. So it's possible to have a track with a **played count** of **0** but an **unplayed** value of **false**.

## Playing a Track

To play a track, you simply need to finger your victim and then give iTunes the **play** command.

Usually, the easiest way to identify the track you want is to use the track's name and the playlist it's in. For example, to play the track called **Almost Summer** in the playlist named **Latest Additions**, you can use this statement:

```
play the track "Almost Summer" of playlist "Latest Additions"
```

If the track is in your library rather than in a particular playlist, no problem—just tell iTunes the track is the Library "playlist" like this:

```
play the track "Treat Me Like Your Mother" of the playlist "Library"
```

To pause playback, use the **playpause** command:

```
playpause
```

To restart playback, use the **playpause** command again—just like clicking the Play/Pause button in the iTunes window (or pressing SPACEBAR).

## Looping Through Multiple Tracks

The only problem with identifying a song in the Library by name comes when the Library contains two or more tracks with the same name. When this happens, iTunes plays the first track it finds, which may not be the one you want.

Following is a short script that works through the different versions of the same track, allowing you to pick the one you want. Here's what happens in the script:

- The script uses a **try** block so that it can catch the error generated by the Cancel button in its dialog box.

- The script assigns to the variable **MyGimmes** all the versions of the track Gimme Shelter that iTunes can dig out of the music library.

- The script then uses a **repeat** loop with a counter (**myCounter**) running from **1** to the **count** of **MyGimmes**—in other words, once for each song.

- The script uses the **play** command to start the first of the tracks playing. The **delay 15** command pauses the script for 15 seconds so that you hear that amount of the song.

- The script then displays a three-button dialog (see Figure 12-1) that lets you choose whether to keep playing this version, go on to the next version, or cancel in disgust.

- If the user clicks the Play The Next Version button, the **next track** command starts the next version playing, and the loop continues. If the user clicks the Keep Playing This Version button, the **else** statement runs the **return** command, which ends the loop. If the user clicks the Cancel button, the error handler gives a **playpause** command to pause playback.

```
tell the application id "com.apple.itunes"
    try
        set MyGimmes to every track whose name is "Gimme Shelter"
        repeat with myCounter from 1 to count of MyGimmes
            play the item myCounter of MyGimmes
            delay 5
            display dialog ¬
                "Keep playing this version, or play the next?" ¬
                buttons {"Keep Playing This Version", ¬
                "Play the Next Version", ¬
                "Cancel"} with title "Gimme Shelter"
```

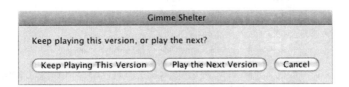

**Figure 12-1**   Using a custom dialog box to choose whether to keep playing the current version of a song or start playing the next version.

```
            if the button returned of the result is ¬
                "Play the Next Version" then
                next track
            else
                return
            end if
        end repeat
    on error number -128
        playpause
    end try
end tell
```

## Changing the Tags for a Track

To keep your library in order and to make iTunes' Smart Playlists work effectively, you'll need to make sure that all the tracks in your library are properly tagged with accurate information. To change the tag information for a track, set the relevant property. For example, the following snippet assigns the tracks from the album **Among My Swan** to the variable **trax** and then uses a **repeat** loop to set the **genre** property, the **year** property, and the **EQ** property of each track:

```
set trax to every track of playlist "Library" ¬
    whose album is "Among My Swan"
repeat with mytrack in trax
    set the genre of mytrack to "Alternative & Punk"
    set the year of mytrack to "1996"
    set EQ of mytrack to "Vocal Booster"
end repeat
```

# Working with Playlists

iTunes uses the **playlist** object to represent a list of tracks or audio streams. Table 12-2 explains the properties of the **playlist** object.

## Creating a New Playlist

To create a new playlist, use a **make new playlist** command, providing the name by adding the **with properties** parameter with the **name** property. For example, the following statement creates a new playlist named **High Desert Rock**:

```
make new playlist with properties {name:"High Desert Rock"}
```

iTunes puts the new playlist at the top level of playlists so that it appears in the Playlists section of the Source list.

| playlist Object Property | Explanation |
|---|---|
| name | The playlist's name |
| duration | An integer giving the total length of the playlist (including all tracks) in seconds. This property is read-only. |
| parent | If the playlist is stored in a folder, the folder's name. This property is read-only. If the playlist is stored at the top level rather than in a folder, checking this property returns error −1728 ("Can't get parent of playlist"). |
| shuffle | **true** to play the songs in random order, **false** to play them in the order in which they're currently sorted. |
| size | A double integer giving the size of the playlist (including all tracks) in bytes—for example, **4.346414914E+9**. This property is read-only. |
| song repeat | Whether the songs are set to repeat all (**all**), repeat one song (**one**), or not repeat (**off**) |
| special kind | A read-only property that indicates whether the playlist is a special one: **none** for a normal playlist; **Audiobooks, folder** for a playlist folder; **Movies, Music, Party Shuffle** (for the iPod DJ feature, which used to be called Party Shuffle); **Podcasts; Purchased Music; TV Shows;** or **Videos** |
| time | The playlist's length (including all songs) in MM:SS format—for example, **"15:13:29"** for a chunky playlist |
| visible | **true** if the playlist appears in the Source list, **false** if it is hidden. This property is read-only. |

**Table 12-2**   Properties of the playlist Object

To get a handle on the new playlist so that you can work with it, assign it to a variable when you create it. You can then add songs to the playlist by using the **duplicate** command, as in the following example:

```
set Listen to make new playlist with properties ¬
    {name:"High Desert Rock", shuffle:true}
duplicate (every track of playlist "Library" ¬
    whose genre is "Stoner Rock") to Listen
```

## Deleting a Playlist

To delete a playlist, use a **delete** command and specify the playlist. For example, the following statement deletes the playlist named **High Desert Rock**:

```
delete playlist "High Desert Rock"
```

**NOTE**
iTunes doesn't confirm the deletion when you take out a playlist using AppleScript.

**Try This** Dealing with All the Songs That Have an Intermediate Rating

I don't know about you, but I find iTunes' rating system to be a great way for slimming down my music library by identifying songs I don't actually listen to. If a song is great, I give it five stars; if it's a keeper, four stars; if I'm undecided, three stars; if I doubt I want to keep it, two stars; and if it's irredeemably wretched, one star. Zero stars indicates a blank slate, a song that hasn't been judged yet.

Every now and then I clear out the one-star and two-star songs—but that leaves the three-star songs in limbo. In this example, you build a script that loops through the three-star songs, playing each in turn and displaying a dialog box (see Figure 12-2) that prompts you to upgrade the rating to four stars or downgrade it to two stars. When you rate the current song, iTunes starts the next playing, and so on until you've waded through all the three-star songs or reached your limit, at which point you click the Cancel button.

**NOTE**
If you use the star rating system differently, change the script to match your needs. For example, if two stars marks your Zone of Terminal Uncertainty, use **every song whose rating is 40**, and then change the rating values of the buttons in the dialog box. If you want to apply a wider range of ratings, use a **choose from list** command rather than the **display dialog** command.

To create the script, follow these steps:

1. In AppleScript Editor, press ⌘-N or choose File | New to create a new script.

2. Start a **tell** block to iTunes, identifying it formally:

```
tell the application id "com.apple.itunes"
end tell
```

**Figure 12-2** The sample script displays a dialog box with buttons for changing the star rating on three-star songs.

3. Inside the **tell** block, add a **with timeout** block to increase the time AppleScript waits before timing out. The default time is two minutes (120 seconds), which is fine for many scripts, but this script needs to be able to wait for the user to listen to almost the whole of a song, which may well be longer than that. The new block appears in boldface here:

```
tell the application id "com.apple.itunes"
    with timeout of 1200 seconds
    end timeout
end tell
```

4. Inside the **timeout** block, add a **try** block, as shown in boldface here. This will let you trap the error that results from clicking the Cancel button in the dialog the script uses.

```
tell the application id "com.apple.itunes"
    with timeout of 1200 seconds
        try
        end try
    end timeout
end tell
```

5. Within the **try** block, create a variable named **three_star_songs** and assign to it every track in the Library whose rating is 60—that is, three stars. The new statement appears in boldface here:

```
tell the application id "com.apple.itunes"
    with timeout of 1200 seconds
        try
            set three_star_songs to every track of ¬
                playlist "Library" whose rating is 60
        end try
    end timeout
end tell
```

6. After that, add a **repeat** loop that uses a **with** structure to run for each song in the **three_star_songs** list, as shown in boldface here:

```
tell the application id "com.apple.itunes"
    with timeout of 1200 seconds
        try
            set three_star_songs to every track of ¬
                playlist "Library" whose rating is 60
            repeat with this_song in three_star_songs
            end repeat
        end timeout
end tell
```

*(continued)*

7. Inside the **repeat** loop, create a variable named **song_details** and add to it the essential details of the current song, which is represented by the **this_song** variable. The new statement appears in boldface here:

```
tell the application id "com.apple.itunes"
    with timeout of 1200 seconds
        try
            set three_star_songs to every track of ¬
                playlist "Library" whose rating is 60
            repeat with this_song in three_star_songs
                set song_details to "Song:" & tab & ¬
name of this_song & return & ¬
                    "Artist:" & tab & artist of this_song & return & ¬
                    "Album:" & tab & album of this_song & return & ¬
                    "Played:" & tab & played count of this_song & return & ¬
                    "Added:" & tab & date added of this_song
            end repeat
        end try
    end timeout
end tell
```

8. Next, add a statement creating the variable **song_length** and setting it to two seconds less than the duration of the song, as shown in boldface here:

```
tell the application id "com.apple.itunes"
    with timeout of 1200 seconds
        try
            set three_star_songs to every track of ¬
                playlist "Library" whose rating is 60
            repeat with this_song in three_star_songs
                set song_details to "Song:" & tab & ¬
                    name of this_song & return & ¬
                    "Artist:" & tab & artist of this_song & return & ¬
                    "Album:" & tab & album of this_song & return & ¬
                    "Played:" & tab & played count of this_song & return & ¬
                    "Added:" & tab & date added of this_song
                set song_length to (duration of this_song) - 2
            end repeat
        end try
    end timeout
end tell
```

9. Use a **play** command to set **this_song** playing, and then display a dialog box that displays the song's information stored in the **song_details** variable and provides buttons for rating the song with two stars, rating it with four stars, and canceling. Set the dialog box to give up after the length of time specified by the **song_length** variable,

so that the dialog box remains displayed until two seconds before the end of the song if the user doesn't click any of the buttons. The new statements appear in boldface here:

```
tell the application id "com.apple.itunes"
    with timeout of 1200 seconds
        try
            set three_star_songs to every track of ¬
                playlist "Library" whose rating is 60
            repeat with this_song in three_star_songs
                set song_details to "Song:" & tab & ¬
                    name of this_song & return & ¬
                    "Artist:" & tab & artist of this_song & return & ¬
                    "Album:" & tab & album of this_song & return & ¬
                    "Played:" & tab & played count of this_song & return & ¬
                    "Added:" & tab & date added of this_song
                set song_length to (duration of this_song) - 2
                play this_song
                display dialog song_details ¬
                    with title "Change Rating of Three-Star Songs" ¬
                    buttons {"Rate As Two Stars **", ¬
                        "Rate As Four Stars ****", ¬
                    "Cancel"} giving up after song_length
            end repeat
        end try
    end timeout
end tell
```

**10.** Use an outer **if** structure to see if the **gave up** property of the dialog box's result is **false** to check whether the user clicked a button in the dialog box. Inside this **if** structure, place a nested **if… then… else if** structure that checks the **button returned** of the dialog box's result and applies a two-star rating for a click of the Rate As Two Stars button or a four-star rating for a click of the Rate As Four Stars button. The outer and nested **if** structures appear in boldface here:

```
tell the application id "com.apple.itunes"
    with timeout of 1200 seconds
        try
            set three_star_songs to every track of ¬
                playlist "Library" whose rating is 60
            repeat with this_song in three_star_songs
                set song_details to "Song:" & tab & ¬
                    name of this_song & return & ¬
                    "Artist:" & tab & artist of this_song & return & ¬
                    "Album:" & tab & album of this_song & return & ¬
                    "Played:" & tab & played count of this_song & return & ¬
                    "Added:" & tab & date added of this_song
                set song_length to (duration of this_song) - 2
                play this_song
                display dialog song_details ¬
```

*(continued)*

```
            with title "Change Rating of Three-Star Songs" ¬
            buttons {"Rate As Two Stars **", ¬
            "Rate As Four Stars ****", ¬
            "Cancel"} giving up after song_length
        if gave up of the result is false then
            if the button returned of the result is ¬
                "Rate As Two Stars **" then
                set the rating of this_song to 40
            else if the button returned of the result is ¬
                "Rate As Four Stars ****" then
                set the rating of this_song to 80
            end if
        end if
    end repeat
end try
end timeout
end tell
```

11. Between the **end repeat** line and the **end try** line, add an **on error** statement that runs with error **number –128** to catch the error generated by clicking the Cancel button in the dialog box. All the error handler needs is a **playpause** command to pause playback in iTunes. The added statements appear in boldface here:

```
tell the application id "com.apple.itunes"
    with timeout of 1200 seconds
        try
            set three_star_songs to every track of ¬
                playlist "Library" whose rating is 60
            repeat with this_song in three_star_songs
                set song_details to "Song:" & tab ¬
                    & name of this_song & return & ¬
                    "Artist:" & tab & artist of this_song & return & ¬
                    "Album:" & tab & album of this_song & return & ¬
                    "Played:" & tab & played count of this_song & return & ¬
                    "Added:" & tab & date added of this_song
                set song_length to (duration of this_song) - 2
                play this_song
                display dialog song_details ¬
                    with title "Change Rating of Three-Star Songs" ¬
                    buttons {"Rate As Two Stars **", ¬
                    "Rate As Four Stars ****", ¬
                    "Cancel"} giving up after song_length
                if gave up of the result is false then
                    if the button returned of the result is ¬
                        "Rate As Two Stars **" then
                        set the rating of this_song to 40
                    else if the button returned of the result is ¬
                        "Rate As Four Stars ****" then
                        set the rating of this_song to 80
                    end if
                end if
```

```
               end repeat
           on error number -128
               playpause
           end try
       end timeout
   end tell
```

12. Save the script under a name of your choice.

13. Press ⌘-R or click the Run button on the toolbar to run the script.

# Working with iPhoto

iPhoto is a terrific application for manipulating and managing your photos manually on your Mac, and you can use much of its functionality via AppleScript too.

Apart from the **application** object, which—like other applications—iPhoto uses to represent the application as a whole, the three main objects you need to know about when working with iPhoto from AppleScript are these:

● **album**    The **album** object represents an album in an iPhoto library.

● **photo**    The **photo** object represents a photo.

● **keyword**    The **keyword** class represents a keyword you can associate with photos.

## Working with Albums and Photos

iPhoto uses the **album** object to represent an album—any kind of album. Table 12-3 explains the properties of the **album** object.

| album Object Property | Explanation |
|---|---|
| name | The album's name |
| id | An integer giving the album's unique ID within iPhoto. This property is read-only. |
| children | A list of the albums that this album contains |
| parent | The name of the parent album that contains this album |
| type | The album type (see Table 12-4). This property is read-only. |
| URL | If you've published the album, or if you've subscribed to it, the URL on which the album is shared |

**Table 12-3**  Properties of the album Object

As you can see, the properties are pretty straightforward, except for the **type** property, which Table 12-4 explains.

### Creating a New Album

To create a new album in iPhoto, use a **new album** command and specify the **name** parameter with a string for thc name. For example, the following statement creates a new album named *Vacation Photos*:

```
new album name "Vacation Photos"
```

When you create a new album like this, iPhoto automatically puts it at the top level of the Albums list, just as it does when you create a new album when working interactively.

| Album Type Constant | Explanation |
|---|---|
| book album | A photo book |
| events album | An Event |
| faces album | An album in Faces |
| flagged album | The "album" containing the photos you've flagged |
| folder album | A folder (for putting other albums in) |
| last import album | The Last Import album in the Recent category |
| last months album | The Last 12 Months album (or however many months you've chosen in General preferences) |
| last rolls album | The Last Roll album used in previous versions of iPhoto |
| photo library album | The Photo Library |
| places album | An album in Places |
| published album | An album you've published |
| regular album | A regular, honest-to-god album |
| shared album | An album you've shared with other iPhoto users on your network |
| shared library | Someone else's shared library to which you've connected |
| slideshow album | A slideshow |
| smart album | A Smart Album |
| subscribed album | Someone else's published album to which you've subscribed |
| trash album | The Trash |
| unknown album type | An album that iPhoto can't recognize |

**Table 12-4** iPhoto's Different Types of Albums

## Seeing Whether an Album Exists

To see whether an album already exists, use an **exists** command. For example, the following snippet checks to see whether an album called **Industrial Seascapes** already exists; if not, the code creates the album. Either way, the code assigns the **Industrial Seascapes** album to the variable **myAlbum** so that you can then work with it.

```
if exists album "Industrial Seascapes" then
    set myAlbum to album "Industrial Seascapes"
else
    set myAlbum to new album name "Industrial Seascapes"
end if
```

## Deleting an Album

To delete an album, use the **remove** command. This gets rid of the album but leaves the photos it contains in iPhoto, just as when you delete an album when working interactively.

For example, the following statement deletes the album named **Lombard Stunts**:

```
remove the album "Lombard Stunts"
```

# Working with Photos

Normally, much of what you'll want to do with iPhoto involves photos. To manipulate photos, you work with the **photo** object. Table 12-5 explains the properties of the **photo** object.

## Setting Properties for a Photo

As you can see in Table 12-5, many of the properties for a photo—for example, the **dimensions** property and the **height** and **width** properties—are read-only. But you can change properties such as the title and rating easily enough, as in this example, which uses the photo assigned to the variable **my_pic**:

```
tell my_pic
    set the rating to 4
    set the title to "Oregon Cliffs"
    set the date to current date
end tell
```

You can identify photos within albums or within the photo library as a whole, but what's often most convenient is to work with a selection of photos you've made manually. To do so, get the **selection** object and assign it to a variable, and then use the **item** object to pick out the object you want. Here's an example:

```
set my_pix to the selection
set my_pic to item 1 of my_pix
```

| photo Object Property | Explanation |
|---|---|
| altitude | An integer giving the GPS altitude in meters. The value 1.79769313486232E+308 means that the altitude isn't available rather than that the camera was orbiting the Horsehead Nebula. |
| comment | The comment attached to the photo |
| date | The date and time the photo was taken |
| dimensions | The photo's width and height in pixels, returned as a list—for example, **{1600.0, 1200.0}**. This property is read-only. |
| height | An integer giving the photo's height in pixels. This property is read-only. |
| id | An integer giving the photo's unique ID. This property is read-only. |
| image filename | The name of the file containing the photo. This property is read-only. |
| image path | The path to the file containing the photo, including the filename. This property is read-only. |
| latitude | An integer giving the GPS latitude of the photo, using the range −90.0 to 90.0. The value 3.40282346638529E+38 means that the latitude isn't available. |
| longitude | An integer giving the GPS longitude of the photo, using the range −180.0 to 180.0. The value 3.40282346638529E+38 means that the longitude isn't available. |
| name | The text assigned to the photo's title. This property returns the same text as the **title** property. |
| original path | The path to the original photo file you imported, including the filename. If you haven't edited the original file, this property may return the same file path as the **image path** property. This property is read-only. |
| rating | An integer giving the star rating, from 0 (no stars) through 5 (five stars) |
| thumbnail filename | The path to the thumbnail file for the photo, including the filename. This property is read-only. |
| thumbnail path | The name of the thumbnail file for the photo, including the filename. This property is read-only. |
| title | The title assigned to the photo. This property returns the same text as the **name** property. |
| width | The photo's width in pixels. This property is read-only. |

**Table 12-5** Properties of the photo Object

### NOTE

You can't pick items out of the selection directly—for example, by using **set myPic to item 1 of the selection**. That fails with the error "Can't make item 1 of selection into type reference." But if you assign the selection to a variable, you can pick out the items just fine.

## Adding Photos to an Album

To add photos to an album, use the **add** command and provide properties that identify the photos you want. Here are three examples of ways of identifying photos:

- **By keyword**   To identify photos by keyword, set a variable to the first **keyword** item that has the name you want. Then use **whose keywords contains** and that keyword to identify the photos. Here's an example:

```
set FamilyKey to item 1 of (every keyword whose name is "Family")
add (every photo in album "Photos" ¬
    whose keywords contains FamilyKey) ¬
    to album "Family Snaps"
```

- **By dimensions**   To identify photos by dimensions, use a statement such as **whose dimensions is equal to** followed by a list of the dimensions—for example, **{320, 480}** for portrait-orientation photos taken on an iPhone:

```
add (every photo whose dimensions is equal to {320, 480}) ¬
    to album "iPhone Photos"
```

- **By rating**   To identify photos by rating, use a statement such as **whose rating is** and the rating you want. For example, the following script adds all the five-star photos to a variable named **all_the_best** and then uses a **repeat** loop to assign 20 of the photos to the album **Best Photos**:

```
tell application "iPhoto"
    set all_the_best to every photo whose rating is 5
    repeat with myCounter from 1 to 20
        add item myCounter of all_the_best ¬
            to the album "Best Photos"
    end repeat
end tell
```

## Removing a Photo from an Album

To remove a photo from an album, use the **remove** command and specify the photo. For example, the following statement removes the first photo from the album named **Best Photos**:

```
remove the first photo of album "Best Photos"
```

# Working with Keywords

The only property of the **keyword** object that's not inherited from the standard **item** class is the **name** property, which is the string assigned to the keyword.

## Finding Out Which Keywords Are Assigned to a Photo

To find out which keywords are assigned to a photo, use a **get every keyword** command for the appropriate **photo** object. For example, the following statement returns every keyword assigned to the first photo:

```
get every keyword of photo 1
```

This statement returns a list such as **{keyword "Europe" of application "iPhoto", keyword "Vacations" of application "iPhoto"}**.

## Applying a Keyword to a Photo

To apply a keyword to a photo, use the **assign keyword** command. This command requires you to select the photo or photos first, which you can do by using the **select** method.

For example, the following statements select the first photo in the album **Industrial Decay** and assign the existing keyword **Urban** to it:

```
select the first photo in album "Industrial Decay"
assign keyword string "Countryside"
```

### *CAUTION*

If you try to assign a keyword that you haven't yet created, iPhoto pretends to apply it but doesn't. iPhoto doesn't throw an error, but the photo doesn't receive the keyword.

## Finding Out Which Keywords Are Available

To find out which keywords exist in iPhoto, return **every keyword**. For example, the following statement assigns every keyword to the variable **all_keywords**:

```
set all_keywords to every keyword
```

The first keyword in iPhoto's default list is **_Favorite_**, which is the special term for the favorite keyword designated by the check mark. To get all the keywords except this one, exclude it by name, like this:

```
set all_keywords to every keyword whose name is not "_Favorite_"
```

## Creating a New Keyword

At this writing, you need to create your keywords manually in iPhoto rather than creating them in AppleScript. A statement such as **make new keyword at end of keywords with properties {name:"Insolvency"}** should work, but it flops with an "AppleEvent handler failed" message.

**Try This**  Creating an Album and Adding Photos to It

In this example, you create a new album in iPhoto and add photos to it. You then choose whether to delete the album.

To create the sample script, follow these steps:

**1.** Open iPhoto if it's not already running.

**2.** Select the photos that you want to use. While AppleScript lets you select photos programmatically, it makes more sense to select them manually for many scripts.

**3.** In AppleScript Editor, press ⌘-N or choose File | New to create a new script.

**4.** Start a **tell** block to iPhoto, addressing it by its formal name:

```
tell the application id "com.apple.iphoto"
end tell
```

**5.** Create the variable named **my_pix** and assign the selected photos to it, as shown in boldface here:

```
tell the application id "com.apple.iphoto"
    set my_pix to the selection
end tell
```

**6.** Create a new album named **ABG Test**, as shown in boldface here:

```
tell the application id "com.apple.iphoto"
    set my_pix to the selection
    new album name "ABG Test"
end tell
```

**7.** Use a **repeat** loop to add each picture (identified by the **my_pic** variable) in **my_pix** to the album, as shown in boldface here:

```
tell the application id "com.apple.iphoto"
    set my_pix to the selection
    new album name "ABG Test"
    repeat with my_pic in my_pix
        add my_pic to album "ABG Test"
    end repeat
end tell
```

**8.** Add a **display dialog** statement to display a dialog box offering to delete the album, and use an **if** statement to delete the album if the user clicks the Yes button. The code appears in boldface here:

```
tell the application id "com.apple.iphoto"
    set my_pix to the selection
```

*(continued)*

```
new album name "ABG Test"
repeat with my_pic in my_pix
    add my_pic to album "ABG Test"
end repeat
display dialog "Delete the ABG Test album?" ¬
    buttons {"Yes", "No"} ¬
    default button "Yes" with icon caution
if the button returned of the result is "Yes" then
    remove the album "ABG Test"
end if
end tell
```

9. Save the script under a name of your choice.

10. Press ⌘-R or click the Run button on the toolbar to run the script. When the dialog box appears (see Figure 12-3), click the Yes button if you want to delete the album. Click the No button if you want to check the album's contents and then delete it manually.

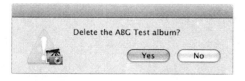

**Figure 12-3**  Choose whether to delete the sample album the script creates.

# Chapter 13

## Automating Apple Mail

## Key Skills & Concepts

- Working with Mail accounts
- Working with mailboxes
- Creating and sending messages
- Dealing with incoming messages
- Working with tasks

Apple's Mail application may come as part of the operating system, but it's a powerful enough e-mail client for anyone who doesn't need the organization power—and cost—of high-end solutions such as Microsoft Entourage. And because you can script Mail using AppleScript, you can automate everything from setting up mail accounts to creating mail messages and dealing with incoming messages.

**NOTE**
Chapter 16 discusses how to bring AppleScript to bear on Microsoft Entourage.

First, you need to know the essentials of how Mail handles messages. This may be obvious once you've thought about it—but if you've just used Mail casually, you may have had no reason to ponder its structure.

# Working with Mail Accounts

To work with Mail, the first object you need to understand is the **account** object. Mail uses this object to represent an e-mail account, and it's the key to getting anything done in Mail.

As you know, before you can start sending or receiving messages with Mail, you need to set up an account in Accounts preferences. The account includes the e-mail address, password, incoming mail server, outgoing mail server, and details of how you want to use the account—for example, whether you want to include this account when you automatically check for new mail.

Similarly, whenever you script Mail to take an action, you need to tell it which account to use. To get to a message, you have to go through the appropriate account to the mailbox in it that contains the message.

| Account Type | Explanation |
|---|---|
| mac | An account on Apple's MobileMe service (which used to be called the .Mac service—hence the name). A MobileMe e-mail address uses the @me.com domain name (or the @mac.com domain name for backward compatibility—both @me.com and @mac.com resolve to the same address). A MobileMe account uses an IMAP mail server. |
| imap | An account that uses the Internet Mail Access Protocol (IMAP). IMAP's big advantage over POP3 is that you can keep your messages on the server rather than downloading them to your Mac. This lets you check your mail from any computer without getting confused about which message is where. |
| pop | An account that uses the Post Office Protocol version 3 (POP3) |
| smtp | An account that uses the Simple Mail Transfer Protocol (SMTP). This account is for sending e-mail only and works alongside the other three types of accounts. |

**Table 13-1**   AppleScript's account type Constants for Mail Accounts

## Understanding the Four Types of Accounts

Mail provides four different types of accounts for connecting to different types of mail servers. Table 13-1 gives the details.

Table 13-2 explains the properties of the **account** object. These properties are largely shared by the four account types, but each account type also has some extra settings of its own.

# Ask the Expert

**Q:**  What is Mail's smtp **account type for?**

**A:**  At first sight, the **smtp** account type is enough to raise your eyebrows. As you probably know from setting up e-mail accounts or arguing with mail servers, the Simple Mail Transfer Protocol (SMTP) is used only for sending messages, not for receiving them.

Mail has the **smtp** account type to dissociate the outgoing mail from the incoming mail. While most ISPs give you a pair of mail servers—an incoming mail server (POP3, IMAP, or HTTP) and an outgoing mail server (SMTP)—many ISPs prevent you from sending mail via that SMTP server unless your computer is logged in to your Internet account with that ISP. This measure, which is intended to cut down on the amount of spam being sent, is only a partial success, but it means that you may need to send mail using a different SMTP server.

| account Property | Explanation |
|---|---|
| account directory | The folder in which the account stores its messages and other items |
| account type | The account type: **mac**, **imap**, **pop**, or **smtp** |
| authentication | The account type used for the account. The basic type is **password**. The other options are **apop**, **kerberos 5**, **ntlm**, **md5**, and **none**. |
| delivery account | The e-mail account used for sending mail from this account. This property returns an **smtp server** object. |
| email addresses | The e-mail address or addresses set up for the account |
| empty junk messages frequency | −1 for never deleting, 0 for deleting when you quit Mail, or a positive integer giving the number of days to wait before deleting junk mail (for example, **3** to wait three days) |
| empty junk messages on quit | **true** to delete messages in the Junk Mail folders (there's a folder for each account) when you quit Mail; **false** to keep the messages until you delete them manually |
| empty sent messages frequency | −1 for never deleting sent messages, 0 for deleting when you quit Mail, or a positive integer giving the number of days to wait before deleting sent messages |
| empty sent messages on quit | **true** to delete sent messages when you quit Mail; **false** to keep the messages until you deal with them manually |
| empty trash frequency | −1 for never emptying the Trash, 0 for emptying it when you quit Mail, or a positive integer specifying how many days to wait before deleting items in the Trash |
| empty trash on quit | **true** to empty the Trash when you quit Mail; **false** to leave the Trash for you to empty manually |
| enabled | **true** if the account is enabled for sending and receiving mail; **false** if it is disabled |
| full name | The full name of the user for the account |
| include when getting new mail | **true** if the account is set for inclusion when you check for new mail; **false** if it is not |
| move deleted messages to trash | **true** if the account is set to move deleted messages to the Trash; **false** if it is not. |
| name | The account's name (for example, **billg@me.com**) |
| password | The account's password. This property is write-only: You can set it using a script, but you can't get it. |
| port | The port on the mail server to which the account connects. Standard ports are **110** (POP3), **143** (IMAP without SSL), and **993** (IMAP with SSL), but an ISP can set any port it chooses. |
| server name | The name of the server to which the account connects—for example, **mail.mac.com** |
| user name | The user name for the account (the name used to connect to the server) |
| uses ssl | **true** if the account is set to use Secure Sockets Layer (SSL) when connecting to the mail server; **false** if it is not |

**Table 13-2** Properties of the account Object

| pop account Property | Explanation |
|---|---|
| big message warning size | Set this property to an integer size to specify the size limit in bytes above which Mail should prompt the user before downloading a large message. For example, set **2048000** to prompt for any message 2MB or larger. Set this property to **−1** to turn off prompting. |
| delayed message deletion interval | Set this property to an integer to specify the number of days to wait before deleting downloaded messages from the server. Set this property to **0** to delete messages as soon as you download them. |
| delete mail on server | Set this property to **true** to tell Mail to delete messages from the server when you download them (this is normally the most useful setting). Set this property to **false** to keep messages on the server—useful when you're accessing your mail from another computer and still want to be able to download it to your main Mac afterward. |
| delete messages when moved from inbox | Set this property to **true** to delete messages from the server when you move them from your inbox—either deleting them or moving them to another folder. This setting lets you keep the messages in your inbox available to multiple computers until you deal with them. Set this property to **false** if you want to keep the messages on the server even when they leave your inbox. |

**Table 13-3**   Extra Properties of the pop account Object

The **pop account** object also has the properties shown in Table 13-3.

The **imap account** object also has the properties shown in Table 13-4. The **mac account** object is an IMAP account, so it also has these properties. (Technically, the **mac account** object inherits these properties from the **imap account** object.)

The **smtp server** object has only these properties: **name**, **password**, **account type**, **authentication**, **enabled**, **user name**, **port**, **server name**, and **uses ssl**.

The following sections provide examples of working with accounts in Mail via AppleScript.

## Checking and Changing the Settings for an E-mail Account

By manipulating the properties of an e-mail account, you can quickly change its settings. Here are some examples of checks and changes you may want to make.

### NOTE
Because you probably don't want to mess with the settings on a live mail account, this section of the chapter does not have a Try This example. But do try any of the following examples that you're comfortable running on your mail accounts.

| imap account Property | Explanation |
|---|---|
| compact mailboxes when closing | Set this property to **true** to make Mail automatically compact the mailbox when you either switch to another mailbox or quit Mail. Set this property to **false** if you prefer to compact manually. |
| message caching | Choose how to cache messages for the account. You can choose **all messages and their attachments**, **all messages but omit attachments**, **do not keep copies of any messages**, or **only messages I have read**. |
| store drafts on server | Set this property to **true** if you want to store draft messages on the IMAP server so that you can access them from any computer. Set this property to **false** to keep the drafts on your Mac. |
| store junk mail on server | Set this property to **true** if you want to store junk mail on the IMAP server. Set it to **false** if you want to store junk mail on your Mac. |
| store sent messages on server | Set this property to **true** if you want to store messages you've sent on the IMAP server. Set it to **false** if you want to store sent messages on your Mac for easy access. |
| store deleted messages on server | Set this property to **true** if you want to store deleted messages on the server. Set it to **false** if you want to store deleted messages on your Mac. |

**Table 13-4**   Extra Properties of the imap account Object and the mac account Object

## Finding Out Where an Account Stores Its Mail

To find out the folder in which an account stores its mail, return the **account directory** property of the **account** object. For example, the following statement returns the account directory of the first account in Mail:

```
get the account directory of the first account
```

This returns a result such as file **"Macintosh HD:Users:pete:Library:Mail:Mac-pete_wright:"**.

## Finding Out the E-mail Address for an Account

To find out the e-mail address associated with an account, get the **e-mail addresses** property of the **account** object. For example, the following statement returns the e-mail addresses for the account named **billg@me.com**:

```
get email addresses of account "billg@me.com"
```

This returns a list of e-mail addresses such as **{"billg@mac.com", "billg@me.com"}**. Most accounts will return a single e-mail address (as a single-item list).

## Setting Mail Not to Check for New Messages on an Account

To prevent Mail from checking for new messages on a particular account, set the **include when getting new mail** property to **false**:

```
set include when getting new mail of the account ".Mac account" to false
```

Set this property back to **true** when you want to start checking for new mail again.

## Setting a Size Limit for Large-Attachment Warnings on a POP3 Account

To set the size limit for warnings about large incoming attachments on a POP3 account, set the **big message size warning** property for the **account** object to the appropriate number of bytes. For example, the following statement sets the trigger level to 2048000 bytes (2MB):

```
tell the account "myEarth"
    set the big message warning size to 2048000
end tell
```

## Setting Up a New SMTP Server for an E-mail Account

To set up a new SMTP server, use a **make new smtp server** command as shown in the next example. This command is ticklish and may require some juggling to make it work correctly. The example assigns the server address (**smtp.acmevirtualindustries.com**) to the variable **smtpserver** and the user name (**w_acme**) to the variable **smtpuser**, and then uses the **make new smtp server** command with the **smtpserver** variable to create the new **smtp server** object. It then uses a **tell** block to set the authentication, the user name, and the password.

```
tell application "Mail"
    set smtpserver to "smtp.acmevirtualindustries.com"
    set smtpuser to "w_acme"
    set mysmtp to make new smtp server with properties ¬
        {server name:smtpserver, uses ssl:false}
    tell mysmtp
        set authentication to password
        set user name to smtpuser
        set password to "beepbeep"
    end tell
end tell
```

## Setting a User Account to Use a Different SMTP Server

When you connect to the Internet via a different connection than your regular ISP, you may need to use a different SMTP server in order to send mail. To change the SMTP server, set the **smtp server** property of the account. Here's an example that retrieves the **smtp server** object from the account named **Roving**, stores it in a variable named **TravelServ**, and then applies the contents of that variable as the **smtp server** for the account named **Main Mail**:

```
set TravelServ to the smtp server of account "Roving"
tell the account "Main Mail"
    set the smtp server to TravelServ
end tell
```

# Working with Mailboxes

Within each account lurk the **mailbox** objects that represent the mailboxes. Though vital, mailboxes are simple objects, with just four properties each, as Table 13-5 explains.

Of these four properties, the ones you'll use the most are the **name** property (which you use to identify the mailbox you want to get a hold of) and the **unread count** property, which lets you see how many new messages the mailbox contains.

## Creating a New Mailbox

To create a new mailbox, use a **make new mailbox** command and use the **with properties** parameter to specify the **name** property. For example, the following statement creates a new mailbox named **Read Later**:

```
make new mailbox with properties {name:"Read Later"}
```

## Renaming a Mailbox

To rename a mailbox, identify it by its current name and set the **name** property to the new name. For example, the following statement renames the mailbox **Odd Messages** to **Holding Zone**:

```
set the name of mailbox "Odd Messages" to "Holding Zone"
```

| mailbox Property | Explanation |
|---|---|
| name | The mailbox's name |
| unread count | An integer giving the number of unread messages in a mailbox |
| account | The account to which the mailbox belongs |
| container | The account to which the mailbox belongs |

**Table 13-5**  Properties of the mailbox Object

## Deleting a Mailbox

To delete a mailbox, use a **delete** command and identify the mailbox by name. For example, the following statement deletes the mailbox named **Holding Zone**:

```
delete the mailbox "Holding Zone"
```

### CAUTION

When you delete a mailbox from AppleScript, Mail deletes the mailbox and the messages it contains without confirmation.

**Try This** Finding the Number of New Messages for Only Some Accounts

The tell-tale number on the Mail icon on the Dock shows the total number of new messages without separating them out into what's hot and what's not. To find out the number of new messages in only one account, or in only some accounts, create a script that returns the **unread count** property of the appropriate **mailbox** object.

Follow these steps to create this script:

**1.** In AppleScript Editor, press ⌘-N or choose File | New to create a new script.

**2.** Start a **tell** block to Mail, addressing it by its **application id**:

```
tell the application id "com.apple.mail"
end tell
```

**3.** Create a variable named **NewCount** and assign to it the **unread count** property of the **mailbox "INBOX"** of the account you want to use. The sample account here is named **Main**, but you'll need to substitute the name of one of your accounts to make the code work. The new statement appears in boldface here:

```
tell the application id "com.apple.mail"
    set NewCount to the unread count of mailbox "INBOX" ¬
    of account "Main"
end tell
```

**4.** Add an **if… then… else if… else** block that checks the value of **NewCount** and assigns suitable text to the variable **myMess**, as shown in boldface here:

```
tell the application id "com.apple.mail"
    set NewCount to the unread count of mailbox "INBOX" ¬
    of account "Main"
    if NewCount is 0 then
```

*(continued)*

```
        set myMess to "Your Inbox contains no new messages."
    else if NewCount is 1 then
        set myMess to "Your Inbox contains 1 new message."
    else
        set myMess to "Your Inbox contains " & NewCount ¬
            & " new messages."
    end if
end tell
```

5. Add a **display dialog** statement to display the **myMess** message in an OK-only dialog box with the title **New Messages**. The new statement appears in boldface here:

```
tell the application id "com.apple.mail"
    set NewCount to the unread count of mailbox "INBOX" ¬
        of account "Main"
    if NewCount is 0 then
        set myMess to "Your Inbox contains no new messages."
    else if NewCount is 1 then
        set myMess to "Your Inbox contains 1 new message."
    else
        set myMess to "Your Inbox contains " & NewCount ¬
            & " new messages."
    end if
    display dialog myMess with title "New Messages" buttons {"OK"}
end tell
```

6. Save the script under a name of your choice.

7. Press ⌘-R or click the Run button on the toolbar to run the script. You'll see a dialog box such as the one shown in Figure 13-1.

8. Click the OK button in the dialog box, and then close the script.

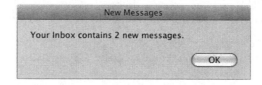

**Figure 13-1** A dialog box that displays the number of unread messages in only one of Mail's accounts.

# Creating and Sending Messages

Mail distinguishes between messages you send, which it calls *outgoing messages,* and messages you receive, which it calls simply *messages.* This section shows you how to work first with outgoing messages and then with incoming messages.

## Creating an Outgoing Message

Mail uses the **outgoing message** object to represent each outgoing message. Table 13-6 explains the properties of the **outgoing message** object.

To create a new outgoing message, you use the **make new outgoing message** command. Normally, you'll want to set the essential properties of the message—the **sender** property, the **subject** property, and the **content** property—in the same command. Here's an example that first assigns the text for the **content** property to a variable to shorten the **make new outgoing message** statement:

```
tell the application id "com.apple.Mail"
    set cust_mess to ¬
    "Thank you for your recent query about our products." ¬
        & return & return & ¬
        "We will send you a full information pack today."
    make new outgoing message with properties ¬
        {sender:"eduardo_sempio@mac.com", ¬
        subject:"Thank You for Your Product Query", ¬
        content:cust_mess, visible:true}
end tell
```

| outgoing message Property | Explanation |
|---|---|
| sender | The sender to use for the outgoing message. Identify the account by name—for example, **steveb@mac.com**. |
| subject | The subject line of the message |
| content | The content of the message's body |
| visible | **true** if the message is displayed on screen; **false** if it is hidden from view. The default setting is **false**. |
| message signature | The signature (if any) applied to the message |
| Id | A unique identifier for this message |

**Table 13-6**  Properties of the outgoing message Object

## Ask the Expert

**Q:** When I use the make new outgoing message **command, nothing happens—but AppleScript doesn't return an error. What's wrong?**

**A:** Most likely, you just need to set the **visible** property of the **outgoing message** object to **true** so that you can see what's happening.

If you don't set the visible property to true, leaving it at its default setting of false, Mail creates a hidden message that you can't check visually. You can kick this message into visibility by trying to quit Mail, at which point the application will prompt you to save the changes to the message.

You'll have noticed that the **outgoing message** object doesn't have a property for the recipient or recipients, let alone recipients of carbon-free copies or blind-carbon copies. Instead, you need to add the recipients separately using a **make new** command and the appropriate ones from the three types of **recipient** objects explained in Table 13-7.

Each of the **recipient** objects has two properties:

- **address**   The e-mail address for the recipient
- **name**   The display name used for the recipient

Without the **address** property, the message can't be sent. But normally, you'll want to use the **name** property as well to make clear who the message is being sent to.

The following example creates a new message, assigns it to the variable **my_mess**, and then uses that variable to add a recipient:

```
tell the application id "com.apple.Mail"
    set my_mess to make new outgoing message with properties ¬
        {sender:"eduardo_sempio@mac.com", subject:"Latest News", ¬
```

| recipient Object | Recipients List | Explanation |
|---|---|---|
| to recipient | to recipients | A recipient in the message's To field |
| cc recipient | cc recipients | A recipient in the message's Cc field |
| bcc recipient | bcc recipients | A recipient in the message's Bcc field |

**Table 13-7**   Mail's Three Types of Recipients

```
        content:"Here is the latest news about our company.", ¬
        visible:true}
    tell my_mess
        make new to recipient at end of to recipients with properties ¬
        {name:"Chris Smith", address:"chris__smith@mac.com"}
    end tell
end tell
```

The following example, which assumes the **my_mess** message has already been created, adds a **to recipient**, a **cc recipient**, and a **bcc recipient**:

```
tell my_mess
    make new to recipient at end of to recipients with properties ¬
        {name:"Chris Smith", address:"chris__smith@mac.com"}
    make new cc recipient at end of cc recipients with properties ¬
        {name:"Jan Ramirez", address:"jan.ramirez44@gmail.com"}
    make new bcc recipient at end of bcc recipients with properties ¬
        {name:"Dan Philps", address:"dan_philps@hotmail.com"}
end tell
```

### NOTE
To add multiple recipients of the same type, use a **make new** statement for each recipient.
You can also use a **repeat** loop.

## Attaching a File to an Outgoing Message
When you need to send a file as an attachment, use a **make new attachment** command to tell the **content** object of the **message** object to add the attachment and where to put it. The **attachment** class has only one property, **file name**, which you use to specify the path and name of the file you want to attach.

For example, the following statement assigns an alias to the file **Macintosh HD: Users:dan:Documents:User Guide.pdf** to a variable named **myFile**, which it then uses to attach the file to the message referenced by the variable **my_mess**:

```
set myFile to alias "Macintosh HD:Users:guy:Documents:User Guide.pdf"
tell my_mess
    tell the content
        make new attachment with properties {file name:myFile} at
after last paragraph
    end tell
end tell
```

To attach multiple files to the same message, use a separate **make new attachment** statement for each file. Alternatively, use a **repeat** loop to add the files.

## Sending the Message

When you've finished creating the message, all you need to do to send it is use the **send** command. For example, the following command sends the message referenced by the variable **my_mess**:

```
send my_mess
```

# Dealing with Incoming Messages

Mail uses the **message** object to represent an incoming message (as opposed to the **outgoing message** object that represents an outgoing message). Table 13-8 explains the properties of the **message** object.

| message Property | Explanation |
|---|---|
| id | A unique integer that identifies the message. Mail assigns this integer, which is read-only. |
| all headers | A read-only property that contains all the headers of the message (including the headers that are normally hidden) |
| background color | The background color for the message. You can use **none** (the best choice), **blue**, **gray**, **green**, **orange**, **purple**, **red**, or **yellow**. In theory, you can also use **other** and specify an RGB color, but this doesn't work properly at this writing. |
| mailbox | The mailbox that contains the message |
| content | The message's text content |
| date received | The date that Mail received the message |
| date sent | The date the message was sent |
| deleted status | **true** if the message is marked as deleted; **false** if it is not |
| flagged status | **true** if the message has a flag set on it; **false** if it does not |
| Junk mail status | **true** if the message is marked as being junk mail; **false** if it is not |
| read status | **true** if the message is marked as having been read; false if it is marked as unread |
| message id | A text ID that uniquely identifies the message—for example, **"BAY113-DAT84 E653D459B1FDEC4D92DB1200@phx.gbl"** |
| sender | The sender of the message—for example, **"Helen Hochwasser <h_wasser@hotmail.com>"** |
| subject | The subject line of the message |
| was forwarded | **true** if the message is marked as having been forwarded; **false** if it is not |
| was redirected | **true** if the message is marked as having been redirected; **false** if it is not |
| was replied to | **true** if the message is marked as having had a reply sent for it; **false** if it is not |

**Table 13-8**  Properties of the Mail message Object

Mail puts messages you receive into the inbox for the account to which they're sent, so this is where you'll usually want to check for them. For example, the following statement returns the name of the sender of the first message in the inbox of the account named **Main Mail**:

```
get the sender of the first message in the mailbox "INBOX" ¬
    of the account "Main Mail"
```

### NOTE
You must refer to the inbox in capitals—**INBOX**—to make Mail understand which mailbox you're referring to.

## Opening a Message in a Separate Window

You can read a message easily enough in the message area of Mail's Message Viewer window, but you may want to open a message in a separate window so that you can give it your undivided attention or scrutinize it alongside another open message.

To open a message, use the **open** command, identifying the message, the mailbox that contains it, and the account that contains the mailbox. For example, the following **tell** block opens the first message in the inbox of the account named **Main Mail**:

```
tell the mailbox "INBOX" of the account "Main Mail" ¬
    open the first message
end tell
```

## Deleting a Message

To delete a message, use the **delete** command. As usual, you need to identify the message, the mailbox that contains it, and the account that contains the mailbox. For example, the following statement deletes the first message in the inbox of the account named **Main Mail**:

```
tell the mailbox "INBOX" of the account "Main Mail" ¬
    to delete the first message
```

### NOTE
Deleting a message puts it in Mail's Trash, from which you can recover it until you empty the Trash.

## Moving a Message to a Folder

To move a message to a folder, you set the **mailbox** property of the appropriate **message** object to the target mailbox. For example:

```
set the mailbox of the first message ¬
    in the mailbox "INBOX" in the account ".Mac account" ¬
    to mailbox "GMSV" of mailbox "Newsletters"
```

**NOTE**
To refer to one mailbox stored inside another, use the name of the nested mailbox, "of," and the name of the mailbox that contains it. For example, use **mailbox "Shauna" of mailbox "Friends"** to refer to the mailbox named **Shauna** stored in the mailbox named **Friends**.

## Dealing with Incoming Attachments

When you receive a file attached to a message, Mail treats the file as a **mail attachment** object. This object has the properties explained in Table 13-9.

To save an attachment to a folder, you can use the standard **save** command with the **name** property of the appropriate item in the **mail attachment** object. For example, the following statement saves the first attached file of the second message in the Inbox folder of the account named **Main Mail** to the folder **Macintosh HD:Users:pik:Downloads**:

```
tell the mailbox "INBOX" of the account "Main Mail"
    save the first item of the mail attachment of the second message ¬
        in "Macintosh HD:Users:pik:Downloads:" & ¬
        name of the first item of the mail attachment ¬
        of the second message
end tell
```

| mail attachment Property | Explanation |
|---|---|
| **name** | The file name or names of the attached files, returned as a list—for example, {"**Literary Trauma.docx**","**Sheep Design in the Rockies.jpg**"} |
| **MIME type** | The MIME type of the attachment—for example, **text/plain** for a text file, **image/jpeg** for a JPEG file, **application/msword** for a Microsoft Word document, **application/pdf** for a PDF file, or **application/zip** for a zip file. This property returns a list—for example, {"application/pdf", "application/zip", "text/plain"} for three attachments. |
| **file size** | The approximate size of the attached file, measured in bytes, as a list—for example, {**228777, 896834, 482525**} for three attachments. Because sending a file as an attachment adds overhead, the attachment's file size is larger than the size of the file you end up removing from the message. |
| **downloaded** | **true** if Mail has downloaded the file from the server; **false** if it has not. Again, you get a list—for example, {**false,false**} for a brace of attachments that are still on the server. |
| **Id** | A text ID that uniquely identifies the attached file within the message (rather than globally)—for example, **1** or **1.2**. Once more, you get a list—for example, {"1"} for a single attachment. |

**Table 13-9**   Properties of the mail attachment Object

This is fine if you know that the message has an attachment. If not, you need to test. The following code shows one way of finding messages with attachments—using a **repeat** loop to walk through the messages in a mailbox one by one, checking each to see if the **name** property of the first item of the mail attachment is not equal to a blank string (""), and then saving it with a similar technique to that described previously.

```
tell the application "Mail"
    set myFolder to "Macintosh HD:Users:guy:Incoming:"
    try
        tell the mailbox "INBOX" of the account "Demon"
            repeat with myCounter from 1 to count of messages
                if the name of item 1 of the mail attachment ¬
                    of the message myCounter as string ¬
                    is not equal to "" then
                    set myAttachments to every mail attachment ¬
                        of message myCounter
                    repeat with Counter2 from 1 ¬
                        to count of items in myAttachments
                        set filename to the name of item Counter2 ¬
                            of myAttachments
                        save item Counter2 of myAttachments ¬
                            in myFolder & filename
                    end repeat
                end if
            end repeat
        end tell
    on error myErrorMessage number myErrorNumber
        if myErrorNumber is -1728 then
            -- the message has no attachment; continue to next message
        end if
    end try
end tell
```

If the message being checked has no attachment, trying to get the name of the first item of the attachment returns an error. The error handler checks for this error (number **–1728**) to allow the script to continue past messages that have no attachments.

# Working with Tasks

To create a new task that appears in your To Do list in Mail's Reminders category, you need to use iCal rather than Mail. iCal uses the **todo** class to represent a task. Table 13-10 explains the properties of the **todo** object.

To create a new task, use a **make new todo** command in iCal. Tell iCal where to place the new item—for example, **at the end of todos** of a particular calendar—and use a **with properties** parameter to set essential properties such as the summary and the due date.

| todo Property | Explanation |
|---|---|
| completion date | The date on which the task was marked as completed |
| due date | The date on which the task is set to be due |
| priority | The task's priority: **no priority, low priority, medium priority,** or **high priority** |
| sequence | A read-only integer that gives the version number of the task |
| stamp date | The date on which the task was modified |
| summary | The name of the task |
| description | The notes added to the task |
| Uid | A unique text identifier that identifies the task |
| url | The URL (if any) associated with the task |

**Table 13-10**  Properties of the iCal todo Object

For example, the following snippet creates a new task in the **Work** calendar with the summary (name) **Mow the Roses** and a due date in July 2010:

```
tell the application "iCal"
    make new todo at the end of todos of the calendar "Work" ¬
        with properties {summary:"Mow the Roses", ¬
        due date:date "Wednesday, July 14, 2010 12:00:00 PM"}
end tell
```

The ideal way to work with a task via AppleScript is to identify it by its **uid** property because this property's uniqueness means you can be sure you've got exactly the item you want. But unless you've just created the task, you're not likely to be able to grab its **uid** property quickly unless you can easily identify it in another way—for example, by virtue of its being the first item in a particular calendar.

The following example shows a way of using the **summary** property of a **todo** object to identify it and then delete it, though you could use the same technique to perform other operations on it—for example, shoving its due date out into the middle distance or ratcheting up its priority to the subpoena level. Here's what the code does:

- First, it declares the **myToDos** variable as containing every **todo** item in the calendar called **Work**.

- Next, it starts a **repeat** loop with a counter variable (**myCounter**) to run from **1** to the **count of myToDos**—in other words, once for each of the **todo** items found in the calendar.

- The third line assigns to a variable named **myToDo** the **item myCounter of myToDos**—the first **todo** on the first iteration of the loop, the second **todo** on the second iteration, and so on.

- If the **summary** of **myToDo** matches the test string, the **delete myToDo** statement deletes the **todo** item, and the **return** statement kicks AppleScript out of the loop so that it doesn't run again.

- If the **summary** of **myToDo** doesn't match the test string, the loop keeps running until either it finds a match or it reaches the last item in **myToDos**:

```
tell the application id "com.apple.ical"
    set myToDos to every todo of the calendar "Work"
    repeat with myCounter from 1 to count of myToDos
        set myToDo to item myCounter of myToDos
        if summary of myToDo as string is "Mow the Park" then
            delete myToDo
            return
        end if
    end repeat
end tell
```

# Chapter 14

## Automating Microsoft Word

## Key Skills & Concepts

- Launching and quitting Word

- Understanding the key Word objects for AppleScript

- Working with documents

- Working with windows and views

- Working with text

- Using sections, page setup, and headers and footers

- Displaying Word's built-in dialog boxes

- Running your scripts from Word

In this chapter, you'll learn the essentials of manipulating Microsoft Word 2008 via AppleScript. We'll start by looking at how to launch Word and quit it, and then move on to examine the key objects that you use for scripting Word. Most likely, your first action will be to choose a document to work on, so I'll show you how to create, save, open, and close documents—and how to print them. We'll then peer at how to work with windows and views, how to add text to a document and format it, and how to set up a document using sections, page setup, and headers and footers. Finally, I'll teach you how to commandeer Word's built-in dialog boxes for use in your scripts, and how to run the scripts directly from Word rather than using the Script menu on the Mac OS X menu bar.

## Launching Word—and Quitting Word

To launch Word, use the **launch** command—for example:

```
tell the application id "com.microsoft.Word" to launch
```

If you want to bring Word to the front, use an **activate** statement as well:

```
tell the application id "com.microsoft.Word"
    launch
    activate
end tell
```

**NOTE**

You can also launch and activate Word by using the **activate** command without the **launch** command. But usually it's better to make explicit what your code does.

You can also launch Word implicitly by telling it to open a document or to create a new document. For example, the first of the following statements tells Word to create a new document, and the second statement activates Word. If Word is not open, the **make new document** command launches Word, because it can't create a document unless it's open.

```
tell the application id "com.microsoft.Word"
    make new document
    activate
end tell
```

To quit Word, use the **quit** command as usual:

```
tell the application id "com.microsoft.com" to quit
```

Before complying with the **quit** command, Word prompts you to save any unsaved changes to documents. We'll look at how to deal with unsaved changes a little later in this chapter.

# Understanding the Key Word Objects for AppleScript

To make Word do your bidding via AppleScript, you work with the objects from which Word is built and the objects it creates. In this chapter, you will work with the most widely useful objects, which include the following:

- The **application** class returns the Word application. You use the **application** class to manipulate Word as a whole—for example, to launch Word or to quit it.

- The **document** class represents an open document. Word organizes the **document** objects into the **documents** list, which you can use to reach any open document.

- The **active document** class returns the active document—the one that currently has the focus. This class is great for scripts that need to manipulate the document that the user is working with.

- The **window** class represents a window that a Word document appears in. Word collects the **window** objects into the **windows** list, which enables you to grab hold of any window.

- The **active window** class returns the active window in the Word application. This class gives you direct access to the window with which the user is working.

- The **selection** class represents the user's current selection in the active document. You use this class to access the text or other object with which the user is working.

# Working with Documents

Chances are that you'll spend most of your Word time working with documents—creating and saving them, opening and closing them, and printing them out on dead trees. This section shows you how to perform these operations with documents. Later sections dig into the details of operations you'll want to perform with documents open, such as adding text to them and formatting them.

## Creating a New Document

To create a new document based on the Normal template, use a **make new document** statement. This statement adds a new document to the **documents** list, where you can work with it.

```
tell the application id "com.microsoft.Word"
    make new document
end tell
```

Sometimes all you'll want to do is create a new document like this and leave it for the user to work with, but what's usually more useful is to assign the new document you create to an object variable so that you can keep tabs on it. For example, the following statement assigns the new document created by the **make new** command to the variable **myDoc**:

```
tell the application id "com.microsoft.Word"
    set myDoc to make new document
end tell
```

You can then use the **myDoc** variable to manipulate the document—for example, to add text or other items to it, to save it, or to close it.

As you'll know if you've worked with Word, the Normal template is a catch-all template used for documents that don't need a specific template. Because each document must have a template attached to it, Word automatically attaches the Normal template unless you tell it to use another template. Word automatically loads the Normal template when you launch the application; it loads any other template when you create or open a document with that template attached, or when you open the template itself.

# Working with the Template Attached to a Document

The first step toward making a document look the way you want is to attach the right template to it. Because a template can contain custom settings from margins to styles, not to mention default content, you can save time by making sure that a document has the appropriate template attached.

## Seeing Which Template Is Currently Attached

To find out which template is attached to a document, check the **attached template** property of the relevant **document** object. For example, the following statement uses the **name** property of the **attached template** object to return the filename of the **document** object referenced by the **myDocument** variable:

```
get name of attached template of myDocument
```

This returns just the filename—for example, **"Post-Modern Report.dotx"**. If you want the full path and filename of the template attached to a document, return the **full name** property of the **attached template** object like this:

```
get full name of attached template of myDocument
```

This returns all the information you need to reach the template—for example, **"Macintosh HD:Users:kat:Templates:Indecipherable Newsletter.dotx"**.

## Attaching a Template to a Document in Word 2008

To change the template attached to a document, set the **attached template** property of the appropriate **document** object to the template you want. For example, the following statement attaches the template named **Over-Arty Flyer.dot** to the front document:

```
set the attached template of the front document to "Macintosh HD:
Users:kat:Templates:Over-Arty Flyer.dot"
```

When you're creating a new document, you can attach a template to it by setting the **template** item in the document's properties to the appropriate template. For example, the following statement assigns to the variable **myDoc** a new document based on the template named **Sudoku Designer.dotx**:

```
set myDoc to make new document with properties {attached template: ¬
    "Macintosh HD:Users:kat:Templates:Sudoku Designer.dotx"}
```

## Attaching a Template to a Document in Word 2004

In Word 2004, the **attached template** property doesn't work consistently. If you find it doesn't work on your copy of Word, try using a **do Visual Basic** statement instead.

## Ask the Expert

**Q:** Can I use the do Visual Basic statement in Word 2008?

**A:** Sadly not.

The **do Visual Basic** statement executes the Visual Basic for Applications (VBA) command that you specify, so it's a great tool to have up your sleeve if you know VBA.

But Office 2008 for Mac doesn't include VBA, so you can't use the **do Visual Basic** command with Word 2008. Supposedly Microsoft will graft VBA back on to the next version of Office for Mac, so **do Visual Basic** may return too.

For example, the following statement attaches the template named **Industrial.dot** to the active document:

```
do Visual Basic "ActiveDocument.AttachedTemplate = \"Macintosh HD:
Users:kat:Templates:Industrial.dot\""
```

One thing to notice there—because AppleScript passes the command to VBA as a string inside double quotes, you have to escape the double-quote characters around the template path and name with backslashes to prevent them from ending the command. This is why the path begins and ends with **\"** rather than a plain double-quote character.

### Finding Out Where the Templates Are

The examples so far have used hard-coded paths, which work fine—as long as you know them. But because the Word templates will likely be stored in different folders on different Macs, you'll normally need to use the paths to the template folders to reach the templates reliably.

Word stores template files in two different folders:

- **User Templates**  This is the folder in which the user stores his or her own templates. The default location is the user's ~/Library/Application Support/Microsoft/Office/User Templates/ folder (where ~ represents the user's home folder). Word sets this folder automatically on installation, but you can change it as needed.

- **Workgroup Templates**  This is the folder an administrator can use to make other templates available to the user. Word doesn't set this folder, so unless someone sets it manually, it may remain blank in the File Locations Preferences. For a networked Mac, it's usually best to locate this folder on a network drive so that the administrator can easily update the templates centrally.

When working interactively, you can set the User Templates location and the Workgroup Templates location by choosing Word | Preferences, clicking the File Locations icon, and then working in the File Locations Preferences window (see Figure 14-1). Click the User Templates item in the File Locations list box, click the Modify button, select the folder you want in the Choose A Folder dialog box, and then click the Choose button. Lather, rinse, and repeat for the Workgroup Templates item, and then click the OK button to close the window.

### NOTE
Even if the File Locations Preferences window shows the Workgroup Templates location to be blank, AppleScript returns a default location, such as /Applications/Microsoft Office 2008/Office/Media/Templates/.

Using AppleScript, you can get or set the template folders by using the **default file path** command and specifying the **user templates path** constant or the **workgroup templates path** constant for the **file path type** parameter. For example, the following statement returns the User Templates path:

```
get default file path file path type user templates path
```

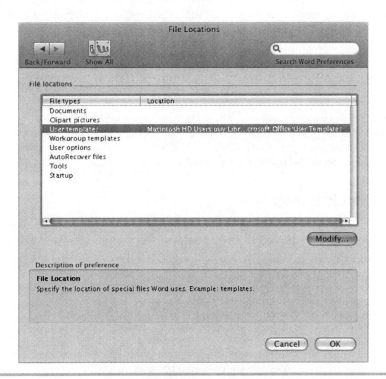

**Figure 14-1**   You can set the User Templates location and Workgroup Templates location manually from the File Locations Preferences.

And the following "path"-heavy statement sets the User Templates path to a networked drive:

```
set default file path file path type workgroup templates path ¬
    path "Server:Templates:Word"
```

### Creating a New Template

To create a new template from AppleScript, create a new document as described earlier in this chapter. Base the document on an existing template if you wish. When you save the document, as discussed later in this chapter, use the **format template** constant for the **file format** parameter, as in this example:

```
save as active document file name ¬
    (get default file path file path type user templates path) & ¬
    ":Example template.dotx" ¬
    file format format template
```

## Opening an Existing Document

You open an existing document by using the **open** command and the filename, including the path to it. For example, the following statement opens the document named Sample Document.docx in the Macintosh HD:Users:Shared:Documents: folder:

```
open "Macintosh HD:Users:Shared:Documents:Sample Document.docx"
```

### TIP

If you want to prevent the document you're opening from appearing on the Recent Documents list in Word, add the parameter **without add to recent files**. This is useful when you prefer your script not to change the user's Recent Documents list. Omit this parameter or use **with add to recent files** to add the document to the Recent Documents list.

## Saving a Document

To save a document for the first time, use the **save as** command with the appropriate **document** object. As when you're saving a document using the Save As dialog box, Word offers various options, including password-protecting the document. These are the three parameters you're most likely to use:

- **file name**   This parameter is optional, but you'll almost always want to provide it—if you don't, Word blandly uses whatever name the document window has, such as Document42. (Arguably, this is marginally better than the alternatives—throwing an error or displaying the Save As dialog box so that the user can choose a more creative name.) Include the folder path in the filename, or else you'll get whichever folder was last used.

- **file format** This parameter is optional, too, but you should always use it to make sure you get the format you want—if you omit **file format**, Word uses the format selected in the Save Word Files As pop-up menu in the Save Preferences window. Table 14-1 explains the 10 most useful file formats you can use.

- **without add to recent files** Add this optional parameter if you want to prevent the document from appearing on the Recent Documents list. This lets you create documents without changing the user's Recent Documents list. Omit this parameter (or use **with add to recent files** for clarity) to add the document to the Recent Documents list—for example, if you want the user to be able to reopen the document easily.

| file format Constant | Format | Extension | Comments |
|---|---|---|---|
| **format document** | Word 2007/2008 document | .docx | The most stable document format, but users with Word 2004, Word 2003, or Word XP will need to install file converters before they can open these documents. |
| **format document97** | Word 97–2004 document | .doc | The most widely used format. Good for general use. |
| **format documentAuto** | (The format set in Save Preferences) | — | Use this setting when you want to follow the user's preferred file format. |
| **format template** | Word 2007/2008 template | .dotx | Use this format for templates you create for Word 2008 or Word 2007. |
| **format template97** | Word 97–2004 template | .dot | The most widely used template format. Good for general use. |
| **format templateAuto** | (The template format matching the document format set in Save Preferences) | — | Use this setting when you want to follow the user's preferred file format for templates. |
| **format Unicode text** | Unicode text | .txt | Use this setting to produce a universally readable text document without formatting. |
| **format rtf** | Rich-text format | .rtf | Use this setting to produce a widely readable RTF document (including formatting and objects such as pictures). |
| **format pdf** | Portable Document Format | .pdf | Use this setting when you need to create a PDF. |
| **format xml** | Extensible Markup Language | .xml | Use this setting to save the Word document in XML format. |

**Table 14-1** Word's 10 Most Useful File Formats

For example, the following statement saves the active document in Word 2007/2008 format in the folder Transfer:Documents:Word with the filename Sad Penguins.docx:

```
save as active document ¬
    file name "Transfer:Documents:Word:Sad Penguins.docx" ¬
    file format format document
```

The following statement saves the front document in the current working folder in Word 97–2004 format with the filename Primate Language.doc, preventing the document from appearing on the Recent Documents list:

```
save as front document file name "Primate Language.doc" ¬
    file format format document97 without add to recent files
```

After you've saved a document with a filename and folder location, you can save it again by using the **save** command with the document but without any further parameters. For example, the following command saves any unsaved changes in the active document:

```
save the active document
```

## Making a Document the Active Document

When you're working via AppleScript, you don't need to activate a document in the way that you need to when you're working interactively. All you need to do is identify the document you want to affect, and then tell AppleScript what to do to the document.

When your scripts need to show a document to the user, however, you can activate the document by using the **activate object** command, the **document** keyword, and the name of the open document you want. Before you do this, you need to use the **activate** command to make sure that Word is the active application—otherwise, the **activate object** command simply doesn't work, instead failing without raising an error.

For example, the following snippet activates the document named **Sample Document.doc**:

```
tell the application id "com.microsoft.word"
    activate
    activate object document "Sample Document.doc"
end tell
```

When you've made a document active, either by using the **activate object** command as described in the previous section or by another means (for example, by creating a new document), that document is the active document. You can then access it by using the **active document** class in Word.

### NOTE

There's only one active document at a time in Word. The **active document** class makes it easy to manipulate the document the user was working with, but you need to be careful because the active document can change during the course of a script. Obviously, if you deliberately activate another document, that document becomes the active document—but so does a new document you create or a document you open. Similarly, if you close the active document, the next document behind it becomes active.

## Closing a Document

To close a document, use the **close** command with the document's name or a variable or object identifying it. For example, the following statement closes the document named **New Document.doc**:

```
tell the application id "com.microsoft.word"
    close the document "New document 1.doc"
end tell
```

If the document contains unsaved changes, Word prompts the user to save them. Sometimes this behavior is convenient, but more often you'll want to take care of any unsaved changes before giving the command to close the document. If you want to save the changes, you can either save the document using the **save** command (as described earlier in this chapter) or set the **saving** parameter of the **close** command to **yes**:

```
close the document "New document 1.doc" saving yes
```

If you need to close the document and lose any unsaved changes without Word prompting the user about them, set the **saving** parameter of the **close** command to **no**:

```
close the document "New document 1.doc" saving no
```

### NOTE

If you try to close a document that has never been saved, Word displays the Save As dialog box unless you've set the **saving** parameter to **no**. For this reason, it's usually best to use the **save** command to explicitly save each new document you create rather than rely on the **saving yes** parameter of the **close** command to save any documents you've neglected to save.

If you want Word to prompt the user to decide whether to save changes, set the **saving** parameter to **ask**:

```
close the document "New document 1.doc" saving ask
```

Setting **saving ask** makes Word display the familiar "Do you want to save the changes you made?" dialog box (see Figure 14-2).

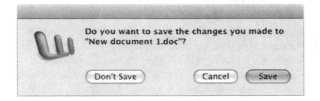

**Figure 14-2** When closing a document that contains unsaved changes, Word asks the user to save them if your code doesn't specify whether to keep the changes or dump them.

### CAUTION

Prompting the user to decide whether to save changes works best when the user knows which changes have been made—for example, if your script needs to close the documents the user has left open so that it can run safely. If the script has changed the document involved, whether to save the changes can be a tricky decision for the user.

To close all open documents, use the **close** command with the **documents** list. As with a single document, you can choose whether to save changes by setting the **saving** parameter to **yes**, **no**, or **ask**, as appropriate. For example, the following statement closes all open documents, saving changes without consulting the user:

```
tell the application id "com.microsoft.word"
    close documents saving yes
end tell
```

### NOTE

Word itself stays open when you close all open documents. To close Word itself, quit it by using the **quit** command.

## Identifying the Document You Want to Work With

When you're working with Word interactively, you always use the active document—the document to which you've given the focus by selecting its window with the keyboard or the mouse.

When you're working with Word from AppleScript, you can work either in the active document or in any other document that's open.

For example, if you want to close the back document without saving changes, use a statement such as this:

```
close the back document saving no
```

Unlike when you're working interactively, you don't need to activate one of the open documents before you can work with it via AppleScript. All you need to do is identify the document to Word.

# Printing a Document

To print a document, use the **print out** command.

The only required parameter for the **print out** command is the direct parameter, which specifies the **document** or **window** you want to print. When you print like this, it's pretty much like clicking the Print button on the toolbar in Word: You get the whole document (and nothing but the document), one copy of it, in page order, printed to either the default printer (if you haven't yet printed in this Word session) or the last printer you used (if you have). For example, the following statement prints the active document in this way:

```
print out active document
```

Often, you'll want to use some of the optional parameters the **print out** command offers. These are the most useful parameters:

- **print out range**   Use this parameter when you need to print out a range of pages. Use the constant **print all document** to print all pages, **print current page** to print the page the selection is on, **print from to** to print a simple range of pages by page numbers or section numbers, **print range of pages** to print a complex range of pages (for example, pages 1, 4, 9–16, 20), or **print selection** to print the current selection.

- **page from**   Use this parameter to set the starting page when you use **print out range print from to**.

- **page to**   Use this parameter to specify the ending page when you use **print out range print from to**.

- **print copies**   Use this parameter to specify the number of copies when you need more than one—for example, **print copies 5** to print five copies.

- **print out page type**   Use this parameter when you need to print out only odd pages (**print odd pages only**) or only even pages (**print even pages only**). You can also use **print out page type print all pages** to print all pages, but there's not much point, because Word does this anyway unless you tell it not to.

For example, the following statement prints the selection in the active document:

```
print out active document print out range print selection
```

**NOTE**

To find out which printer is active, get the **active printer** property of the **application** class. Set the **active printer** property to change the printer.

The following statement prints the even pages from the document referenced by the variable **pDoc**:

```
print out pDoc print out page type print even pages only
```

**NOTE**

Another option is to display the Print dialog box so that the user can print the document as needed. See the end of the chapter for details on displaying Word's built-in dialog boxes.

## Try This    Creating, Saving, and Closing a Document

In this example, you create a script that launches Word by creating a new document based on the Normal template. The script then saves the document and closes it, leaving a blank document that you will use again in examples later in this chapter.

Follow these steps to create the script:

1. Quit Word if it's currently running. (Go on—you can do without it for a couple of minutes. Trust me.)

2. In AppleScript Editor, press ⌘-N or choose File | New to create a new script.

3. Start a **tell** block to Word, identifying it by its **application id** string, **com.microsoft.Word**:

```
tell the application id "com.microsoft.Word"
end tell
```

4. Inside the **tell** block, add a **make new document** statement and assign it to the variable **new_doc**, as shown in boldface here:

```
tell the application id "com.microsoft.Word"
    set new_doc to make new document
end tell
```

5. Add an **activate** statement, as shown in boldface here, to make Word reveal itself and the new document to you. If you don't do this, you won't see what's happening.

```
tell the application id "com.microsoft.Word"
    set new_doc to make new document
    activate
end tell
```

6. Use a **save as** command to save the **new_doc** document under the filename **Sample Document.docx** using the Word 2007/8 document format (**file format format document**). Adapt the file path to suit your file system. The new command appears in boldface here:

```
tell the application id "com.microsoft.Word"
    set new_doc to make new document
    activate
    save as new_doc file name ¬
        "Macintosh HD:Users:kev:Documents:Sample Document.docx" ¬
        file format format document
end tell
```

7. Add a three-second delay to prevent AppleScript from trying to execute the commands more quickly than Word can handle; then close the document and quit Word. The new statements appear in boldface here:

```
tell the application id "com.microsoft.Word"
    set new_doc to make new document
    activate
    save as new_doc file name ¬
        "Macintosh HD:Users:kev:Documents:Sample Document.docx" ¬
        file format format document
    delay 3
    close the document "Sample Document.docx"
    quit
end tell
```

8. Save the script under a name of your choice.

9. Press ⌘-R or click the Run button on the toolbar to run the script. You'll see Word open, create a new document and then display **Sample Document** in the title bar, and then close the document and quit.

# Ask the Expert

**Q:** What happens if my code tries to save a document in a folder that doesn't exist?

**A:** This depends on the version of Word—but it's worth avoiding in any case.

- Word 2008 falls back to the default Documents folder set in File Locations preferences or (if none is set) your ~/Documents folder. This is sane and helpful, but even so, it can cause some surprises.
- Word 2004 throws an error.

# Working with Windows and Views

To present documents helpfully on screen, you'll often need to open, close, and resize windows. You will also need to change the view and zoom it to a suitable degree.

## Working with Windows

To work with windows, you use the **windows** list, which contains a **window** object for each open window. Word treats the windows as being in a stack, with the active window at the front, so you can access the windows in various ways.

- **By the window's position in the stack**   For example, use **the front window** or **window 1** to return the front window.

- **By the window's caption**   The **caption** property of a **window** object returns the text that's displayed in the window's title bar. You can use this property to identify the window you want. For example, the following **if** block checks to see if the caption of the window identified by the **myWindow** variable is **Papal Bull.docx**; if the caption matches, the code activates Word and then activates the window.

```
if the caption of myWindow is "Papal Bull.docx" then
    activate
    activate object myWindow
end if
```

- **By using the active window class**   The **active window** class lets you grab the active window—the window the user is actually using.

## Zooming a Window

To zoom a window up, set the **window state** property of the **window** object to **window state maximize**; to zoom it back down, set the **window state** property to **window state normal**. For example, the following **tell** block toggles the front window between zoomed up and zoomed down, assuming it is in one of those states to start with:

```
tell the application id "com.microsoft.Word"
    tell the front window
        if the window state is window state maximize then
            set the window state to window state normal
        else if the window state is window state normal then
            set the window state to window state maximize
        end if
    end tell
end tell
```

The third state, which the previous example doesn't use, is **window state minimize**. Set the **window state** property to **window state minimize** to minimize a window down to an icon on the Dock.

### CAUTION

The word "zoom" here has the Mac meaning of making the window the size that Mac OS X thinks best fits its contents, or of returning the window from that size to its previous size—the same as clicking the green button in the upper-left corner of the window or choosing Window | Zoom. This is not the same as maximizing the window on Windows.

## Minimizing and Restoring a Window

To minimize a window, set its **collapsed** property to **true**. For example, the following statement minimizes the first window of the document referenced by the variable **myDoc**:

```
set collapsed of window 1 of myDoc to true
```

To restore a window, set the **collapsed** property to **false**. For example, the following statement restores the same window:

```
set collapsed of window 1 of myDoc to false
```

## Resizing, Repositioning, and Arranging Windows

To resize a window, set the **left position**, **top**, **width**, and **height** properties of the appropriate **window** object. Each of these properties takes an integer value of pixels. For example, the following **tell** blocks position the front window in the upper-left corner of the primary monitor and make it 1024 wide by 800 pixels high:

```
tell the application "Microsoft Word"
    tell the front window
        set left position to 0
        set top to 0
        set height to 800
        set width to 1024
    end tell
end tell
```

To reposition a window without resizing it, set the **left position** property and the **top** property to suitable pixel values. For example, the following **tell** block makes Word position the upper-left corner of the front window 400 pixels from the left edge of the screen and 200 pixels from the top edge:

```
tell the application "Microsoft Word"
    set left position of front window to 400
    set top of front window to 200
end tell
```

**NOTE**

Word includes an **arrange windows** command with an **arrange style** parameter that you can set to **tiled** or **icons**. At this writing, this command doesn't work as it should. For example, **arrange windows arrange style tiled** should tile all the open windows across the screen, giving each as equal a share of the space as possible. In practice, the tiling is amusingly random but not much practical use.

# Working with Views

To set up a document so that it's right for reading or for working with, you can set the view type and the zoom. AppleScript uses the **view** object to represent the view, and the **zoom** object to represent the zoom.

## Setting the View in the Window

To work with the view in the window, you use the **view** object of the appropriate window. What you'll probably want to do first is learn which view the window is currently using. To find out the view, check the **view type** property of the **view** object of the appropriate **window** object.

```
get view type of view of active window
```

This returns one of the view types explained in Table 14-2.

To change the view, set the **view type** property of the **view** object of the **window** object. For example, the following statement applies Print Layout view to the first window of the active document:

```
set view type of view of the first window of the active document ¬
    to page view
```

| AppleScript Term | Word View Type | Notes |
|---|---|---|
| **page view** | Print Layout view | — |
| **outline view** | Outline view | — |
| **master view** | Master Document view | This is Outline view with Master Document view turned on. |
| **online view** | Web Layout view | — |
| **draft view** | Draft view | This was Normal view in Word 2004 and earlier versions. |
| **publishing view** | Publishing Layout view | This view is not available in Word 2004. |
| **wordnote view** | Notebook Layout view | — |

**Table 14-2** AppleScript Terms for Word's Views

## Finding Out the Current Zoom of the Window

To find out the current zoom of the window, return the **percentage** property of the **zoom** object of the **view** object of the appropriate window. For example, the following statement returns the zoom percentage of the active window:

```
get percentage of zoom of view of active window
```

## Zooming the Contents of a Window In or Out

To zoom the contents of a window in so that the user can see every pore of the fonts or zoom them out until the letters are just flyspecks on the screen, you use the **zoom** property of the **view** object.

To zoom to a percentage, use a **set** command with the **percentage** property of the **zoom** object. For example, the following statement zooms the first window of the front document to 150 percent:

```
set percentage of zoom of view of the first window ¬
    of the front document to 150
```

If the document is in Page Layout view, you can use the **page fit full page** constant to display the whole page in the window. For example, the following statements switch the active window to Page Layout view and then display the whole page in the window:

```
set the view type of the view of the active window to page view
set page fit of zoom of view of active window to page fit full page
```

## Zooming to the Full Page or the Page Width

To zoom so that the full page appears in the Word window, set the **page fit** property of the **zoom** object to **page fit full page**. To zoom so that the page appears at its full width in the Word window, set the **page fit** property of the **zoom** object to **page fit best fit**. To remove fitting the full page or the page width, set the **page fit** property of the **zoom** object to **page fit none**.

For example, the following statement zooms the active window to the page width:

```
set page fit of zoom of view of active window to page fit best fit
```

## Zooming to Display Multiple Pages at the Same Time

One of Word's neatest tricks is to zoom in or out so that you can see two or more full pages at the same time. This is especially handy when you need to see two full pages at once for layout purposes or see a whole slew of pages—eight pages, say, or 16 pages—to get an overview of a larger document.

To zoom the display to show multiple pages at the same time, use the **page columns** property of the **zoom** object to set the number of columns of pages and the **page rows** property of the **zoom** object to set the number of rows of pages. For example, the following statements set the active window to display two rows of four columns each:

```
set view type of view of the active window to page view
set page rows of zoom of view of active window to 2
set page columns of zoom of view of active window to 4
```

As in the example, you'll need to make sure that the window is in Print Layout view first—otherwise, you'll get an error when you try to set the **page rows** property or the **page columns** property.

# Working with Text

Most Word documents contain text—usually, plenty of it. That means it's important to know how to work with text in your scripts. This section shows you how to come to grips with the text in Word's documents and smaller objects, how to work with the **selection** object, how to work with ranges, and how to enter text in a document.

## Returning a Text Object and Reaching Its Contents

To work with text, you use the **text object** property of an object to return the text in that object. The **text object** property returns a **text range** object—an object that represents a range of text.

A **document** object has a **text object**, as do the **bookmark** object (which represents a bookmark) and the **cell** object (which represents a cell in a table). But usually the most useful way to get at the text in a document is to return the **text object** of a **paragraph** object.

For example, to return a **text range** object referring to the first paragraph of the active document, you can use the **text object** property of the first **paragraph** object in the **active document** object. The following statement returns this **text range** object and assigns it to the variable **para1**:

```
set para1 to the text object of the first paragraph ¬
    of the active document
```

To reach the text in the text range, you use the **content** property of the **text object** class. For example, the following statement returns the text in the first paragraph of the active document:

```
get the content of the text object of the first paragraph ¬
    of the active document
```

To change the text in the text range, use a **set** statement with the **content** property of the **text object** class. For example, the first of the following statements assigns to the variable **para1** the **text range** object of the first paragraph of the active document. The second statement sets the content of **para1** to New Industrial Policy, a carriage return, and its existing contents, thus creating a new paragraph before the existing first paragraph:

```
set para1 to the text object of the first paragraph of the active
document
set the content of para1 to "New Industrial Policy" & return & the
content of para1
```

Apart from the **content** property, the **text range** object has many other properties that you can use to work with different aspects of the text range. Here are three of the most useful properties:

- The **font object** property returns or sets the **font object** class for the text range, which you can use to set the font, font size, and other font options. (More on this later in the chapter.)

- The **paragraph format** property returns or sets the **paragraph format** class for the text range, which you can use to set paragraph formatting, such as the alignment and line spacing. (More on this, too, later.)

- The **style** property returns or sets the Word style applied to the text range. (Likewise.)

# Working with the Selection Object

If your script needs to work with an object the user has selected in the active document, use the **selection** object. For example, if you have the user select some text and then run a script to manipulate it, the script will need to work with the **selection** object. You can also create your own selection by using the **select** command—for example, your script may need to highlight text or another object so that the user can gaze on it with fascination or (more usefully) do something with it.

The **selection** object represents the selection or insertion point in the active document. If something—one or more characters, for example—is selected, the **selection** object returns that selection; if nothing is selected, the selection is considered to be collapsed to an insertion point, and the **selection** object returns that instead.

## Finding Out What Type of Selection You Have

Before you do anything to the selection, it's a good idea to check which kind of selection it is. This helps you avoid awkward surprises, such as inserting text over priceless content that the user has selected, or trying to check the spelling of a non-text object.

Table 14-3 explains Word's different types of selections.

| selection type | Explanation |
|---|---|
| no selection | This is a mystery value that is hard to generate. What you might expect it to mean—that there's no selection because the selection is collapsed to an insertion point—actually has another name. |
| selection ip | No object is selected, and the selection is collapsed to an insertion point. |
| selection block | This is a "block" selection—part of one or more paragraphs is selected. This is the type of selection you get by OPTION-dragging through part of several paragraphs (for example, to remove leading spaces from several one-line paragraphs). |
| selection normal | This is a "normal" selection—for example, a word, a paragraph, or several paragraphs. |
| selection column | Part or all of one or more columns in a table is selected. |
| selection row | One or more full rows in a table is selected. |
| selection frame | A frame is selected. |
| selection shape | A floating shape or text box is selected. |
| selection inline shape | An inline shape is selected. |

**Table 14-3** Word's Different Types of Selections

For example, the following code checks to see if the selection is collapsed to an insertion point. If it's not, the code checks further. If the selection is a block selection, the nested **if** statement collapses the selection to its start; if it's a normal selection, the **else if** statement collapses it to its end. If it's a different kind of selection, the script displays an alert saying it's the wrong kind of selection and prompting the user to make the right kind (see Figure 14-3).

```
tell the application id "com.microsoft.word"
    if selection type of selection is not selection ip then
        if selection type of selection is selection block then
            collapse range text object of selection ¬
                direction collapse start
        else if selection type of selection is selection normal then
            collapse range text object of selection ¬
                direction collapse end
        else
            display alert "Wrong type of selection" ¬
                message "Please click in text where you want ¬
                to insert the address." buttons {"OK"}
        end if
    end if
end tell
```

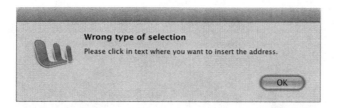

**Wrong type of selection**
Please click in text where you want to insert the address.

OK

**Figure 14-3**    For safety, check what the user has selected before taking action with a script.

As you can see from the previous example, you can collapse a selection to either its start or its end by using the **collapse range** command and using either **direction collapse start** or **direction collapse end**.

- Collapsing a selection to its start is like pressing the LEFT ARROW key when working interactively:

```
collapse range text object of selection direction collapse start
```

- Similarly, collapsing a selection to its end is like pressing RIGHT ARROW:

```
collapse range text object of selection direction collapse end:
```

## Finding Out Which Part of the Document the Selection Is In

Each Word document consists of 11 different parts, which Word calls *stories*—for example, the main text part of the document is called the *main text story*. To find out which part of the document the selection is in, you get the **story type** property. Table 14-4 explains the constants used for the stories.

For example, the following snippet checks to see whether the selection is in the main text story. If the selection is in another story, the code displays a dialog box asking the user to select a paragraph in the main text and then run the script again.

```
if story type of selection is not main text story then
    display dialog "Please select a paragraph in the
        main text of the document and run this script again."
end if
```

## Getting Information About the Current Selection

When you're working with the selection in a document, it's usually a good idea to check that the selection is what your script expects it to be. For example, if your script is trying to manipulate a text object but the user has selected a picture, you'll get unexpected results.

| Word story type | Part of the Document |
|---|---|
| main text story | The main text |
| text frame story | The text in text boxes |
| comments story | The comments |
| endnotes story | The endnotes |
| footnotes story | The footnotes |
| primary header story | The primary header or the odd-page header (for a document with different even-page headers) |
| even pages header story | The even-page header |
| first page header story | The first-page header |
| primary footer story | The primary footer or the odd-page footer (for a document with different even-page footers) |
| even pages footer story | The even-page footer |
| first page footer story | The first-page footer |

**Table 14-4** Word's 11 Story Types

To return information about the selection, use the **get information selection** command. Table 14-5 explains the different information you can return.

For example, the following snippet turns off the Track Changes feature if it is currently on. The **if** statement checks the **selection information type revision marking**; if this returns **true**, the **set track revisions of active document to false** statement turns off Track Changes for the active document.

```
if (get selection information selection information type ¬
    revision marking) is "true" then
    set track revisions of active document to false
end if
```

The following example checks to make sure the selection is within a table. If it's not, the code displays an alert message (see Figure 14-4) explaining the problem.

```
if (get selection information ¬
    selection information type with in table) is "false" then
    display alert "This script requires a table" ¬
        message "Please click in the table you want to process, ¬
        and then run this script again." ¬
        buttons {"OK"}
end if
```

| information type Item | Explanation of What the Item Returns |
|---|---|
| **General Information** | |
| **info caps lock** | **true** if Caps Lock is on; **false** if it is off |
| **info num lock** | **true** if Num Lock is on; **false** if it is off |
| **over type** | **true** if Overtype mode is on; **false** if it is off |
| **revision marking** | **true** if Track Changes is on; **false** if it is off |
| **selection mode** | **0** for the normal selection mode (what you use most of the time); **1** for Extend mode (selecting by pressing the F8 key); **2** for Column-selection mode (selecting columns of multiple lines by OPTION-dragging) |
| **Zoom percentage** | The zoom percentage used for the document |
| **Information About the Selection and the Insertion Point** | |
| **active end adjusted page number** | The page number of the page on which the active end of the selection falls. If you change the starting page number, Word adjusts this number, but not the **active end page number** item. |
| **active end page number** | The page number of the page on which the active end of the selection falls |
| **active end section number** | The section number of the section in which the active end of the selection falls |
| **first character column number** | The number of characters between the left margin and the first character in the selection or the character to the right of the insertion point |
| **first character line number** | In layout views, the line number of the first character in the selection. In Draft mode, this item returns **−1**. |
| **frame is selected** | **true** if the selection or range is a whole frame or whole text box; **false** otherwise (including if the selection or range is *in* a frame or text box) |
| **header footer type** | A number indicating which type of header or footer the selection or range is in: **−1** means the selection or range is not in a header or footer; **0** means the even-page header or footer; **1** means the primary header (in a document that doesn't have different odd- and even-page headers) or an odd-page header; **4** means the first-page header; **2** means the even-page footer; **3** means the primary footer (in a document that doesn't have different odd- and even-page footers) or an odd-page footer; and **5** means the first-page footer |
| **horizontal position relative to page** | The distance from the left edge of the selection or range to the left edge of the page, measured in twips. (A *twip* is $1/20$ of a point, or $1/1440$ of an inch.) Returns **−1** if the selection or range isn't in the screen area. |

**Table 14-5**   Information About the selection Object

| information type Item | Explanation of What the Item Returns |
|---|---|
| horizontal position relative to text boundary | The distance from the left edge of the selection or range to the left edge of the text boundary it is within. This, too, is measured in twips and returns −1 if the selection or range isn't in the screen area. |
| in clipboard | **true** if the selection or range is on the Clipboard |
| in comment pane | **true** if the selection or range is in the document's comment pane |
| in endnote | **true** if the selection or range is in an endnote. This works in both the endnote pane (in Draft view) and the endnote area (in layout views). |
| in footnote | **true** if the selection or range is in a footnote. This works both in the footnote pane (in Draft view) and the footnote area at the bottom of the page in Print view. |
| in footnote endnote pane | **true** if the selection or range is in either a footnote or an endnote, either in the footnote pane or endnote pane (in Draft view), or in the footnote area or endnote area in a layout view |
| in header footer | **true** if the selection or range is in a header or a footer |
| in master document | **true** if the selection or range is in a master document (the master document must contain one or more subdocuments) |
| in word mail | (Applies only on the PC.) Whether the selection or range is in a WordMail send note (1), in a WordMail read note (2), or not in a WordMail message (0). |
| number of pages in document | The number of pages in the document that contains the selection or range |
| reference of type | A value indicating whether the selection or range is in or near a reference to a footnote, endnote, or comment. −1 means the selection includes a reference but also includes other material; 0 indicates that the selection or range is not before a reference; 1 indicates that the selection or range is before a footnote reference; 2 indicates it's before an endnote reference; and 3 indicates it's before a comment reference. |
| vertical position relative to page | The distance from the top edge of the selection or range to the top edge of the page, measured in twips. Returns −1 if the selection or range isn't in the screen area. |
| vertical position relative to page boundary | The distance from the top edge of the selection or range to the top edge of the text boundary it is within. This, too, is measured in twips and returns −1 if the selection or range isn't in the screen area. |

**Table 14-5** Information About the selection Object *(continued)*

| information type Item | Explanation of What the Item Returns |
|---|---|
| **Information About Tables** | |
| **is in table** | The selection or insertion point is in a table. |
| **maximum number of columns** | The maximum number of columns in the table |
| **maximum number of rows** | The maximum number of rows in the table |
| **start_of_range column number** | The number of the column that contains the start of the selection or range |
| **start_of_range row number** | The number of the row that contains the start of the selection or range |
| **end_of range column number** | The number of the column that contains the end of the selection or range |
| **end_of range row number** | The number of the row that contains the end of the selection or range |
| **at end of row marker** | **true** if the selection is at the end-of-row marker in a table (the marker *after* the border of the last cell in the row) |

**Table 14-5**   Information About the selection Object *(continued)*

## Creating a Text Range

The **selection** object is great for scripts that start from an item the user has selected. But when your script itself chooses the parts of the document to work with, you don't need to create your own selection by selecting objects with the **select** command. Instead, you can create one or more **text range** objects that refer to the part of the document you want to affect.

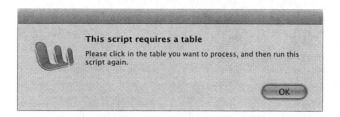

**Figure 14-4**   If checking reveals the selection to be of the wrong type, you can tell the user which type of selection is needed.

Using **text range** objects has four main advantages over using the **selection** object:

● First, you can create as many **text range** objects as you need.

● Second, you can create and use **text range** objects in any open document—you're not confined to using the active document.

● Third, you can redefine a **text range** object as needed, extending it to contain more or reducing it to contain less, or simply moving it to a different location.

● Fourth, **text range** objects are entirely separate from the selection. This means you can use text ranges to change a document without affecting the user's selection. Or you can assign the selection to a **text range** object, work with the **selection** object, and then select that **text range** object, giving the user back the original selection at the end of the script.

To create a text range, you use a **set** statement, the variable name to which you want to assign the range, and the details of the range to which you want to set it. For example, the following statement assigns the **text** object of the first paragraph of the active document to the variable **first_paragraph**:

```
set first_paragraph to the text object of the first paragraph ¬
    of the active document
```

That example uses the active document, but you can use any open document. For example, the following statement assigns the last **word** object in the rearmost document to the variable **last_word**:

```
set last_word to the last word of the back document
```

You can also assign the current contents of a text range to another text range. For example, the following statement assigns the contents of the range referenced by the **first_paragraph** variable to the **doc_opening** variable, and then uses a **select** statement to select the range referenced by **doc_opening**. This is useful when you need to change the text range or manipulate part of it.

```
set doc_opening to first_paragraph
select doc_opening
```

**NOTE**

You can also create a text range by using the **create range** command, as you'll see in the next section. This command isn't entirely reliable, so the method of creating text ranges described previously is preferable.

By selecting a text range or other object, you can also present the user with a selection to work with.

## Extending, Shortening, or Moving a Range

After creating a range, you can extend it, shorten it, or move it as needed. For example:

- The following statement extends the **doc_opening** range to the end of the fourth paragraph by moving the end of the range by three paragraphs:

```
set doc_opening to move end of range doc_opening ¬
    by a paragraph item count 3
```

- The following statement shortens the **doc_opening** range to the end of the second paragraph by moving the end of the range back by two paragraphs (**by a paragraph item count –2**):

```
set doc_opening to move end of range doc_opening ¬
    by a paragraph item count -2
```

- The following statement uses the **create range** command to redefine the **doc_opening** range to the position before the first character of the document. Here, the **create range** command takes a direct parameter (**active document**) specifying the document, a **start** parameter specifying the start position (character position **0**), and an end parameter specifying the end position (also character position **0**, making the range a single point right at the beginning of the document).

```
set doc_opening to create range active document start 0 end 0
```

## Entering Text in a Document

To insert text, use the **insert text** command and specify where to insert the text. For example, the following statement inserts text and a carriage return (to create a new paragraph) at the beginning of the **selection** object:

```
insert text "New Caledonian Tour Plans" & return at the beginning ¬
    of the text object of the selection
```

The following statement inserts a new paragraph after the third paragraph of the active document:

```
insert text return & "Industrial Policy" & return at the end of the ¬
    text object of the third paragraph of the active document
```

You can insert a new paragraph by using the **return** constant with the **insert text** command, as in the last two examples, but you can also use the **insert paragraph** command. For example:

```
insert paragraph at the beginning of the text object ¬
    of the fifth paragraph of the active document
```

# Formatting Text

You can use AppleScript to apply any of Word's many types of formatting. Just as when you're working interactively, the most efficient way of formatting a document via AppleScript is to use styles, but you can also apply direct font formatting (such as boldface or italic) or direct paragraph formatting as needed.

## Applying a Style

To apply a style, set the **style** property of the **paragraph** object or the **text range** object you want to affect, putting the style name inside double quotation marks. For example, the following statement applies the Heading 1 style to the first paragraph of the active document:

```
set the style of the first paragraph of the active document ¬
    to "Heading 1"
```

## Applying Font Formatting

As you know, Word provides enough font formatting to stun a charging rhinoceros, including little-used options such as Emboss, Engrave, and Kerning. AppleScript gives you access to all these options through the **font** object; here are the types of formatting that are generally most useful:

- To change the font, set the **name** property of the **font** object to the font you want. For example, to use the Times New Roman font on the selection:

  ```
  set name of font object of the text object of the selection ¬
      to "Times New Roman"
  ```

- To change the font size, set the **font size** property of the font object to the size you need. For example, to use 36-point font:

  ```
  set the font size of the font object of the text object ¬
      of the selection to "36"
  ```

## Applying Paragraph Formatting

As with font formatting, Word provides more paragraph-formatting options than most people need or want. Some items use the **paragraph** object itself, while others use the **paragraph format** object, which contains all the formatting for the paragraph.

Here are examples of the most widely useful types of paragraph formatting:

- To align a paragraph, set the **alignment** property of the **paragraph format** object of the selection or range to the appropriate value (see Table 14-6). For example, the following statement aligns the paragraphs in the range named **range1** with the right margin:

```
set alignment of paragraph format of range1 ¬
    to align paragraph right
```

- To check or change the amount of space before a paragraph, get or set the **space before** property of the **paragraph** object, as in the following statement. To change the amount of space after a paragraph, set the **space after** property of the **paragraph** object.

```
set space before of paragraph 1 of active document ¬
    to (inches to points inches 1.0)
```

- To check or change the first-line indent for a paragraph, get or set the **first line indent** property of the **paragraph format** object. Using a positive value creates an indent, while using a negative value creates a hanging indent (or "outdent" if you can stand the word). For example, the following statement returns the first-line indent for the second paragraph of the active document:

```
get the first line indent of the second paragraph ¬
    of the active document
```

- To check or change the line spacing for a paragraph, you work with the **line spacing rule** property and the **line spacing** property of the **paragraph format** object. Set the **line spacing rule** property to the appropriate constant from Table 14-7, and then set the **line spacing** property if you've chosen **line space at least**, **line space exactly**, or **line spacing multiple**. For example, the following statement sets the third paragraph of the active document to use double spacing:

```
set the line spacing rule of the third paragraph ¬
    of the active document to line space double
```

| alignment Type | alignment Constant |
|---|---|
| Left alignment | **align paragraph left** |
| Center | **align paragraph center** |
| Right alignment | **align paragraph right** |
| Justified | **align paragraph justify** |

**Table 14-6** Constants for the alignment Property of the paragraph format Object

| line spacing rule Constant | Sets This Line Spacing | line spacing Setting |
|---|---|---|
| line space single | Single spacing | — |
| line space1 pt5 | Line-and-a-half (1.5-line) spacing | — |
| line space double | Double spacing | — |
| line space at least | Minimum line spacing | The minimum number of points you want |
| line space exactly | Exact line spacing | The exact number of points you want |
| line spacing multiple | Multiple-line spacing | The line spacing in points. To set it in lines, use **lines to points lines** and the number—for example, **lines to points lines 3**. |

**Table 14-7**   Details for Setting Line Spacing via AppleScript

## Try This  Entering and Formatting Text in a Document

In this example, you open the document you created in the first example, add text to it, apply some formatting, and then save it. Follow these steps:

1. In AppleScript Editor, press ⌘-N or choose File | New to create a new script.

2. Start a **tell** block to Word, identifying it by its name this time for variety, and tell it to activate:

```
tell the application "Microsoft Word"
    activate
end tell
```

3. Open the document as shown in boldface here. Change the file path as needed for your Mac's file system.

```
tell the application "Microsoft Word"
    activate
    open "Macintosh HD:Users:kev:Documents:Sample Document.docx"
end tell
```

4. Insert two paragraphs at the beginning of the active document, as shown in boldface here. It's easier to repeat the command than to use a **repeat** loop here, even if it's not especially pretty.

```
tell the application "Microsoft Word"
    activate
    open "Macintosh HD:Users:guy:Documents:Sample Document.docx"
    insert paragraph at the beginning of the text object ¬
```

```
            of the active document
        insert paragraph at the beginning of the text object ¬
        of the active document
    end tell
```

**5.** Assign the first paragraph to a variable named **para1**, and the second paragraph to a variable named **para2**, as shown in boldface here:

```
tell the application "Microsoft Word"
    activate
    open "Macintosh HD:Users:guy:Documents:Sample Document.docx"
    insert paragraph at the beginning of the text object ¬
        of the active document
    insert paragraph at the beginning of the text object ¬
        of the active document
    set para1 to the first paragraph of the active document
    set para2 to the second paragraph of the active document
end tell
```

**6.** Create a **tell** block to **para1** that assigns text to it and sets the style to Heading 1, as shown in boldface here:

```
tell the application "Microsoft Word"
    activate
    open "Macintosh HD:Users:guy:Documents:Sample Document.docx"
    insert paragraph at the beginning of the text object ¬
        of the active document
    insert paragraph at the beginning of the text object ¬
        of the active document
    set para1 to the first paragraph of the active document
    set para2 to the second paragraph of the active document
    tell para1
        set the content of the text object to "Canine Forensics"
        set the style to "Heading 1"
    end tell
end tell
```

**7.** Create a **tell** block to **para2** that assigns text to it and sets its font size, as shown in boldface here:

```
tell the application "Microsoft Word"
    activate
    open "Macintosh HD:Users:guy:Documents:Sample Document.docx"
    insert paragraph at the beginning of the text object ¬
        of the active document
    insert paragraph at the beginning of the text object ¬
        of the active document
    set para1 to the first paragraph of the active document
    set para2 to the second paragraph of the active document
```

*(continued)*

```
    tell para1
        set the content of the text object to "Canine Forensics"
        set the style to "Heading 1"
    end tell
  tell para2
        set the content of the text object to ¬
            "We show you how to begin a power-packed career" ¬
            & "in this rapidly developing area."
        set the font size of the font object of the text object ¬
            to "12"
    end tell
```

8. Add a **save the active document** statement to save the document, as shown in boldface here:

```
tell the application "Microsoft Word"
    activate
    open "Macintosh HD:Users:guy:Documents:Sample Document.docx"
    insert paragraph at the beginning of the text object ¬
        of the active document
    insert paragraph at the beginning of the text object ¬
        of the active document
    set para1 to the first paragraph of the active document
    set para2 to the second paragraph of the active document
    tell para1
        set the content of the text object to "Canine Forensics"
        set the style to "Heading 1"
    end tell
  tell para2
        set the content of the text object to ¬
            "We show you how to begin a power-packed career " ¬
            & "in this rapidly developing area."
        set the font size of the font object of the text object ¬
            to "12"
    end tell
    save the active document
end tell
```

9. Save the script under a name of your choice.

10. Press ⌘-R or click the Run button on the toolbar to run the script. Word opens the sample document, adds the text and formatting, and then saves the document. Leave the document open for the next Try This section.

# Using Sections, Page Setup, and Headers and Footers

To make your documents look right, you'll probably need to set the margins and orientation, and add headers and footers, as discussed in this section.

To use different margins or different headers or footers in different parts of the same document, you need to break the document into sections—so we'll start there.

## Breaking a Document into Sections

To break the documents into logical parts, you'll need to use Word's sections. Each section can have its own layout (for example, different margins or a different number of columns) and its own headers and footers.

Each document starts off as a single section, but you can add other sections as needed by using the **insert break** command. Table 14-8 explains the **break type** constants you can use, including the non-section break types.

For example, the following statement collapses the current selection to its start and then inserts a next-page section break before it:

```
set myText to text object of selection
set myIP to collapse range myText direction collapse start
insert break at myIP break type section break next page
```

To work with a section, identify the section of the document—for example, **section 3 of active document**.

| break type Constant | Type of Break |
|---|---|
| line break | Line break (forcing a new line without starting a new paragraph) |
| page break | Page break (for forcing a new page) |
| column break | Column break (for forcing a new column) |
| section break next page | Section break with the new section starting on the next page |
| section break continuous | Section break with the new section starting immediately after the end of the previous section |
| section break even page | Section break with the new section starting on the next even-numbered page |
| section break odd page | Section break with the new section starting on the next odd-numbered page |

**Table 14-8** AppleScript's break type Constants

## Choosing Page Setup

To control the page setup, use the **page setup** object of either the **document** object (if you want to affect the whole of the document) or the **section** object (if you want to affect just a section).

To set the margins, set the **top margin** property, **bottom margin** property, **left margin** property, and **right margin** property to the appropriate numbers of points. For example, the following snippet sets each of the margins in the first section of the active document to 100 points:

```
tell the active document to tell the page setup of section 1
    set the top margin to 100
    set the bottom margin to 100
    set the left margin to 100
    set the right margin to 100
end tell
```

### NOTE

To create mirrored margins, where the margins on facing pages look like reflections of each other, first set the **mirror margins** property of the **section** object to **true**. Then set the **left margin** property to the number of points you want for the inside margins (where the pages meet) and the **right margin** property to the number of points for the outside margins.

To set the orientation for the document or section, set the **orientation** property to **orient portrait** for portrait orientation (taller than wide) or **orient landscape** for landscape orientation (wider than tall). For example, the following statement sets the second section of the active document to landscape orientation:

```
set the orientation of the page setup of section 2 ¬
    of the active document to orient landscape
```

## Adding Headers, Footers, and Page Numbers

Most printed documents need information in header sections at the top of each page and footer sections at the bottom of each page to make their identity clear. You'll also usually want to add page numbers so that the reader knows how many pages the document contains and can keep the pages in the right order.

### Understanding How Word Handles Headers and Footers

You can simply create the same header (or footer, or both) on every page of the document—but most documents need different headers and footers on different pages.

If you've created documents interactively in Word, you're probably familiar with its confusing way of handling headers and footers. But in case you're not, here's what you need to know:

- Headers and footers are part of section formatting.

- Word gives you three basic types of headers and footers: a header and footer for the first page of the section, a header and footer for the even-numbered pages, and a header and footer for the odd-numbered pages. So if you need your two-page spreads to have different headers and footers (as this book does), you can set those up within the same section.

- Headers and footers are always present in your document, but they don't appear until you activate them. For example, a blank document doesn't show a header or footer area until you activate the area (working interactively) or add text or other objects to it (working via AppleScript). When you do that, you get the primary header or footer; the first-page, even-numbered, and odd-numbered headers and footers lurk in the background until you summon them.

- When you create different headers for even-numbered pages and odd-numbered pages, the primary header becomes the odd-numbered page header Fsooters work in the same way.

- Any section in the document can have a different set of headers and footers than each other section. So you must start a new section whenever you need to give the document a new set of headers and footers. See the previous section for instructions for creating sections using AppleScript. Working manually, you choose Insert | Break, and then choose one of the Section Break commands—for example, Insert | Break | Section Break (Continuous).

- Word links a section's headers and footers to the previous section's headers and footers until you unlink them. So when you create a new section, it picks up the headers and footers from the previous section until you break the link and change the headers and footers.

## Returning the Header or Footer You Want

To work with a header or a footer, you use the appropriate **header footer** object for the section of the document you want to affect. Word organizes the **header footer** objects into the **header footers** list, and you return a **header footer** object by using the **get header** command (for a header) or the **get footer** command (for a footer), together with the keyword **index** and the constant for the type of header or footer.

Calling every header and footer a "header footer" makes you want to rap your forehead against the wall, but it must have made sense to somebody at Microsoft. Use the commands and constants shown in Table 14-9 to tell Word which header or footer you want.

For example, the next statement creates the variable **myHeader** and assigns the primary header of the first section of the active document to it:

```
set myHeader to (get header section 1 of active document ¬
    index header footer primary)
```

## Adding Text to Headers and Footers

Once you've grabbed hold of the **header footer** object, you can manipulate it using the techniques described earlier in this chapter. For example, the **text** object contains the text in the header or footer, so you can add text to the header or footer by using the **content** property of the **text** object.

For example, the following statement works with the **myHeader** variable created in the previous section to assign text to the header:

```
set content of text object of myHeader to ¬
    "AppleScript: A Beginner's Guide" & tab & tab & "Chapter 14"
```

## Setting Up Different Headers or Footers in a Section

To set up a different first-page header or footer, or different even-numbered page and odd-numbered page headers or footers, you work with the **page setup** object of the **document** object.

To turn on different first-page headers and footers for a section, you set the **different first page header footer** property of the **page setup** object to **true**. For example, the following statement turns on different first-page headers and footers for the first section of the active document:

```
set different first page header footer of page setup ¬
    of section 1 of active document to true
```

| Header or Footer | Command | Constant |
|---|---|---|
| Primary header | **get header** | header footer primary |
| First-page header | **get header** | header footer first page |
| Even-numbered page header | **get header** | header footer even pages |
| Primary footer | **get footer** | header footer primary |
| First-page footer | **get footer** | header footer first page |
| Even-numbered page footer | **get footer** | header footer even pages |

**Table 14-9** Commands and Constants for Returning header footer Objects

To turn on different headers and footers for the odd-numbered pages and even-numbered pages, set the **odd and even pages header footer** property of the **page setup** object to **true**. For example, the following statement turns on different odd- and even-numbered page headers for the second section of the document referenced by the variable **myDoc**:

```
set odd and even pages header footer of page setup ¬
    of section 2 of myDoc to true
```

## Adding Page Numbers to a Document

To add page numbers to a document, you normally place them in either the header or the footer so that they repeat automatically on the relevant pages of the document.

Use the **make new page number** command to add a new **page number** object to the **page numbers** list. For example, the following statement adds page numbers to the footer of the even-numbered pages in the first section of the document referenced by the variable **myDoc**:

```
make new page number at ¬
    (get footer section 1 of myDoc index header footer even pages)
```

# Displaying Word's Built-in Dialog Boxes

Often it's useful to be able to display one of Word's built-in dialog boxes in a script. For example, you can display the Open dialog box to let the user choose a document for the script to work on, the Save As dialog box to let the user save a document under a name and location of the user's choice, or the Page Setup dialog box to let the user pick a suitable fix for a formatting problem.

### NOTE

You can also use AppleScript's built-in dialog boxes as usual. For example, use the **choose from list** dialog box when you need to let the user select one item from a list, the **choose file** dialog box to have the user choose a file, or the **choose folder** dialog box when you need the user to pick a folder.

To display one of Word's built-in dialog boxes, you use the **dialog** command and specify the appropriate **dialog type** constant for the dialog box you want. Table 14-10 lists the most useful couple of dozen of Word's built-in dialog boxes.

### CAUTION

At this writing, the **dialog edit replace** constant displays the Find tab of the Find And Replace dialog box rather than the Replace tab—and the Replace tab button is grayed out so that you can't access it.

| Dialog Box | Menu Command | AppleScript dialog type Constant |
|---|---|---|
| Open | File \| Open | **file open** |
| Project Gallery | File \| Project Gallery | **file new** |
| Print | File \| Print | **file print** |
| Save | File \| Save *or* File \| Save As | **file save as** |
| Document | File \| Page Setup | **file page setup** |
| Paste | Edit \| Paste Special | **edit paste special** |
| Find And Replace, Find tab | Edit \| Find | **edit find** |
| Find And Replace, Replace tab | Edit \| Replace | **edit replace** |
| Find And Replace, Go To tab | Edit \| Go To | **edit go to** |
| Zoom | View \| Zoom | **view zoom** |
| Font | Format \| Font | **format font** |
| Paragraph | Format \| Paragraph | **format paragraph** |
| Bullets And Numbering | Format \| Bullets And Numbering | **format bullets and numbering** |
| Borders And Shading | Format \| Borders And Shading | **format borders and shading** |
| Tabs | Format \| Tabs | **format tabs** |
| Style | Format \| Style | **format style** |
| Spelling And Grammar | Tools \| Spelling And Grammar | **tools spelling and grammar** |
| Word Count | Tools \| Word Count | **tools word count** |
| Highlight Changes | Tools \| Track Changes \| Highlight Changes | **tools revisions** |
| Word Preferences | Word \| Preferences | **tools options** |
| Templates And Add-ins | Tools \| Templates And Add-ins | **tools templates** |
| Language | Tools \| Language | **tools language** |
| AutoCorrect | Tools \| AutoCorrect | **tools auto manager** |

**Table 14-10**   AppleScript dialog type Constants for Built-in Dialog Boxes

For example, the following statement displays the Open dialog box by using the **file open** constant:

```
show (get dialog dialog file open)
```

## TIP

To change the folder that Word displays in the Open dialog box, use the **change file open directory** command with the **path** parameter and the folder path. For example, to set the folder to the **Server:Documents:Word** folder, use **change file open directory path "Server:Documents:Word"**.

If the dialog box contains different tabs, you can display the tab you want by assigning the dialog box to a variable and then using the **default dialog tab** property to specify the tab you want. For example, the following snippet displays the AutoText tab of the AutoCorrect dialog box:

```
set autoDB to get dialog dialog tools auto manager
set default dialog tab of autoDB to ¬
    dialog tools auto manager tab auto text
show autoDB
```

## NOTE

Open the Word dictionary in AppleScript Editor and look at the **dialog** object to find a list of Word's dialogs and their **default dialog tab** constants.

## Try This Adding a Header, Adjusting Margins, and Displaying a Dialog Box

In this example, you finish off the document you created in the previous Try This sections. Here, you add a header to the document, adjust its margins, and then display the Save As dialog box so that the user—okay, *you*—can save the document under a different name.

Follow these steps to create the script:

1. In Word, make the Sample Document.docx document the active window. If you closed the document earlier, open it again.

2. In AppleScript Editor, press ⌘-N or choose File | New to create a new script.

3. Start a **tell** block to Word:

```
tell the application id "com.microsoft.Word"
end tell
```

*(continued)*

4. Activate Word and switch the first window of the active document to Print Layout view, as shown in boldface here:

```
tell the application id "com.microsoft.word"
    activate
    set view type of the first window of the active document ¬
        to page view
    end tell
```

5. Add text to the primary header—the only header in the document, because you haven't set the document to have any others. The new command appears in boldface here:

```
tell the application id "com.microsoft.word"
    activate
    set view type of the first window of the active document
to page view
    set content of text object of ¬
        (get header section 1 of active document ¬
        index header footer primary) to ¬
        "Canine Forensics" & tab & ¬
        "Expert Guidance for the Gullible" & tab & "Chapter 1"
    end tell
```

6. Add a **tell** block to the **page setup** object of **section 1 of the active document**; then set each margin to 72 points inside it, as shown in boldface here:

```
tell the application id "com.microsoft.word"
    activate
    set view type of the first window of the active document ¬
        to page view
    set content of text object of ¬
        (get header section 1 of active document ¬
        index header footer primary) to ¬
        "Canine Forensics" & tab & ¬
        "Expert Guidance for the Gullible" & tab & "Chapter 1"
    tell page setup of section 1 of the active document
        set top margin to 72
        set bottom margin to 72
        set left margin to 72
        set right margin to 72
    end tell
    end tell
```

7. Finally, add the **show** command for displaying the Save As dialog (**dialog file save as**), as shown in boldface here:

```
tell the application id "com.microsoft.word"
    activate
    set view type of the first window of the active document ¬
```

```
        to page view
    set content of text object of ¬
        (get header section 1 of active document ¬
        index header footer primary) to ¬
        "Canine Forensics" & tab & ¬
        "Expert Guidance for the Gullible" & tab & "Chapter 1"
    tell page setup of section 1 of the active document
        set top margin to 72
        set bottom margin to 72
        set left margin to 72
        set right margin to 72
    end tell
    show (get dialog dialog file save as)
end tell
```

8. Save the script under a name of your choice.

9. Press ⌘-R or click the Run button on the toolbar to run the script. Word adds the header, changes the margins, and then displays the Save As dialog box.

10. Save the document under a name of your choice, and then close it.

# Running Your Scripts from Word

Rather than running your scripts from the Script menu on the Mac OS X menu bar (or from AppleScript Editor), you'll probably want to run them directly from Word. You can do this by using Word's own Script menu or by assigning a keyboard shortcut to each script.

## Adding a Script to Word's Script Menu

Word's Script menu appears to the right of the Help menu on the menu bar. To add your scripts to the Script menu, you simply move or copy them to the right folder (or, if you prefer, save them there in the first place). That folder is the ~/Documents/Microsoft User Data/Word Script Menu Items/ folder.

Follow these steps to add scripts to the Word Script Menu Items folder:

1. Click the Scripts menu, and then click About This Menu. Word displays the information dialog box shown in Figure 14-5.

2. Click the Open Folder button. Word opens a Finder window to the Word Script Menu Items folder.

3. Copy or move your Word-related scripts to this window, and then close it.

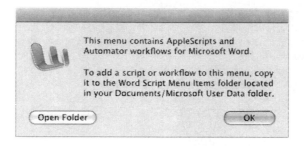

This menu contains AppleScripts and Automator workflows for Microsoft Word.

To add a script or workflow to this menu, copy it to the Word Script Menu Items folder located in your Documents/Microsoft User Data folder.

Open Folder          OK

**Figure 14-5** The easiest way to open the Word Scripts folder is by choosing About This Menu from the Scripts menu and then clicking the Open Folder button.

*TIP*
You can create folders in the Word Script Menu Items folder to make the Script menu display submenus. This is a great way of organizing your scripts into different categories and keeping the Script menu manageable. Put your most-used scripts directly on the Script menu so you don't have to go to a subfolder to open them.

Now, when you open the Scripts menu, your scripts appear on it. Click the script you want to run.

## Creating a Keyboard Shortcut to Run a Script

If you like to use the keyboard, the easiest way to run a script is to create a keyboard shortcut for it. You can either assign a keyboard shortcut in System Preferences (as discussed in Chapter 11) or change the script's name to include a keyboard shortcut.

The simple way of creating a keyboard shortcut is to tack the shortcut onto the script's name. The best time to do this is when you add the script to the Word Script Menu Items folder.

At the end of the script's name, add a backslash character (\) followed by the keypress you want. Use the letters shown here for the ⌘, OPTION, and CONTROL modifier keys, followed by the letter or number you want to use. If you want to include the SHIFT key, type the shifted character—for example, type **P** instead of **p** to include SHIFT.

| Modifier Key | Character to Use |
|---|---|
| ⌘ | m |
| OPTION | o |
| CONTROL | c |

Here are two examples:

- Add **\mcc** to the end of the script's name to use ⌘-CONTROL-C as the keyboard shortcut.
- Add **\moP** to the end of the script's name to use ⌘-OPTION-SHIFT-P as the keyboard shortcut.

### *TIP*

When creating custom keyboard shortcuts, avoid stepping on any of Word's existing keyboard shortcuts that you value. If you don't remember them, you can create a list easily. Chose File | Print to open the Print dialog box. Open the pop-up menu in the middle and choose Microsoft Word to display the Word options. In the Print What pop-up menu, choose Key Assignments, and then print the document—or save the forests by clicking the PDF button and making a virtual printout instead.

# Chapter 15

## Automating
## Microsoft Excel

## Key Skills & Concepts

- Understanding Excel's main objects
- Launching and quitting Excel
- Creating, saving, opening, and closing workbooks
- Working with worksheets and other sheets
- Creating and using ranges of cells
- Using charts in your workbooks
- Working with Excel windows and views
- Using Find and Replace in your scripts

This chapter shows you how to bring the power of AppleScript to bear on Microsoft Excel, the widely used spreadsheet application. You'll learn how to launch Excel (and quit it when you're done), create workbooks, and manipulate the worksheets and other sheets inside them. After that, I'll show you how to create ranges of cells and work with them and build charts automatically in your workbooks. Finally, we'll look at how to work with windows and views in Excel, and how to use the Find and Replace features in scripts.

First, let's take a quick look at the main objects you will work with when you automate Excel.

# Understanding Excel's Main Objects

These are the main objects you will work with to automate Excel using AppleScript:

- The **application** class represents the Excel application as a whole. You use the **application** class for launching Excel, quitting it, setting options, and performing other tasks that involve the whole application rather than a workbook or a smaller component.

- The **workbook** class represents an open workbook. As usual, Excel marshals the **workbook** objects into the **workbooks** list, which you can use to work with all the open workbooks together. For example, you can save all the open workbooks that contain unsaved changes, or you can close all the open workbooks, saving changes or not (more on this shortly).

● Within a workbook, the **worksheet** class represents a worksheet. Excel groups the **worksheet** objects together into the **worksheets** list. This collection works as usual, but you have to bear in mind that Excel also has chart sheets (discussed next), list sheets, macro sheets, and dialog sheets—and all these appear in another collection, **sheets**.

● The **chart sheet** object represents a chart sheet (a chart on its own sheet—not a chart on a worksheet). Excel groups the **chart sheet** objects with the **worksheet** objects in the **sheets** list.

● The **active sheet** object represents the active sheet in the active workbook.

● As in most applications, the **window** object represents an open window. All the **window** objects together make up the **windows** list.

# Launching and Quitting Excel

To launch Excel, use the **launch** command, followed by the **activate** command if you want to bring Excel to the front so that you can see what's happening—often useful when you're developing your scripts or when you want the user to see what the script does. For example:

```
tell the application id "com.microsoft.Excel"
    launch
    activate
end tell
```

### NOTE
If you prefer, you can omit the **launch** command—the **activate** command on its own will launch Excel if it's not already running. But your code will be clearer if you include **launch** if you're intending to launch the application. If the application is running already, using **launch** doesn't return an error.

You can also launch Excel if it's not running by telling it to open a workbook or to create a new workbook. For example, the following snippet launches Excel if it's not running, as the **make new workbook** command requires Excel to be open:

```
tell the application id "com.microsoft.excel"
    make new workbook
end tell
```

To quit Excel, use the **quit** command:

```
tell the application id "com.microsoft.Excel"
    quit
end tell
```

Before agreeing to quit, Excel prompts you to save any unsaved changes to workbooks. You'll see how to handle unsaved changes later in this chapter.

# Working with Workbooks

To get things done in Excel—either via AppleScript or when working interactively—you'll need to use workbooks. So our next move here is to see how you create and save workbooks, open and close them, share them with others, and protect them against unwanted interference.

## Creating a New Blank Workbook

To create a new workbook based on the Blank Document workbook, like you get when you press ⌘-N when working interactively, use the **make new workbook** command. Excel adds a new workbook to the **workbooks** list, where you can work with it.

```
tell the application id "com.microsoft.Excel"
    make new workbook
end tell
```

### NOTE

When you create a new workbook using AppleScript, Excel names the new workbook **Sheet1** (or the next unused number—**Sheet2**, **Sheet3**, or whatever) rather than using the **Workbook1** name (or the next unused number) it uses when you give a New Workbook command interactively (for example, choosing File | New Workbook). Excel also marks the new workbook as *dirty*, meaning that it contains unsaved changes—even though you haven't changed anything in it yet.

To give yourself a direct handle on the new workbook, use a **set** statement to assign it to a variable, as in the next example, which uses the **x_book** variable. You can then use the variable to refer to the workbook rather than finding it through the **workbooks** list.

```
tell the application id "com.microsoft.Excel"
    set x_book to make new workbook
end tell
```

A blank workbook can be good when you're starting from scratch, but often you'll want to give your workbook a head start by basing it on either a template or on an existing workbook. Let's look at how to do that next.

## Creating a New Workbook Based on a Template

To create a new workbook based on a template, you don't use a **make new workbook** command with a **template** parameter or property as you might expect. Instead, all you need to do is to tell Excel to open the template. This makes Excel create a new workbook based on the template.

For example, the following statement creates a new workbook based on the Event Budget.xlxs spreadsheet template:

```
open "Macintosh HD:Applications:Microsoft Office 2008:Office:Media:
Templates:Ledger Sheets:Budgets:Event Budget.xlsx"
```

The new workbook's title bar shows the template's name, so this command is confusing. But when you try to save the new workbook, Excel prompts you to choose a new name, just as when you're saving a workbook that appears new in the conventional way.

The **open** command you're using here is in AppleScript's Standard Suite—commands available to every application under the sun. This command doesn't return a result, so you can't assign the new workbook you create to a variable that will let you access it easily. To assign the workbook to a variable, you need to use Excel's **open workbook** command instead. This command takes the parameter **workbook file name** followed by the filename. Here's an example of an **open workbook** command that assigns the new document created to a variable:

```
set myBudget to open workbook workbook file name ¬
    "Macintosh HD:Applications:Microsoft Office 2008:Office:Media:
Templates:Ledger Sheets:Budgets:Event Budget.xlsx"
```

## Saving a Workbook

To save a workbook, use the **save workbook as** command. Put the workbook, or a variable referring to it, as the direct parameter, followed by the **filename** parameter and the path and filename you want to use. For example, the following statements declare a variable called **myfilename**, assign a path and filename to it, and then save the workbook referenced by the variable **WB** to that location:

```
set myfilename to (path to desktop as string) & "2012 Budget.xlsx"
save workbook as WB filename myfilename
```

Apart from the **filename** parameter, which you'll want to use every time you save a new workbook or save an existing workbook under a different name, the **save workbook as** command offers various parameters that correspond to choices you can make in the Save As dialog box. The following parameters are the most useful:

- **file format**  Add this parameter if you want to control the file format Excel uses for the workbook—usually a good idea. If you omit the **file format** parameter, Excel uses the format selected in the Save Files In This Format pop-up menu in the Compatibility Preferences. Table 15-1 explains the most useful of Excel's many file formats.

- **add to most recently used list**  Add this optional parameter and set it to **true** if you want the workbook to appear on the Recent Documents list—for example, so that the user can reopen the workbook quickly from the File menu. If you don't want the workbook to appear on the Recent Documents list, either set this parameter to **false** or simply omit it—the default value is **false**.

- **create backup**  Add this optional parameter set to **with create backup** to make Excel create a backup copy of the file.

For example, the following statement saves the active workbook in Excel 2007/2008 format in the folder **Shared:Spreads:Excel** with the filename **Production Statistics.xlsx**, setting Excel to create a backup:

```
save workbook as active workbook filename ¬
    "Shared:Spreads:Excel:Production Statistics.xlsx" ¬
    file format Excel XML file format with create backup
```

The following statement saves the workbook referenced by the variable **this_book** in Excel 97–2004 format in the folder **Shared:Spreads:Excel** with the filename **Recruitment Tactics.xls**, explicitly preventing the workbook from being added to the Recent Documents list:

```
save workbook as this_book ¬
    filename "Shared:Spreads:Excel:Recruitment Tactics.xls" ¬
    file format Excel98to2004 file format ¬
    without add to most recently used list
```

After you've saved a workbook with a filename and folder location, you can save it again by using the **save** command with the **workbook** object (so Excel knows which workbook you're referring to) but without any further parameters. For example, the following command saves any unsaved changes in the active workbook:

```
save the active workbook
```

| file format Constant | Format | Extension | Comments |
|---|---|---|---|
| Excel XML file format | Excel Workbook | .xlsx | This is Excel 2007/Excel 2008's default workbook format (unless someone changes it in the Compatibility Preferences). Users with earlier versions of Excel will need to install file converters to read this format. Files in this format cannot contain macros. |
| template file format | Excel Template | .xltx | This is Excel 2007/2008's default template format. Users with earlier versions of Excel will need to install file converters to read this format. Templates in this format cannot contain macros. |
| Excel binary file format | Excel Binary Workbook | .xlsb | This is Excel 2007/2008's new binary file format. It's good for use with Excel 2007 and 2008, but not with earlier versions of other applications. |
| Excel98to2004 file format | Excel 97–2004 Workbook | .xls | This is the default format for versions of Excel from Excel 97 (for Windows) and Excel 98 (for Mac) through Excel 2003 (for Windows) and Excel 2004 (for Mac). This is the best choice for workbook compatibility. |
| Excel98to2004 template file format | Excel 97-2004 Template | .xlt | This is the default template format for versions of Excel from Excel 97 (for Windows) and Excel 98 (for Mac) through Excel 2003 (for Windows) and Excel 2004 (for Mac). This is the best choice for template compatibility. |
| macro enabled XML file format | Excel Macro-Enabled Workbook | .xlsm | The version of the Excel 2007/Excel 2008 file format that can contain macros. Users with earlier versions of Excel will need to install file converters to read this format. |
| macro enabled template file format | Excel Macro-Enabled Template | .xltm | The version of the Excel 2007/Excel 2008 template format that can contain macros. Users with earlier versions of Excel will need to install file converters to read this format. |
| CSV file format | Comma Separated Values | .csv | This is the standard format that contains only the text of a spreadsheet and uses commas to separate the cell contents. Universally compatible with spreadsheet applications and text editors. |
| PDF file format | PDF | .pdf | This creates a Portable Document Format file, which is good for sharing a spreadsheet for reading rather than for use. |

**Table 15-1**   Excel's Most Useful File Formats

## Opening an Existing Workbook

The standard way of opening a workbook is to use the **open** command in AppleScript's Standard Suite of commands. For example, the following statement opens the workbook named **Amortization.xlsx** in the **Server:Shared:Sheets** folder:

```
open "Server:Shared:Sheets:Amortization.xlsx"
```

As mentioned earlier in this chapter, the **open** command in AppleScript's Standard Suite doesn't return a result, so you can't assign the workbook you're opening to a variable. If you need to assign the workbook you're opening to a variable, use Excel's **open workbook** command, which returns a result that you can assign to a variable. This command takes the parameter **workbook file name** followed by the filename.

For example, the following statement opens the workbook named **Amortization.xlsx** in the **Server:Shared:Sheets** folder and assigns it to the variable **amort**:

```
set amort to open workbook ¬
    workbook file name "Transfer:Examples:Excel:Amortization.xlsx"
```

## Closing a Workbook

To close a workbook, use the **close** command with the **workbook** keyword and the workbook's name or a variable or object identifying the workbook. For example, the following statement closes the workbook named **Product Goal-Seeking.xlsb**:

```
close workbook "Product Goal-Seeking.xlsb"
```

If the workbook contains unsaved changes, Excel prompts the user to save them. Sometimes you'll want the user to decide whether to keep the changes (for example, if it's a workbook they've been editing), but often you'll want to take care of any unsaved changes automatically in the script. You can either use the **save** command (discussed earlier in this chapter) before using the **close** command, or set the **saving** parameter of the **close** command to **yes**:

```
close workbook "Product Goal-Seeking.xlsb" saving yes
```

If you need to close the workbook and lose any unsaved changes without Excel prompting the user about them, set the **saving** parameter of the **close** command to **no**:

```
close workbook "Product Goal-Seeking.xlsb" saving no
```

**NOTE**

If you try to close a workbook that has never been saved, Excel displays the Save As dialog box unless you've set the **saving** parameter to **no**. Unless you can be sure that the workbook has already been saved, use the **save** command to explicitly save each new workbook you create rather than rely on the **saving yes** parameter of the **close** command.

If you want Excel to prompt the user to save changes, set the **saving** parameter to **ask** so that the user sees the "Do you want to save the changes you made?" dialog box (see Figure 15-1).

```
close workbook "Product Goal-Seeking.xlsb" saving ask
```

To close all open workbooks, use the **close** command with the **workbooks** list. As with a single workbook, you can set the **saving** parameter to **yes**, **no**, or **ask** to control what happens to unsaved changes. For example, the following statement closes all open workbooks, saving any unsaved changes automatically:

```
tell the application id "com.microsoft.Excel"
    close the workbooks saving yes
end tell
```

After you close all the open workbooks, Excel stays open until you explicitly quit it.

## Sharing a Workbook with Others

When you need to share a workbook with other people so that two or more people can edit the workbook at the same time without tripping over one another's changes, save the workbook as a shared workbook. To do so, use the **save workbook as** command and set the **access mode** property to **shared**.

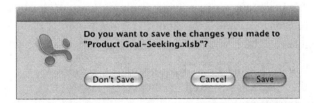

**Figure 15-1**    Setting the saving parameter to ask—or omitting it—makes Excel prompt the user to decide whether to save any unsaved changes in the workbook your script is closing.

For example, the following statement saves the open workbook named **Amortization .xlsx** as a shared workbook under the same filename:

```
save workbook as workbook ("Amortization.xlsx") ¬
    filename "Transfer:Examples:Excel:Amortization.xlsx" ¬
    access mode shared
```

### NOTE
To remove sharing from a shared workbook, use the **save workbook as** command but set the **access mode** property to **exclusive**.

To check whether a workbook is shared, get the **multi user editing** property of the **workbook** object. If this property returns **true**, the workbook is shared; if it returns **false**, the workbook is single-user.

## Protecting a Workbook Against Changes

To protect a workbook against changes, run the **protect workbook** command on the appropriate **workbook** object. This command has three parameters; each is optional, but you'll normally want to set at least the first of them.

- **password**  Use this parameter to lock down the protection with a password. If you don't apply a password, the protection is worthless, as anyone can remove it without effort.

### CAUTION
Even with a password, Excel's protection is relatively easy to break, especially as there are plenty of password crackers just a search away on the Internet. The best way to prevent anyone untrustworthy from changing your workbooks is to keep the workbooks away from them—for example, on a secure area of your network.

- **structure**  Add the parameter **with structure** to protect the workbook's structure, preventing your colleagues (or yourself) from moving the sheets around. Applying structure protection to a shared workbook is usually a good idea. The default value is **without structure**, which you can specify if you want to make your code explicit.

- **windows**  Add the parameter **with windows** if you want to protect the workbook's windows so that they remain fixed in place. How helpful this is depends on what you and your colleagues are trying to do with the workbook; locking the window immovably to the screen tends to make people think Excel has crashed, so it's a good idea to warn the user that you're locking the windows. The default value is **without windows**; again, you can specify this for full disclosure.

For example, the following statement protects the workbook named **Budget Strategy .xlsx** with a password you should never use, protecting the structure but not the windows:

```
protect workbook workbook ("Budget Strategy.xlsx") password "lockdown" ¬
    with structure without windows
```

**NOTE**

You can also protect a worksheet, as discussed later in this chapter.

To unprotect a workbook, use the **unprotect** command, specify the **workbook** object, and give the password if you used one. For example, the following statement unprotects the active workbook:

```
unprotect active workbook password "lockdown"
```

## Using the active workbook Class

When you're working from AppleScript, you don't need to activate a workbook as you do when you're working manually in Excel. Instead, you can tell AppleScript which workbook you want to manipulate and which actions to take with it. For example, you can work with a workbook that the user cannot see without disturbing the active workbook, the workbook they've been using.

Other times, you'll want to work with the active workbook so that you can interact with the user's data and the user can see what's happening. To access the active workbook via AppleScript, use the **active workbook** class.

## Ask the Expert

**Q:** Can I safely use the active workbook **class in just about any script?**

**A:** Yes—up to a point. Only one workbook is active at a time in Excel—the workbook that has the focus, accepting the mouse clicks and the keystrokes.

This is all very straightforward when you're using Excel interactively. But when you're using the **active workbook** class in a script, it's a good idea to assign the result to a variable so that you can manipulate it easily.

This is because the active workbook can change during the course of a script—for example, if you open a workbook or create a new workbook, that workbook becomes the active workbook. And if you close the active workbook, the next workbook behind it becomes active. It's easy to miss these switches of focus when you're creating code, and they can give your workbooks some uncomfortable surprises.

To make a workbook the active workbook, give the **activate** command to Excel itself, and then give the **activate object** command followed by the **workbook** object. For example, the following statements activate the workbook named **Widget Output.xls**:

```
activate
activate object workbook "Widget Output.xls"
```

## Try This  Creating, Saving, and Closing a Workbook

In this example, you create a script that launches Excel by creating a new workbook based on the Blank Document template. The script then saves the workbook and closes it, leaving a workbook that you will use again in examples later in this chapter.

To create the script, follow these steps:

1. If Excel is running at the moment, quit it in your preferred way. For example, press ⌘-Q.

2. In AppleScript Editor, press ⌘-N or choose File | New to create a new script.

3. Start a **tell** block to Excel, addressing it by its **application id** string, **com.microsoft.Excel**:

```
tell the application id "com.microsoft.Excel"
end tell
```

4. Inside the **tell** block, type a **make new workbook** statement and assign it to the variable **xbook**, as shown in boldface here:

```
tell the application id "com.microsoft.Excel"
    set xbook to make new workbook
end tell
```

5. Add an **activate** statement, as shown in boldface here, so that you will see Excel and the new workbook you create. (Otherwise, they remain hidden.)

```
tell the application id "com.microsoft.Excel"
    set xbook to make new workbook
    activate
end tell
```

6. Add a **save workbook as** command to save the **xbook** workbook under the filename **ABG Book.xlsx** using the Excel 2007/8 workbook format (**file format Excel XML file format**). This example saves the workbook to the Desktop, but you can change it to any path that works for your Mac's file system. The new command appears in boldface here:

```
tell the application id "com.microsoft.Excel"
    set xbook to make new workbook
    activate
```

```
    save workbook as xbook ¬
        filename (path to desktop as string) & "ABG Book.xlsx" ¬
        file format Excel XML file format
end tell
```

**7.** Add a **delay 3** command to insert a pause in the script to give the file system a chance to handle the save operation. Then close the workbook and quit Excel. The new statements appear in boldface here:

```
tell the application id "com.microsoft.Excel"
    set xbook to make new workbook
    activate
    save workbook as xbook ¬
        filename (path to desktop as string) & "ABG Book.xlsx" ¬
        file format Excel XML file format
    delay 3
    close the workbook "ABG Book.xlsx"
    quit
end tell
```

**8.** Save the script under a name of your choice.

**9.** Press ⌘-R or click the Run button on the toolbar to run the script. You'll see Excel open, create the new workbook, display the name "ABG Book" in the title bar after it saves the workbook, and then close the workbook and quit.

# Working with Worksheets and Other Sheets

You can't do much in Excel without using sheets, be they worksheets, list sheets, chart sheets, or dialog or macro sheets. As mentioned earlier in this chapter, Excel uses a **sheet** object to represent each sheet in an open workbook and gathers the sheets together into the **sheets** list.

As usual, you can refer to a sheet by its name or by its index number, with the leftmost sheet in the workbook being the first sheet. Each type of sheet has its own index numbering, so the first worksheet (**worksheet 1**) is different from the first chart sheet (**chart sheet 1**), and so on.

This section shows you how to insert and delete worksheets, rename them, move and copy them, protect them, and print them. You'll also learn to find out which kind of sheet you grabbed hold of and how to use the **active worksheet** class to work with the active worksheet.

## Inserting a Worksheet in a Workbook

To insert a worksheet in a workbook, use the **make new worksheet** command, either the **at** keyword or (more naturally) the **in** keyword, and the workbook to which you want to add it. For example, the following statement adds a new worksheet at the beginning of the open workbook named **Budget Strategy.xlsx**:

```
make new worksheet in workbook "Budget Strategy.xlsx"
```

If you use the command on its own like that, you get a new worksheet named **Sheet1** (or the next unused name—**Sheet42** or whatever) at the beginning of the workbook. Sometimes this naming and placement is convenient, but usually you'll want to set at least the worksheet's **name** property and specify where to put it.

To set the name for the new worksheet, add a **with properties** statement and put the **name** property and its values within braces, as in this example:

```
make new worksheet in workbook "Budget Strategy.xlsx" ¬
    with properties {name:"2014 Planning"}
```

### NOTE

If the name you try to set is already in use, Excel uses the next available **Sheetn** name without comment—it doesn't return an error.

Your choices on this are somewhat constrained, because the commands for specifying where to put the worksheet don't always work as they should. The parameters **at beginning of** and **at end of** work, but the parameters **at before** and **at after** don't work reliably. Because the default placement is at the beginning of the workbook, there's little point in adding **at beginning of** unless you need to be explicit—so **at end of** is the parameter you're most likely to need. For example, the following statement adds a new worksheet named **2015 Planning** to the end of the **Budget Strategy.xlsx** workbook:

```
make new worksheet at end of workbook "Budget Strategy.xlsx" ¬
    with properties {name:"2015 Planning"}
```

If you need to place a new worksheet in a particular position, your best bet is to place it at the beginning or the end (your choice) and then use the **move** command to move the worksheet to the required position. With the **move** command, the **before** and **after** parameters work as they should. For example, the following statements add the same new worksheet (**2015 Planning**) to the same workbook (**Budget Strategy.xlsx**), but then move the new worksheet to the position after the second worksheet:

```
tell the workbook "Budget Strategy.xlsx"
    make new worksheet at end with properties {name:"2015 Planning"}
    move the last sheet to before sheet 2
end tell
```

### CAUTION
AppleScript's commands for inserting and moving worksheets are delicate, and many operations that should logically work (such as assigning a new worksheet you add to a variable and then moving the sheet referenced by that variable) fail with errors. To save time, stick with a simple approach, such as the previous one, if you find a more elegant approach throws unexpected errors.

## Renaming a Worksheet
To rename a worksheet, use a **set** statement to change the **name** property of the sheet object. For example, the following statement changes the name of the sheet called **Sheet1** to **2013 Planning**:

```
tell the active workbook
    set name of sheet "Sheet1" to "2017 Planning"
end tell
```

Each sheet name must be unique within a workbook, so if there's already a sheet with the name you try to use, the rename operation fails, but with no error message. To avoid this giving you awkward surprises, use **exists** to test whether a sheet already has the name you're planning to use, as in this example:

```
tell the active workbook
    if not (exists sheet ("2014 Planning")) then
        set name of sheet "Sheet4" to "2014 Planning"
    end if
end tell
```

## Deleting a Worksheet
To delete a worksheet, use the **delete** command and specify the sheet in the workbook. For example, the following statement deletes the first sheet in the active workbook:

```
delete the first sheet in the active workbook
```

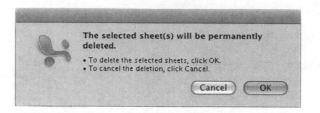

**Figure 15-2** To avoid Excel confirming the deletion of a sheet with the user like this, you have to suppress alerts before deleting a sheet.

When a script deletes a worksheet (or chart sheet, or other type of sheet) like this, Excel prompts the user for confirmation of the deletion (see Figure 15-2).

If you don't want the user to be able to prevent the script from deleting the sheet, set the **display alerts** property of the Excel **application** object to **false** before issuing the **delete** command, and then set **display alerts** back to **true**. Here's an example:

```
set display alerts to false
delete the first sheet in the active workbook
set display alerts to true
```

This way, Excel deletes the sheet without displaying the confirmation dialog box.

## Moving or Copying a Worksheet

To move a worksheet, use the **move** command, identify the **sheet** object, and tell Excel where to put it by using **at beginning of**, **at end of**, **at before**, or **at after**, as appropriate. For example, the following statement moves the sheet named **Chart5** in the active workbook to after the sheet named **2015 Planning**:

```
tell the active workbook
    move sheet "Chart5" to after sheet "2015 Planning"
end tell
```

To copy a worksheet, use the **copy worksheet** command, identify the **sheet** object, and tell Excel the destination by using the **before** parameter or the **after** parameter and the name of the target sheet. For example, the following statement copies the worksheet named **Personnel** in the active workbook to after the worksheet named **2014 Planning**:

```
tell the active workbook
    copy worksheet sheet "2016 Planning" after sheet "2017 planning"
end tell
```

### NOTE

The **copy worksheet** command uses either the **after** parameter or the **before** parameter, not **at after** or **at before**. Don't ask; I won't tell.

Excel gives the copied sheet the same name as the original sheet, followed by a space and the number 2 or the next unused number in parentheses. For example, the first copy of the sheet **2016 Planning** is named **2016 Planning (2)**, the second copy is named **2016 Planning (3)**, and so on. You can then rename the copied sheet by using this name to identify it—for example:

```
set name of sheet "2016 Planning (2)" to "2018 Planning"
```

To copy a worksheet to a new workbook, use a **copy worksheet** command with the worksheet name but without either the **before** parameter or the **after** parameter. For example, the following statement copies the worksheet named **Materials** from the active workbook to a new workbook:

```
tell the active workbook to copy worksheet sheet "Materials"
```

This gives you a new workbook that's the active workbook. You can then either work with it directly as the active workbook (for example, you'll probably want to save it) or assign it to a variable so that you can keep track of it.

## Finding Out Which Kind of Sheet You're Dealing With

To find out which type of sheet you're dealing with, check the **worksheet type** property of the **sheet** object. Table 15-2 explains the five kinds of **worksheet type** that this property returns.

For example, the following snippet checks the **worksheet type** property of the active sheet and displays an alert (see Figure 15-3) if it is not a worksheet:

```
if worksheet type of active sheet is not sheet type worksheet then
    display alert "Please select a worksheet" ¬
        message "This script works only on worksheets, ¬
        not on other types of sheets."
end if
```

| worksheet type Constant | Type of Worksheet |
|---|---|
| sheet type worksheet | Worksheet |
| sheet type chart | Chart sheet |
| sheet type dialog sheet (but returns missing value) | Dialog sheet |
| sheet type excel 4 macro sheet | Excel 4 macro sheet |
| sheet type excel 4 intl macro sheet | Excel 4 International macro sheet |

**Table 15-2** AppleScript worksheet type Constants

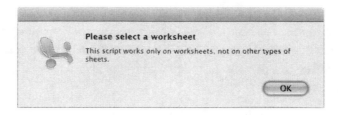

**Figure 15-3** It's a good idea to check the worksheet type before trying to perform actions on the worksheet.

## Protecting a Worksheet

To protect a worksheet, use the **protect worksheet** command, specify the sheet, and add the parameters for the type of protection you want. The following list explains the parameters; each is optional, but you'll normally want to at least set a password to make the protection effective.

● **password** Use this parameter to secure the protection with a password. If you don't apply a password, anybody can remove the protection with two clicks of the mouse.

● **drawing objects** Set this parameter to **with drawing objects** to protect the shapes in the worksheet. Set this parameter to **without drawing objects**, or omit it, to leave shapes unprotected.

● **worksheet contents** Set this parameter to **with worksheet contents**, or simply omit it to get the default value of **true**, to protect the worksheet contents. Set this parameter to **without worksheet contents** if you want to leave the worksheet contents unprotected.

● **scenarios** Set this parameter to **with scenarios**, or omit the parameter to get the default value of **true**, to protect the scenarios in the worksheet. Set this parameter to **without scenarios** if you need to let users change the scenarios.

● **user interface only** Set this parameter to **with user interface only** if you want to protect the drawing objects, worksheet contents, and scenarios (using the parameters chosen previously) while leaving macros unprotected. Omit this argument if you want the protection to apply to macros as well as to the user interface items.

For example, the following statement protects everything in sight (and the macros) on the active worksheet and applies a token password:

```
protect worksheet active sheet password "abcd1234" ¬
    with drawing objects, worksheet contents and scenarios
```

To remove protection from a worksheet, use the **unprotect** command, identify the worksheet, and provide the password if the protection uses one. For example, the following statement unprotects the active sheet:

```
unprotect active sheet password "abcd1234"
```

# Using the active worksheet Class

The **active worksheet** class represents the active worksheet in the active workbook. This class lets you work directly with the worksheet the user has selected.

You can set a worksheet to be the active worksheet by using an **activate** command on Excel (unless it's already activated) and then using an **activate object** command on the worksheet. For example, the following statements activate Excel, the workbook named **Budget Strategy.xlsb**, and then the worksheet named **2013 Planning**:

```
activate
activate object workbook "Budget Strategy.xlsb"
activate object worksheet "2013 Planning"
```

You can also activate a worksheet by adding a new worksheet—the new worksheet becomes the active worksheet.

### TIP

When creating a script that uses the active worksheet, assign the active worksheet to a variable so that you can easily restore it. Once you've done this, you can add new worksheets or activate other worksheets as needed, and then still restore the user's original active worksheet at the end of the script.

# Printing a Worksheet

To print a worksheet, use the **print out** command with the appropriate **sheet** object. You can set the following parameters, all of which are optional:

- **from**   Use this parameter with the page number at which you want to start printing. If you omit this parameter, Excel starts printing from the beginning of the sheet or object.

### NOTE

You can also use the **print out** command to print out a **workbook** object or the contents of a **window** object, but usually a worksheet is the most useful item to print.

- **to**   Use this parameter with the page number at which you want to stop printing. If you omit this parameter, Excel prints to the end of the sheet or other object.

- **copies**   Use this parameter with an integer number (for example, **copies 3**) when you need more than the single copy that Excel prints by default.

- **preview**  Set this parameter to **true** to display the sheet or other object in Print Preview before printing it.

- **collate**  When you're printing multiple copies of the same item, set this parameter to **true** to make Excel collate the copies.

### NOTE
The **print out** command has two parameters that Excel 2008 doesn't yet support: **active printer** (for changing the printer) and **print to file** (for printing to a file that you can then print on a different printer).

For example, the following statement prints the sheet named **2011 Budget** from the workbook named **Budget Strategy.xlsx**:

```
print out sheet "2011 Budget" of workbook "Budget Strategy.xlsx"
```

## Try This  Opening a Workbook and Adding a Worksheet to It

In this example, you open the workbook you created in the first example (earlier in this chapter), rename its existing worksheet, and add a worksheet to it before saving the workbook.

To create the script, follow these steps:

1. In AppleScript Editor, press ⌘-N or choose File | New to create a new script.

2. Start a **tell** block to Excel, addressing it by its name for variety:

```
tell the application "Microsoft Excel"
end tell
```

3. Inside the **tell** block, type an **open workbook** command that opens the workbook **ABG Book.xlsx** and assigns it to the variable **abook**. The new statement appears in boldface here; if you changed the path in the previous example, you'll need to change it here as well:

```
tell the application "Microsoft Excel"
    set abook to open workbook workbook ¬
        file name (path to desktop as string) & "ABG Book.xlsx"
end tell
```

4. Use a **set** statement to change the **name** property of **Sheet1** to **Sales**. The new statement appears in boldface here:

```
tell the application "Microsoft Excel"
    set abook to open workbook workbook ¬
```

```
        file name (path to desktop as string) & "ABG Book.xlsx"
    set the name of sheet "Sheet1" of abook to "Sales"
    make new worksheet at end of active workbook ¬
    with properties {name:"Results"}
end tell
```

5. Use a **make new worksheet** to insert a new worksheet at the end of the active
   workbook (the workbook is active because you just opened it), giving it the name
   **Results**, as shown in boldface here:

```
tell the application "Microsoft Excel"
    set abook to open workbook workbook ¬
        file name (path to desktop as string) & "ABG Book.xlsx"
    set the name of sheet "Sheet1" of abook to "Sales"
    make new worksheet at end of active workbook ¬
        with properties {name:"Results"}
end tell
```

6. Add a **save** command to save **abook**, as shown in boldface here:

```
tell the application "Microsoft Excel"
    set abook to open workbook workbook ¬
        file name (path to desktop as string) & "ABG Book.xlsx"
    set the name of sheet "Sheet1" of abook to "Sales"
    make new worksheet at end of active workbook ¬
        with properties {name:"Profits"}
    save abook
end tell
```

7. Save the script under a name of your choice.

8. Press ⌘-R or click the Run button on the toolbar to run the script. You'll see the ABG
   Book.xlsx workbook open, change the name of the first worksheet, and then add
   another worksheet with the name Profits.

9. Leave the workbook open so that you can use it in the next example.

# Creating and Using Ranges of Cells

When you're working on a worksheet, you can work directly with the active cell or
the cells that the user has selected, but you can also choose your own ranges of cells to
manipulate. This section shows you how to do both and how to use Excel's special cells in
your scripts.

## Working with the Active Cell or the Selection

To work with the cell the user has selected in the active worksheet in the active workbook, use the **active cell** class. For example, to return the contents of the active cell, get its **value** property:

```
get the value of the active cell
```

To change the contents of the active cell, set its **value** property:

```
set the value of the active cell to "Albuquerque"
```

To change the active cell, use an **activate object** command to activate the **worksheet** object, and then use another **activate object** command to activate the **range** object for the cell. For example, the following statements make cell C5 on the worksheet named **Materials** the active cell:

```
activate object worksheet "Materials"
activate object range "C5"
```

To select the area around the active cell, use a **select** command with the **current region** property of the **active cell** object like this:

```
select current region of active cell
```

Excel uses the **selection** object to represent the current selection—all the cells that are selected. The selection can be a single cell (in which case it is the same as the active cell) or one or more blocks of cells (in which case the active cell is the first cell in the first block).

### NOTE

To find out how many cells the current selection contains, return the **count** property of the **cells** collection in the **selection** object: **get count of cells in selection**.

## Ask the Expert

**Q:** What is the *current region* in Excel?

**A:** The current region is the block of cells that contains data around the cell you're referring to (for example, the active cell). The current region begins after the previous blank column and row, and ends before the next blank column and row.

For example, if cell E5 is the active cell, columns B and K are blank, and rows 2 and 8 are blank, the current region is C3:J7.

## Referring to a Range of Cells

To refer to a range of cells, use the **range** class and provide the reference for the cells as a string. For example, the following statement selects the range **C1:F25**:

```
select range "C1:F25"
```

To refer to a complex range, use Excel's normal syntax—for example:

```
select range "A4,B5,C8:E12,F15"
```

Often, you'll want to assign a range of cells to a variable so that you can refer to it easily throughout a script. For example, the following statement assigns the range **B2:E9** to the variable **range1**:

```
set range1 to range "B2:E9"
```

## Using Named Ranges for Easy Reference

When you need to work with several ranges, define names for the ranges. To define a name, set the **name** property of the **range** object to a string containing the name you want. For example, the following statement applies the name **Essential_Info** to the range **B2:C4** in the active worksheet in the active workbook:

```
set the name of the range "B2:C4" ¬
    of active sheet of active workbook to "Essential_Info"
```

After creating the name, you can refer to the range by the name. For example, the following statement selects the **Essential_Info** range:

```
select range "Essential_Info"
```

To remove a name from a range, delete the **named item** for the name. For example, the following statement deletes the **Essential_Info** name:

```
delete named item "Essential_Info" of active workbook
```

## Working with a Worksheet's Used Range

To work with all a worksheet's cells that contain data, use the **used range** property of the **sheet** object. The *used range* is the smallest rectangle that includes all the cells that contain data.

For example, the following statement selects the used range on the active worksheet:

```
select the used range of the active sheet
```

## Using Excel's Special Cells

In your scripts, you may need to work with only certain types of cells in a range or on a worksheet—for example, only the cells that contain formulas, or only the cells that are blank.

To save you having to round up these cells manually (or programmatically), Excel provides the **special cells** command, which gives you direct access to the various types of special cells.

When using the **special cells** command, you need to provide two or three pieces of information. The first is the range on which you want the command to work—for example, **cells of active sheet** to find the special cells on the active worksheet.

The second piece of information is the type of special cells you want. To tell Excel this, you use one of the **type** constants explained in Table 15-3.

If you're using the **cell type constants** type or the **cell type formulas** type, you can also use the **value** parameter to tell Excel which constants or formulas to return. Table 15-4 shows the values you can use.

For example, the following statement selects all the cells containing formulas in the used range of the active worksheet:

```
select (special cells of used range of active sheet ¬
    type cell type formulas)
```

| cell type Constant for Special Cells | Returns These Cells |
|---|---|
| cell type all format conditions | Cells that have formatting conditions applied |
| cell type all validation | Cells that have data validation applied |
| cell type blanks | Blank cells |
| cell type comments | Cells with comments attached to them |
| cell type constants | Cells that contain constants |
| cell type formulas | Cells that contain formulas |
| cell type last cell | The last cell in the used range of the sheet |
| cell type same format conditions | Cells that have the same format conditions applied |
| cell type same validation | Cells that have the same data validation applied |
| cell type visible | All visible cells |

**Table 15-3** AppleScript's cell type Constants for Accessing Special Cells

| value Constant | Returns These Cells |
|---|---|
| errors | Cells containing errors |
| logical | Cells containing logical values |
| numbers | Cells containing numbers |
| text values | Cells containing text values |

**Table 15-4** AppleScript's value Constants for Accessing Special Cells

## Inserting a Formula in a Cell

To insert a formula in a cell, set the **formula** property of the **range** object that represents the cell. For example, the following statement inserts the formula **=AVERAGE(C2:C22)** in cell **C23** of the worksheet named **2011 Budget**:

```
set the formula of range "C23" of worksheet "2011 Budget" ¬
    to "=AVERAGE(C2:C22)"
```

## Try This Adding Data to a Workbook

In this example, you add some data to the workbook you created earlier in this chapter. Follow these steps to create the script:

1. In AppleScript Editor, press ⌘-N or choose File | New to create a new script.

2. Start a **tell** block to Excel, addressing it by its **application id** string, **com.microsoft.Excel**:

```
tell the application id "com.microsoft.Excel"
end tell
```

3. Inside the **tell** block, start a nested **tell** block to the **Sales** sheet, as shown in boldface here:

```
tell the application id "com.microsoft.excel"
    tell sheet "Sales"
    end tell
end tell
```

4. Inside the nested **tell** block, set the **value** property of the **range** object **A1** to the string **"California"**, as shown in boldface here:

```
tell the application id "com.microsoft.excel"
    tell sheet "Sales"
```

*(continued)*

```
            set the value of range "A1" to "California"
        end tell
    end tell
```

5. Similarly, add three other states to cells **A2**, **A3**, and **A4**, and add a corresponding value to the cells **B1**, **B2**, **B3**, and **B4**. The new statements appear in boldface here:

```
tell the application id "com.microsoft.excel"
    tell sheet "Sales"
        set the value of range "A1" to "California"
        set the value of range "A2" to "Oregon"
        set the value of range "A3" to "Nebraska"
        set the value of range "A4" to "Wyoming"
        set the value of range "B1" to 453
        set the value of range "B2" to 861
        set the value of range "B3" to 102
        set the value of range "B4" to 649
    end tell
end tell
```

6. After the nested **tell** block but inside the outer **tell** block, add a **save the workbook** statement, as shown in boldface here:

```
tell the application id "com.microsoft.excel"
    tell sheet "Sales"
        set the value of range "A1" to "California"
        set the value of range "A2" to "Oregon"
        set the value of range "A3" to "Nebraska"
        set the value of range "A4" to "Wyoming"
        set the value of range "B1" to 453
        set the value of range "B2" to 861
        set the value of range "B3" to 102
        set the value of range "B4" to 649
    end tell
    save the workbook
end tell
```

7. Save the script under a name of your choice.

8. Display the Sales sheet of the **ABG Book.xlsx** workbook so that you can watch what happens. (If you closed this workbook earlier, open it now.)

9. Press ⌘-R or click the Run button on the toolbar to run the script. You'll see the range A1:B4 take on values.

   Leave the workbook open so that you can use it in the next example, in which you create charts using the data you just entered.

# Using Charts in Your Workbooks

Excel's great for crunching numbers, but when you need to make your data snap, crackle, and pop, turn it into a chart.

As you'll know if you've used them when working manually, Excel offers a full range of chart types and chart options. You can also create charts automatically from AppleScript, as described in this section. You have total control over the charts you create this way, but for the greatest effect, you may need to tweak them manually afterward to enhance the points you wish to make.

## Understanding How to Create a Chart from AppleScript

Excel lets you create a chart either on its own chart sheet or as a chart object on a worksheet. Using a separate chart sheet is often the better choice, as it gives you more space for creating and editing the chart, but placing a chart object on a worksheet can be useful when you need to see the chart together with its source data.

The first step in creating a chart from AppleScript is to either choose data and then add a chart sheet to the workbook, or identify a chart object to a worksheet and then tell it which source data to use. You can then set the chart type, format the axes, and add other items such as a chart title and a legend.

## Adding a Chart Sheet to a Workbook

The easiest way to create a new chart sheet and add a chart to it is to select the source data for the chart first. Just as when you're working interactively, Excel then grabs that data and uses it for the chart, automatically linking the two. (If you prefer, you can build the chart by adding data series, as described later in this chapter.)

To create a new chart sheet, use a **make new** command to create a new object of the **chart sheet** class. As when creating a worksheet, use either **at** or **in** and the name or identity of the workbook in which you want to create the chart.

For example, the following statement adds a chart sheet to the active workbook:

```
make new chart sheet in active workbook
```

By default, Excel places the chart sheet before the current worksheet in the workbook. To choose a different position, you can use one of these designations:

- **at beginning of** and the **workbook** object
- **at end of** and the **workbook** object

- **at before** and a **sheet** object

- **at after** and a **sheet** object

### NOTE

Unlike with **worksheet** objects, the **at before** and **at after** parameters work correctly for **chart sheet** objects at this writing.

The following example adds a chart sheet after the sheet named **2013 Planning** in the active workbook:

```
make new chart sheet at before sheet "2013 Planning" of active workbook
```

## Adding a Chart Object to a Worksheet

To add a chart object to a worksheet, you create a new object of the **chart object** class on the worksheet. Use a **make new chart object** command to create the new chart object. Usually, you'll want to assign the chart object to a variable so that you can easily manipulate it. The following example shows code for creating a new chart object in the active worksheet, assigning it to a variable, setting its position (using the **top** property and the **left position** property) and size (using the **height** property and the **width** property), and selecting it:

```
set myChart to make new chart object at active sheet
set top of myChart to 100
set left position of myChart to 200
set height of myChart to 500
set width of myChart to 800
select myChart
```

When you create a chart like this, Excel creates a blank chart, even if you selected the data beforehand. So your next move is to specify its source data. To do so, you use the **set source data** command, which takes one required parameter and one optional parameter.

- **range**    This required argument tells Excel which range to draw the chart's data from.

- **plot by**    This optional argument lets you tell Excel how to plot the chart's data—by columns (use **plot by columns**) or by rows (use **plot by rows**).

For example, the following statement sets the source data of the active chart to the range **A1:C13** on the worksheet named **Temperatures**. Note that the range is in double quotation marks and that the reference starts with an equal sign:

```
set source data active chart source range "=Temperatures!A1:C13"
```

## Setting the Chart Type

To set the chart type, set the **chart type** property of the **chart** object to the appropriate constant. Table 15-5 shows the constants you can use, broken down by the category of the charts they create.

For example, the following statement sets the chart type of the active chart to a stacked bar chart:

```
set chart type of active chart to bar stacked
```

| Chart Category | AppleScript chart type Constants |
|---|---|
| Area chart | area chart, area stacked, area stacked 100, ThreeD area, ThreeD area stacked, ThreeD area stacked 100 |
| Bar chart | bar clustered, bar stacked, bar stacked 100, ThreeD bar clustered, ThreeD bar stacked, ThreeD back stacked 100, cylinder bar clustered, cylinder bar stacked, cylinder bar stacked 100, cone bar clustered, cone bar stacked, cone bar stacked 100, pyramid bar clustered, pyramid bar stacked, pyramid bar stacked 100 |
| Bubble chart | bubble, bubble ThreeD effectstock HLC |
| Column chart | column clustered, column stacked, column stacked 100, ThreeD column, ThreeD column clustered, ThreeD column stacked, ThreeD column stacked 100, cylinder column, cylinder column clustered, cylinder column stacked, cylinder column stacked 100, cone column, cone column clustered, cone column stacked, cone column stacked 100, pyramid column, pyramid column clustered, pyramid column stacked, pyramid column stacked 100 |
| Doughnut chart | doughnut, doughnut exploded |
| Line chart | line chart, line stacked, line stacked 100, line markers, line markers stacked, line markers stacked100, ThreeD line |
| Pie chart | pie chart, pie of pie, pie exploded, ThreeD pie, ThreeD pie exploded, bar of pie |
| Radar chart | radar, radar markers, radar filled |
| Scatter chart | xyscatter, xy scatter smooth, xy scatter smooth no markers, xy scatter lines, xy scatter lines no markers |
| Stock chart | stock OHLC, stock VHLC, stock VOHLC |
| Surface chart | surface, surface wireframe, surface top view, surface top view wireframe |

**Table 15-5** Excel's chart type Constants by Chart Category

## Add a Series to the Chart

If you've set up the data for the chart as described earlier in this chapter, you're probably all set with the chart's contents. But if necessary, you can add a data series to the chart by using the **make new series** command. You specify where to add the series—for example, **at beginning** or **at end**—and use the properties to provide the series values, the xvalues, and name. Here's an example:

```
set mySeries to make new series at end ¬
    with properties {series values:"E4:E20", xvalues:"A4:A20", ¬
    name:"Bay Area"}
```

## Adding a Caption to an Axis

To add a caption to a chart axis, first use the **get axis** command to return the axis you want. The **get axis** command takes two parameters.

- **axis type**   This required parameter tells Excel which axis you want. Use **category axis** to return the category axis, **series axis** to return the series axis (only on 3-D charts), or **value axis** to return the value axis.

- **which axis**   This optional parameter lets you specify which axis group you want: **primary axis** or **secondary axis**. Excel uses the primary axis if you omit this parameter.

For example, the following statement returns the category axis of the chart referenced by the **myChart** variable and assigns it to the **catax** variable:

```
set catax to get axis axis type category axis which axis primary axis
```

Once you've grabbed hold of the axis, set its **has title** property to **true**. You can then tell the **axis title** object to set its **caption** property to the text you want, or tell the **font** object to change the font name (the **name** property), the font size (the **font size** property), or other properties such as bold and italic.

For example, the following snippet adds a title to the axis identified by the **catax** variable and applies font formatting to it:

```
tell catax
    set has title to true
    tell its axis title
        set caption to "Cities"
        tell the font object
```

```
        set the font size to 14
        set the name to "Trebuchet"
    end tell
  end tell
end tell
```

## Adding a Chart Title

To add a chart title, set the **has title** property to **true**, and then set the **caption** property of the **chart title** object to the text you want the title to have. You can also use the **font** object of the **chart title** object to apply font formatting to the chart title.

The following example adds a title (**Latest Sales Figures**) to the chart referenced by the variable **myChart** and then sets the font size of the chart title to 22 points:

```
tell myChart
    set has title to true
    tell its chart title
        set caption to "Latest Sales Figures"
        tell the font object to set the font size to 22
    end tell
end tell
```

### NOTE

When you're referring to the **chart title** property, you need to use **its chart title** to make the chart notice the changes. Don't ask.

## Adding a Legend

To add a chart legend, set the **has legend** property to **true**:

```
tell myChart
    set has legend to true
end tell
```

To control the position of the legend, set the **position** property of the **legend object** item to the position you want: **legend position top**, **legend position bottom**, **legend position left**, or **legend position right**. For example, the following boldface statement positions the legend on the left:

```
tell myChart
    set has legend to true
    set the position of the legend object to legend position left
end tell
```

**Try This** Creating a Chart

In this example, you create a small chart using the data entered by the script you wrote in the previous example.

To create the script, follow these steps:

1. In AppleScript Editor, press ⌘-N or choose File | New to create a new script.

2. Start a **tell** block to Excel, addressing it by its **application id** string, **com.microsoft.Excel**:

```
tell the application id "com.microsoft.Excel"
end tell
```

3. Inside the **tell** block, add a **select** statement that selects the range **A1:B4** on the sheet named **Sales**, the range that contains the data for the chart. The new statement appears in boldface here:

```
tell the application id "com.microsoft.excel"
    select (range "A1:B4")
end tell
```

4. Add a **make new chart sheet** command to insert a new chart sheet at the beginning of the active workbook, giving the sheet the name **Sales Chart**. The new statement appears in boldface here:

```
tell the application id "com.microsoft.excel"
    select (range "A1:B4")
    make new chart sheet at beginning of active workbook ¬
        with properties {name:"Sales Chart"}
end tell
```

5. Add a **tell** block to the **chart** object on the chart sheet you just created, setting its type to **cylinder column**, setting its **has title** property to **true**, and then setting the **caption** property of the **chart title** object to **Sales Results** and making it 36-point font. The new statement appears in boldface here:

```
tell the application id "com.microsoft.excel"
    select (range "A1:B4")
    make new chart sheet at beginning of active workbook ¬
        with properties {name:"Sales Chart"}
    tell the chart of sheet "Sales Chart"
        set the chart type to cylinder column
        set has title to true
        tell its chart title
            set the caption to "Sales Results"
            tell the font object
                set the font size to 36
```

```
            end tell
        end tell
    end tell
end tell
```

6. Turn off the display of the legend by setting the **has legend** property to **false**, as shown in boldface here:

```
tell the application id "com.microsoft.excel"
    select (range "A1:B4")
    make new chart sheet at beginning of active workbook ¬
        with properties {name:"Sales Chart"}
    tell the chart of sheet "Sales Chart"
        set the chart type to cylinder column
        set has title to true
        tell its chart title
            set the caption to "Sales Results"
            tell the font object
                set the font size to 36
            end tell
        end tell
        set has legend to false
    end tell
end tell
```

7. Use a **get axis** command with **axis type category axis**, and assign the result to the variable **myaxis**. Then use a nested **tell** block to **myaxis** to set its **has title** property to **true** and a further nested **tell** block to set the **caption** property of the **axis title** object to **States**. Right inside the Russian doll, use a **tell** statement to set the **font size** property to **20** points. The new statements appear in boldface here:

```
tell the application id "com.microsoft.excel"
    select (range "A1:B4")
    make new chart sheet at beginning of active workbook ¬
        with properties {name:"Sales Chart"}
    tell the chart of sheet "Sales Chart"
        set the chart type to cylinder column
        set has title to true
        tell its chart title
            set the caption to "Sales Results"
            tell the font object
                set the font size to 36
            end tell
        end tell
        set has legend to false
        set myaxis to get axis axis type category axis ¬
            which axis primary axis
        tell myaxis
```

*(continued)*

```
                    set has title to true
                    tell its axis title
                        set caption to "States"
                        tell the font object to set the font size to 20
                      end tell
                  end tell
              end tell
          end tell
```

8. Finally, set the **name** property of the first **series** object to **Sales by State**, as shown in boldface here:

```
tell the application id "com.microsoft.excel"
    select (range "A1:B4")
    make new chart sheet at beginning of active workbook ¬
        with properties {name:"Sales Chart"}
    tell the chart of sheet "Sales Chart"
        set the chart type to cylinder column
        set has title to true
        tell its chart title
            set the caption to "Sales Results"
            tell the font object
                set the font size to 36
            end tell
        end tell
        set has legend to false
        set myaxis to get axis axis type category axis ¬
            which axis primary axis
        tell myaxis
            set has title to true
            tell its axis title
                set caption to "States"
                tell the font object to set the font size to 20
              end tell
        end tell
        set the name of the first series to "Sales by State"
    end tell
  end tell
```

9. Save the script under a name of your choice.

10. Press ⌘-R or click the Run button on the toolbar to run the script. You'll see Excel add a new chart sheet, name it, and build the chart on it.

11. Save the workbook and close it.

# Working with Excel Windows and Views

When your scripts open or create workbooks for the user, you'll need to open, close, and resize windows. You will also need to switch views as needed and zoom in or out to show the appropriate amount of a sheet.

To work with windows, you use the **windows** list, which contains all **window** objects for each open window. As usual, Excel treats the windows as being in a stack, with the active window at the front, so you can access the windows in various ways.

- **By the window's position in the stack**   For example, use **the front window** or **window 1** to return the front window.

- **By the window's caption**   The **caption** property of a **window** object returns the text that's displayed in the window's title bar. You can use this property to identify the window you want. You'll see an example of this in just a moment.

- **By using the active window class**   The **active window** class lets you grab the active window—the window the user is actually using.

## Opening a New Window

To open a new window on a workbook, use the **new window on workbook** command. This command takes the **workbook** parameter with the workbook for which you want the new window. For example, the following statement opens a new window on the workbook named **Migration Patterns.xlsx**:

```
new window on workbook workbook "Migration Patterns.xlsx"
```

What you'll normally want to do is assign the new window to a variable so that you can easily resize or reposition it, as discussed later in this section. For example, the following statement assigns the new window created by the **new window on workbook** command to the variable **myWindow**:

```
set myWindow to new window on workbook workbook "Migration Patterns.xlsx"
```

## Activating a Window

To activate a window, use an **activate** command first on the Excel **application** object and then on the **window** object. For example, the following **repeat** block activates the window with the caption **Amortization.xlsx** by going through the open windows until it finds the one with the right caption:

```
repeat with i from 1 to count of windows
    if the caption of window i is "Amortization.xlsx" then
        activate
        activate object window i
        return
    end if
end repeat
```

## Closing a Window

To close a window, use a **close** command and identify the window by its caption, its position in the stack, or by another means. For example, the following statement closes the window with the caption **Migration Patterns.xlsx:1**:

```
close the window "Migration Patterns.xlsx:1"
```

## Repositioning and Resizing Windows

To resize a window, set the **left position**, **top**, **width**, and **height** properties of the appropriate **window** object. Each of these properties takes an integer value of pixels. For example, the following **tell** blocks position the front window in the upper-left corner of the primary monitor and make it 800 wide by 600 pixels high:

```
tell the application id "com.microsoft.Excel"
    tell the front window
        set left position to 0
        set top to 0
        set width to 800
        set height to 600
    end tell
end tell
```

To reposition a window without resizing it, set the **left position** property and the **top** property to suitable pixel values. For example, the following **tell** block makes Excel position the upper-left corner of the front window 600 pixels from the left edge of the screen and 300 pixels from the top edge:

```
tell the application id "com.microsoft.Excel"
    set left position of front window to 600
    set top of front window to 300
end tell
```

# Rearranging Excel Windows

To rearrange the open Excel windows, use the **arrange_windows** command. Without any parameters, this command tiles all visible windows, giving each as equal a share of the screen space as possible. But you can also use the following parameters, all of which are optional:

- **arrange style**    Use this parameter to tell Excel how to arrange the windows. Table 15-6 explains your options.

- **active workbook**    Set this parameter to **with active workbook** to arrange only the windows of the active workbook. This parameter is most useful when you're synchronizing the scrolling of the workbook's windows, as described next, but you can also use it when you want to affect only the active workbook. Set this parameter to **without active workbook**, or simply omit it, to arrange the windows of all the open workbooks.

- **sync horizontal**    This parameter applies only when you're using **with active workbook**. Then you can set this parameter to **with sync horizontal** (giving you **with active workbook and sync horizontal**) to synchronize horizontal scrolling in the windows, allowing you to scroll two or more windows in tandem.

- **sync vertical**    This parameter applies only when you're using **with active workbook**. Then you can set this parameter to **with sync vertical** (giving you **with active workbook and sync vertical** or **with active workbook, sync horizontal and sync vertical**) to synchronize vertical scrolling in the windows.

| arrange style Constant | Explanation |
|---|---|
| arrange style cascade | Arranges the windows in an overlapping cascade so that you can see part of each window. This command doesn't work at this writing. |
| arrange style horizontal | Arranges the windows horizontally—for example, one at the top of the screen and one at the bottom. |
| arrange style tiled | Tiles the windows, sharing the screen space as equally as possible among them. This is the default arrangement if you don't use the **arrange style** parameter. |
| arrange style vertical | Arranges the windows vertically—for example, one on the left of the screen and one on the right. |

**Table 15-6**  AppleScript arrange style Constants for Arranging Windows

For example, the following statement tiles all open windows:

```
arrange_windows
```

The following statement arranges the windows of the active workbook horizontally, setting up synchronized scrolling both horizontally and vertically:

```
arrange_windows arrange style horizontal ¬
    with active workbook, sync horizontal and sync vertical
```

## Changing the View

To change the view in a window, set the **view** property of the appropriate **window** object to **page layout view** (for Page Layout view) or **normal view** (three guesses). For example, the following statement makes sure the active window is in Page Layout view:

```
set the view of the active window to page layout view
```

> **NOTE**
>
> The active window in the last example may already be using Page Layout view—the code doesn't check, because there's no point in doing so.

## Zooming a Window

To zoom a window in or out, set its **zoom** property to the percentage you want. Excel supports zoom percentages from 10 percent to 400 percent. For example, the following statement zooms the active window to 200 percent:

```
set zoom of active window to 200
```

# Using Find and Replace in Your Scripts

When you need to find data in a workbook, you can harness Excel's built-in Find capabilities. Similarly, you can use Excel's Replace tools to replace data, formatting, or both.

## Using find to Search for Data

To search for data, you use the **find** command. This command takes two required parameters and can take up to seven optional parameters.

The two required parameters are straightforward enough.

- **range**   This parameter gives the range in which to search for the data—for example, the active worksheet.

- **what**   This parameter specifies what you're searching for—a particular word or value, for example.

These are the optional parameters you can use:

- **after** Use this parameter to specify the cell after which you want to begin the search. This must be a single cell rather than a range of cells.

- **look in** Set this parameter to **formulas** if you want to search only formulas, **values** to search only values, or **comments** to search only in comments. Omit this parameter to search everything.

- **look at** Set this parameter to **whole** if you want to find entire cells only. Set it to **part** if you'll take a partial match.

- **search order** Set this parameter to **by rows** if you want to search down and then across. Set it to **by columns** if you want to search across and then down.

- **match case** Set this parameter to **with match case** if you want to use case-sensitive matching. If case doesn't matter, omit this parameter or set it to **without match case**.

- **match byte** (Japanese versions of Excel only.) Set this parameter to **with match byte** if you want to accept only matches of double-byte characters to double-byte characters rather than double-byte characters matching their single-byte equivalents.

For example, the following statement searches for the word **density** in the range **A1:Z26** of the worksheet named **Sheet1**, ignoring case:

```
find (range "A1:Z26" of worksheet "Sheet1") ¬
    what "density" without match case
```

### CAUTION

The **look in** parameter, **look at** parameter, **search order** parameter, **match case** parameter, and **match byte** parameter (if you use it) remain in effect from one search to the next. This means it's a good idea to set these settings explicitly to avoid getting surprised by the settings used by whoever searched before you.

## Continuing a Search

To continue a search, you can use the **find next** command to find the next instance of the search item or the **find previous** command to find the previous instance. Each of these commands takes the following two parameters:

- **range** This required parameter specifies the range through which you want to search.

- **after** This optional parameter specifies the cell after which you want the search to start. This works in the same way as the **after** parameter for the **find** command itself, except that for the **find previous** command, "after" actually means "before," because the search is going backward.

For example, the following statement continues questing forward for the next instance of the search target:

```
find next (range "A1:Z26" of worksheet "Sheet1")
```

## Using replace to Replace Data

To perform replace operations using AppleScript, use the **replace** command. This command uses the same parameters as the **find** command (discussed previously) except that it also has the **replacement** parameter, which specifies the replacement text you want to use.

For example, the following statement replaces the first instance of the word **industry** in the range **A1:Z26** of the worksheet named **Sheet1** with the word **company**:

```
replace (range "A1:Z26" of worksheet "Sheet1") ¬
    what "industry" replacement "company"
```

The **replace** command returns **true** if it replaces an item. There's no command for replacing all instances via AppleScript the way there is in the user interface, so if you need to make multiple replacements, create a repeat loop that runs through the region until it finds no more instances.

# Chapter 16

## Automating Microsoft Entourage

## Key Skills & Concepts

- Creating Entourage accounts
- Creating and sending e-mail messages
- Dealing with incoming e-mail messages
- Working with contacts
- Working with events
- Working with tasks
- Working with notes

In this chapter, you'll learn how to use AppleScript to automate essential tasks in Microsoft Entourage, the Mac equivalent of the Windows-based Microsoft Outlook desktop information manager application. I'll show you how to create and send e-mail messages and attachments; deal with incoming e-mail messages (with or without attachments); and work with contacts, events, tasks, and notes.

Before you can get anything done in Entourage, you need to set up one or more accounts—so that's where we'll start with AppleScript as well.

### NOTE

To help you avoid messing up your Entourage setup, this chapter doesn't provide any Try This examples—but do feel free to try any of the sample scripts presented, adapting them to your needs. If you practice setting up or configuring e-mail accounts, work on a test Mac rather than on your production machine.

## Creating Entourage Accounts

Entourage supports four different types of messaging accounts:

- **Exchange account**   An account for accessing a server running Microsoft Exchange
- **IMAP account**   An account for accessing an Internet Mail Access Protocol (IMAP) server for incoming mail. Many ISPs use IMAP servers. Apple's MobileMe service uses IMAP servers.

- **POP account** An account for accessing a Post Office Protocol (POP) server for incoming mail. Most ISPs who don't use IMAP servers use POP servers.

- **Hotmail account** An account for accessing Microsoft's Windows Live Hotmail service. Entourage works only with the Hotmail Plus account type—the type you have to pay for. It doesn't work with free Hotmail accounts.

Because of the different mail servers involved, the different account types have different properties—but the Exchange account, IMAP account, and POP account share a central core of properties. Table 16-1 explains these properties, showing which account type has which of them.

Each of these three account types also has properties that it doesn't share, as explained in the next three sections.

| account Object Property | Explanation | POP | IMAP | Exchange |
|---|---|:---:|:---:|:---:|
| name | The account name | ✓ | ✓ | ✓ |
| ID | An integer containing the unique ID for the account. This property is read-only. | ✓ | ✓ | ✓ |
| full name | The user's full name | ✓ | ✓ | ✓ |
| email address | The account's e-mail address | ✓ | ✓ | ✓ |
| additional headers | Text giving any extra headers to add to messages you're sending | ✓ | ✓ | ✓ |
| default signature type | **none** to use no signature, **random** to use a random signature, **other** to use a signature specified by the **default signature choice** property | ✓ | ✓ | ✓ |
| default signature choice | The signature to use when the **default signature type** property is set to **other** | ✓ | ✓ | ✓ |
| SMTP server | The SMTP server the account uses for sending mail | ✓ | ✓ | |
| password | The password the account uses for the incoming mail server | ✓ | ✓ | |
| include in send and receive all | **true** to include this account when sending and receiving all mail; **false** to exclude it | ✓ | ✓ | |
| send secure password | **true** to send the password securely; **false** to send the password in the clear if requested | ✓ | ✓ | |

**Table 16-1** Properties Shared Among the Exchange account, IMAP account, and POP account Objects

| account Object Property | Explanation | POP | IMAP | Exchange |
|---|---|:---:|:---:|---|
| **SMTP requires SSL** | **true** if the SMTP server requires an SSL connection; **false** if it does not. | ✓ | ✓ | |
| **SMTP port** | An integer showing the port on which to connect to the SMTP server | ✓ | ✓ | |
| **SMTP requires authentication** | **true** if the SMTP server requires authentication; **false** if it does not | ✓ | ✓ | |
| **SMTP uses account settings** | **true** if the SMTP server uses the same account ID and password as the incoming mail server; **false** if the SMTP server requires different credentials | ✓ | ✓ | |
| **SMTP account id** | The account ID for the SMTP server when this server requires authentication and uses different settings from the incoming mail server | ✓ | ✓ | |
| **SMTP password** | The password for the SMTP server when this server requires authentication and uses different settings from the incoming mail server | ✓ | ✓ | |
| **last SMTP authentication method** | The last authentication method Entourage used when connecting to the SMTP server | ✓ | ✓ | |
| **last authentication method** | The last authentication method Entourage used when connecting to the incoming mail server | ✓ | ✓ | |

**Table 16-1** Properties Shared Among the Exchange account, IMAP account, and POP account Objects *(continued)*

## Creating an Exchange Account

Apart from the shared properties shown in Table 16-1, the **Exchange account** object also has the properties explained in Table 16-2.

To set up an Exchange account, use a **make new Exchange account** command. The easiest way to set the key properties for the account is to specify them in the **with properties** parameter, as in the following script:

```
tell the application id "com.microsoft.Entourage"
    set XAcc to make new Exchange account with properties ¬
        {name:"jsmith", Exchange server: ¬
        "server1.acmevirtualindustries.com", ¬
```

| Exchange account Property | Explanation |
|---|---|
| Exchange ID | The user's Exchange ID |
| domain | The Exchange domain name |
| Exchange server settings | A **server settings** object containing the settings for accessing the Exchange server via DAV (Digital Authoring and Versioning) |
| inbox folder | The folder that contains the inbox. This property is read-only. |
| sent items folder | The folder that contains the Sent Items folder. This property is read-only. |
| deleted items folder | The folder that contains the Deleted Items folder. This property is read-only. |
| drafts folder | The folder that contains the Drafts folder. This property is read-only. |
| junk mail folder | The folder that contains the Junk Mail folder. This property is read-only. |
| favorites folder | The folder that contains the Favorites folder. This property is read-only. |
| primary calendar | The calendar for the Exchange mailbox. This property is read-only. |
| primary address book | The primary address book for the Exchange mailbox. This property is read-only. |
| total size | The amount of space the account is occupying on the Exchange server. This property is read-only. |
| Exchange subfolders | A record containing the account's subfolders and the amount of storage they consume |
| LDAP server settings | A **server settings** object containing the settings for the LDAP server |
| LDAP requires authentication | **true** if the account provides a user name and password to the LDAP server |
| partially retrieve messages | **true** to download only the first part of large messages; **false** to download entire messages no matter how lardy they are |
| partially retrieve messages size | An integer giving the maximum size in KB for message downloads |
| partially retrieve messages on dialup only | **true** to download only the first part of large messages when using a dial-up connection; **false** to download the full messages even on dial-up |
| requires Kerberos | **true** if the Exchange account requires Kerberos; **false** if it does not |
| principal | Text giving the GSSAPI (Generic Security Services Application Program Interface) principal name for Kerberos v5 |
| search base | The search base used for LDAP queries |
| maximum entries | An integer specifying the maximum number of entries an LDAP query should return |

**Table 16-2**   Properties Peculiar to the Exchange account Object

| Exchange account Property | Explanation |
|---|---|
| public folder server settings | A **server settings** object containing the Public Folder server's settings |
| GAL | A **folder** object that represents either the Exchange global address list (GAL) or LDAP search |
| out of office | **true** if the out-of-office auto-reply is turned on; **false** if it is not |
| out of office auto reply | The text used for the out-of-office auto-reply message |
| free busy server | The Exchange free/busy server |
| Exchange server | The Exchange server's address |
| DAV requires SSL | **true** if DAV access requires SSL; **false** if it does not |
| DAV port | The port number on which to connect to the Exchange server via DAV |
| LDAP server | The address of the LDAP server used |
| requires authentication | **true** if the account provides a user name and password when logging into the LDAP server; **false** if not |
| LDAP requires SSL | **true** if the LDAP server requires an SSL connection; **false** if it does not |
| LDAP port | The number of the port to connect to on the LDAP server |

**Table 16-2** Properties Peculiar to the Exchange account Object *(continued)*

```
        Exchange ID:"jsmith", domain:"acmevirtualindustries.com", ¬
        free busy server:"server1.acmevirtualindustries.co/public/", ¬
        full name:"Jean Smith", ¬
        email address:"jsmith@acmevirtualindustries.com", ¬
        LDAP server:"ldap.acmevirtualindustries.com", LDAP port:3628, ¬
        search base:"", maximum entries:100, ¬
        partially retrieve messages:true, ¬
        partially retrieve messages size:40000}
end tell
```

### NOTE
If you have Office 2008 Home & Student edition, your version of Entourage doesn't support Exchange accounts.

## Creating an IMAP Account
Apart from the shared properties shown in Table 16-1, the **IMAP account** object also has the properties explained in Table 16-3.

| IMAP account Property | Explanation |
|---|---|
| IMAP server | The IMAP server the account uses for receiving mail |
| IMAP ID | The account's ID for the IMAP server |
| IMAP requires SSL | **true** if the IMAP server requires an SSL connection; **false** if it does not |
| IMAP port | An integer showing the port on which to connect to the IMAP server |
| root folder path | The path to the root folder on the IMAP server |
| send commands to IMAP server simultaneously | **true** for standard sending; **false** to send commands individually to avoid confusing unreliable IMAP servers |
| download complete messages in IMAP Inbox | **true** to download entire messages in the inbox; **false** to download only the headers |
| partially retrieve messages | **true** to retrieve parts of messages up to the maximum size allowed; **false** otherwise |
| partially retrieve messages size | An integer giving the maximum size in KB for downloading messages |
| IMAP live sync | **true** to turn on the IMAP Live Sync feature; **false** to turn it off |
| IMAP live sync only connect to inbox | **true** to use IMAP Live Sync only for the inbox; **false** not to |
| IMAP live sync connect on launch | **true** to run IMAP Live Sync immediately on launching Entourage; **false** not to |
| enable IMAP live sync timeout | **true** to make Live Sync quit after the period of inactivity specified by the **IMAP live sync timeout** property |
| IMAP inbox folder | The path to the IMAP inbox. This property is read-only. |
| store messages in IMAP sent items folder | **true** to store the messages you've sent in the Sent Items folder; **false** not to store them |
| IMAP sent items folder | The folder in which to store sent items (if the **store messages in IMAP sent items folder** property is set to **true**) |
| store messages in IMAP drafts folder | **true** to store incomplete messages in the Drafts folder so that you can work on them from any computer; **false** not to |
| IMAP drafts folder | The folder in which to store draft messages |
| move messages to the IMAP deleted items folder | **true** to move deleted messages to the Deleted Items folder; **false** not to |
| IMAP deleted items folder | The folder in which to store deleted messages |
| empty IMAP deleted items folder on quit | **true** to empty the Deleted Items folder when you quit Entourage; **false** not to empty the folder |

**Table 16-3**  Properties Peculiar to the IMAP account Object

| IMAP account Property | Explanation |
|---|---|
| delete expired IMAP messages on quit | **true** to delete messages older than the number of days specified by the **delete expired IMAP messages on quit after** property when you quit Entourage; **false** to keep the messages that have passed their best-before date |
| delete expired IMAP messages on quit after | An integer giving the number of days after which to delete IMAP messages |
| delete all expired IMAP messages on quit | **true** to delete all expired messages from the Deleted Items folder when you quit Entourage |

**Table 16-3** Properties Peculiar to the IMAP account Object *(continued)*

For example, the following script creates a new IMAP account for the MobileMe service. The script assigns the new account to the **new_account** variable, which it then uses to set five properties one by one (as opposed to using a **tell** block to **new_account**).

```
tell the application id "com.microsoft.Entourage"
    set new_account to make new IMAP account with properties ¬
        {name:"MobileMe", full name:"Chris P. Smith", ¬
        email address:"chris_p_smith@mac.com", ¬
        SMTP server:"smtp.mac.com", ¬
        IMAP server:"mail.mac.com", IMAP ID:"chris__smith", ¬
        password:"dontreadthis", include in send and receive all:true, ¬
        send secure password:false, default signature type:none}
    set send commands to IMAP server simultaneously of new_account ¬
        to true
    set store messages in IMAP sent items folder of new_account to true
    set store messages in IMAP drafts folder of new_account to true
    set move messages to the IMAP deleted items folder of new_account ¬
        to true
    set empty IMAP deleted items folder on quit of new_account to true
end tell
```

## Creating a POP Account

Apart from the shared properties shown in Table 16-1, the **POP account** object also has the properties explained in Table 16-4.

For example, the following script creates a new POP account, assigns it to the variable **PopAcc**, and sets the most important properties for the account by using the

| POP account Property | Explanation |
|---|---|
| POP server | The POP3 server the account uses for receiving mail |
| POP ID | The account's ID for the POP3 server |
| allow online access | **true** to allow Entourage to access this account and display it in the folder list; **false** to prevent Entourage from accessing and displaying the account |
| leave on server | **true** to leave a copy of each read message on the server (useful if you're checking the same mailbox from multiple computers); **false** to remove messages from the server when you read them |
| POP requires SSL | **true** if the POP server requires an SSL connection; **false** if it does not |
| POP port | An integer showing the port on which to connect to the POP server |
| maximum message size | An integer giving the maximum message size for incoming messages (measured in KB) |
| delete messages from server after | An integer giving the number of days after which to delete messages from the mail server |
| delete messages from server when deleted from computer | **true** to delete messages from the mail server when you delete them in Entourage; **false** to keep them on the server |

**Table 16-4**   Properties Peculiar to the POP account Object

with properties parameter in the **make new POP account** statement. It then uses a **tell** block to **PopAcc** to set five properties that are peculiar to the **POP account** object.

```
tell the application id "com.microsoft.Entourage"
    set PopAcc to make new POP account with properties ¬
        {name:"Main Mail", full name:"Wilson Collins", ¬
        email address:"wcollins@acmevirtualindustries.com", ¬
        SMTP server:"smtp.acmevirtualindustries.com", ¬
        POP server:"pop.acmevirtualindustries.com", ¬
        POP ID:"wcollins", password:"abcd0987", ¬
        include in send and receive all:true, ¬
        send secure password:false, default signature type:none}
    tell PopAcc
        set allow online access to true
        set leave on server to false
        set maximum message size to 3072
        set delete messages from server when deleted from computer ¬
            to true
        set delete messages from server after to 7
    end tell
end tell
```

## Creating a Hotmail Account

The **Hotmail account** object shares several properties with the other account types, but it has many fewer properties overall, Table 16-5 explains all of them.

The following example uses the **make new Hotmail account** command to create a new Hotmail account:

```
tell the application id "com.microsoft.entourage"
    set myAcc to make new Hotmail account with properties ¬
        {name:"Hotmail Plus", full name:"John Brown", ¬
        email address:"the_real_john_brown@hotmail.com", ¬
        Hotmail ID:"the_real_john_brown@hotmail.com", ¬
        password:"donttrythis@home", ¬
        include in send and receive all:true, ¬
        save in server sent items:true, ¬
        default signature type:none}
end tell
```

### NOTE

The **make new Hotmail account** command doesn't always work as it should—even if the code contains nothing wrong, it may fail with an error. If this happens, check everything and try again, putting the command together again from scratch. You may find it works the next time—even if you haven't changed anything.

| Hotmail account Object Property | Explanation |
| --- | --- |
| name | The name you want to give the account—for example, **Hotmail Plus** |
| ID | An integer giving the unique ID number for the account within Entourage. This property is read-only. |
| full name | The name you're using as your full name on Hotmail |
| email address | Your Hotmail address |
| Hotmail ID | Your Windows Live Hotmail ID |
| password | Your Windows Live Hotmail password |
| include in send and receive all | **true** to include this account when sending and receiving all mail; **false** to exclude it |
| save in server sent items | **true** to save sent items on the server; **false** to save them on your Mac |
| additional headers | Text giving any extra headers you want to add to messages you send |
| default signature type | **none** to use no signature; **random** to use a random signature; **other** to use a signature specified by the **default signature choice** property |
| default signature choice | The signature to use when the **default signature type** property is set to **other** |

**Table 16-5** Properties of the Hotmail account Object

# Creating and Sending E-mail Messages

As you no doubt well know, e-mail is probably Entourage's most widely used feature—even people who shirk tasks and appointments tend to send and receive messages. This section explains the **message** object that forms the basis of both outgoing messages and incoming messages, and then shows you how to use AppleScript to make Entourage send and receive messages.

## Understanding the message Object

Table 16-6 explains the many properties of the **message** object.

| message Property | Explanation |
|---|---|
| ID | An ID number that uniquely identifies the message—for example, 2023 |
| subject | The subject line of the message |
| content | The content of the message's body |
| time received | The time when the message was received |
| time sent | The time when the message was sent |
| storage | The folder that currently contains the message |
| sender | The address of the sender of the message |
| priority | The message's priority: **lowest**, **low**, **normal**, **high**, or **highest**. The default priority is **normal**. |
| Exchange post | **true** if the message is an Exchange post message; **false** if it is not |
| account | The account that contains the message |
| headers | The full headers of the message |
| source | The message's raw source text (including formatting codes) |
| character set | The character set the message uses |
| color | The color Entourage uses for the message when displaying it in lists. This is an RGB color—for example, {5250, 47184, 5244}. |
| has html | **true** if the message contains HTML text; **false** if it does not |
| online status | Whether the message has been downloaded from the server: **not on server**, **headers only**, **partially downloaded**, or **fully downloaded** |
| connection action | What Entourage is set to do about the message at the next connection. The options are **keep on server**, **download on next connection**, or **remove at next connection**. |
| read status | **untouched** if the message has not been read; **read** if it has been read |
| replied to | **true** if you have replied to the message; **false** if you have not |

**Table 16-6**   Properties of the message Object

| message Property | Explanation |
|---|---|
| forwarded | **true** if you have forwarded the message; **false** if you have not |
| redirected | **true** if the message has been redirected; **false** if it has not |
| flagged | **true** if the message has been flagged for follow-up; **false** if it has not. This is an old property; use the **flag state** property instead, as it offers three options rather than two. |
| flag state | **flag** if the message has been flagged; **complete** if it has been completed; **unflag** if it has no flag |
| edited | **true** if the message has been edited since you received it; **false** if it has not |
| modification date | The date on which the message was last modified |
| category | The list of categories to which the message belongs |
| project list | The list of projects to which the message belongs |
| project sharing list | The list of projects that share this message |
| links | The list of items that are linked to this message |
| properties | A property that enables you to set a list of properties |
| has start date | **true** if the incoming message is a To Do item that has a start date; otherwise **false** |
| start date | The start date and time for a To Do item. If you set the **start date** property, Entourage automatically sets the **flag state** property to **flag**. |
| completed date | The completed date and time of a To Do item |
| has reminder | **true** for a To Do item that contains a reminder; otherwise **false** |
| has due date | **true** for a To Do item that contains a due date; otherwise **false** |
| remind date and time | The date and time to display a reminder for a To Do item. If you set this property, Entourage automatically sets the **flag state** property to **flag**. |
| SMIME signed | **true** if the message is signed with SMIME (Secure Multipurpose Internet Mail Extensions); **false** if it is not |
| SMIME encrypted | **true** if the message is encrypted with SMIME; false if it is not |

**Table 16-6** Properties of the message Object *(continued)*

## Creating and Sending an E-mail Message

Entourage uses the **outgoing message** object to represent a message you're sending. The **outgoing message** object has all the properties of the **message** object, plus the extra properties explained in Table 16-7.

| outgoing message Property | Explanation |
|---|---|
| delivery status | **sent** if the message has been sent; **unsent** if it has not |
| resent | **true** if the message has been resent; **false** if it has not |
| encoding | The means of encoding used for any attachments: **binhex**, **base64**, **uuencode**, or **AppleDouble** |
| compression type | **ZIP compression** if the attachments have compression applied; **no compression** if they are uncompressed |
| send attachments to cc recipients | **true** if the message's attachments are to be sent to Carbon Copy and Blind Carbon Copy recipients; **false** if the attachments are to go only to the To recipients |
| use Windows file names | **true** to send the attachments with Windows file extensions on the filenames so that Windows PCs can identify the files more accurately; **false** to omit the Windows file extensions |

**Table 16-7**   Additional Properties of the outgoing message Object

## Creating an Outgoing Message

To create an e-mail message, you use a **make new outgoing message** command. You can either use the **with properties** parameter to set the properties for the message when you create it—which is usually easiest—or set them afterward as needed.

For example, the following statement creates a new outgoing message, adds text to its **subject** property and to its **content** property, and assigns the message to the variable **myMessage**:

```
set myMessage to make new outgoing message with properties ¬
    {subject:"New Documentation for HR Trials", ¬
    content:"Here is the new documentation for the HR trials next week."}
```

## Adding Recipients to an Outgoing Message

To add recipients to a message you're sending, you create a **recipient** object for each recipient. The **recipient** object has two properties:

- **recipient type**   A recipient in the To field is a **to recipient**, a recipient in the Cc field is a **cc recipient**, and a recipient in the Bcc field is a **bcc recipient**. Entourage also supports a fourth type, the **newsgroup recipient**, which you don't use with messages.

- **address**   This property returns an **address** object that contains the name and e-mail address for the recipient. Each of these has a straightforward property name: **display name** for the name, and **address** for the e-mail address.

For example, the first of the following statements creates a To recipient and assigns it to the variable **recipient1**. The second statement creates a Cc recipient and assigns it to the variable **recipient2**.

```
set recipient1 to {recipient type:to recipient, ¬
    address:{display name:"Chris Smith", ¬
    address:"csmith@acmevirtualindustries.com"}}
set recipient2 to {recipient type:cc recipient, ¬
    address:{display name:"Ed Sempio", ¬
    address:"esempio@acmevirtualindustries.com"}}
```

Once you've got your recipients, you can easily assign them to the **recipient** property of the **outgoing message** object. Here's an example using the **recipient1** variable and the **recipient2** variable:

```
set myRecipients to {recipient1, recipient2}
set myMessage to make new outgoing message with properties ¬
    {recipient:myRecipients, subject:"New Documentation for HR Trials", ¬
    content:"Here is the new documentation for the HR trials next week."}
```

### NOTE

There's no need to assign recipients to variables—you can put them directly in the **make new outgoing message** command if you don't mind nesting several levels of braces. For example, **make new outgoing message with properties {recipient:{recipient type:cc recipient, address:{display name:"Ed Sempio", address:"esempio@acmevirtualindustries.com"}}}** works fine, but most people find it harder to read.

## Sending a Message

To send the message, use a **send** command and specify the message. For example, the following statement uses the variable **myMessage** to refer to the message:

```
send myMessage
```

To cut down on spam, Entourage warns the user when a script is trying to send a message (see Figure 16-1) and makes the user click the Send button before the message goes on its way. It's a good idea to warn users that they will see this dialog box ahead of time so that they know the message is above-board and don't click the Cancel button instead. You may choose to warn them by displaying an information dialog box at the beginning of the script or just before the warning appears, or by educating them in general about the scripts you provide.

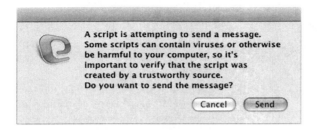

**Figure 16-1**   When a script is trying to send a message, Entourage warns the user and lets them decide whether to send it.

## Creating an E-mail Message for the User to Work With

When you want to begin an e-mail message so that the user can review it, complete it as necessary, and then send it, use a **draft window** object rather than an **outgoing message** object. The **draft window** object has the properties explained in Table 16-8. Roughly half the properties come from the **message** object and the **outgoing message** object, while the rest come from the **window** object that controls the window in which the draft message appears.

| draft window Property | Explanation |
|---|---|
| subject | The subject line of the message |
| content | The content of the message's body |
| account | The account that contains the message |
| priority | The message's priority: **lowest**, **low**, **normal**, **high**, or **highest**. The default priority is **normal**. |
| to recipients | The To recipients of the message |
| CC recipients | The Cc recipients of the message |
| BCC recipients | The Bcc recipients of the message |
| signature type | The type of signature applied to the message: **none** for no signature, **random** for a random signature (seldom wise), or **other** for a signature specified by the **other signature choice** property |
| other signature choice | The signature to apply if the **signature type** property is set to **other** |
| encoding | The means of encoding used for any attachments: **binhex**, **base64**, **uuencode**, or **AppleDouble** |
| compression type | **ZIP compression** if the attachments have compression applied; **no compression** if they are uncompressed |

**Table 16-8**   Properties of the draft window Object

| draft window Property | Explanation |
|---|---|
| send attachments to cc recipients | **true** if the message's attachments are to be sent to Carbon Copy and Blind Carbon Copy recipients; **false** if the attachments are to go only to the To recipients |
| use Windows file names | **true** to send the attachments with Windows file extensions on the filenames so that Windows PCs can identify the files more accurately; **false** to omit the Windows file extensions |
| class | A read-only property that returns the class of the window (**cDfW** for a draft message window) |
| bounds | The boundary coordinates of the four edges of the window |
| closeable | **true** if the window has a close box; **false** if it does not |
| titled | **true** if the window has a title bar; **false** if it does not. This property is read-only. |
| index | An integer giving the index position of the window. For example, the index of the front window is **1** and the index of the window behind it is **2**. |
| floating | **true** if the window is floating; **false** if it is not. This property is read-only. |
| modal | **true** if the window is modal, blocking other windows until the user deals with it; **false** if it is a normal window. This property is read-only. |
| resizable | **true** if the user can resize the window, **false** if they cannot. This property is read-only. |
| zoomable | **true** if the user can zoom the window; **false** if they cannot. This property is read-only. |
| zoomed | **true** if the window is zoomed; **false** if it is not. |
| name | The text that appears in the title bar of the window (if the title bar is displayed). This property is read-only; for a draft message, it shows the **subject** property (if it has been set) or **untitled**. |
| visible | **true** if the window is visible, as a draft message window is. This property is read-only. |
| position | The coordinates of the upper-left corner of the window. This property is read-only, but you can change it by setting the **bounds** property. |
| displayed message | A pointer to the message being displayed in the window. This property is not relevant to draft messages. |
| displayed feature | A pointer to the folder or server being displayed in the window. This property is not relevant to draft messages. |
| content | The body text of the message in the window |

**Table 16-8**   Properties of the draft window Object *(continued)*

For example, the following snippet uses the **draft window** object to create a draft message, which it assigns to the variable **myDraft**:

```
set myMessage to make new draft window with properties ¬
    {subject:"New Documentation for HR Trials", ¬
    content:"Here is the new documentation for the HR trials next week."}
```

Figure 16-2 shows an example of the draft window this creates. The user can then add recipients, edit the content, attach files, and make any other changes the message needs.

After creating a draft message like this, you'll normally want to let the user review it and send it in their own good time. But if your script does need to send it, you can simply use the **send** command and a reference to the message (for example, **send myMessage**).

# Setting a Signature for an E-mail Message

To give the reader essential information about the sender of the message (and perhaps about the sender's company as well), you can add a signature to it. As you'd expect, this works with both an **outgoing message** object and a **draft window** object.

## Creating a Signature

Normally, you'll want to create a signature manually to make sure it contains exactly the information you want and that (if you include formatting) it looks precisely right. But you

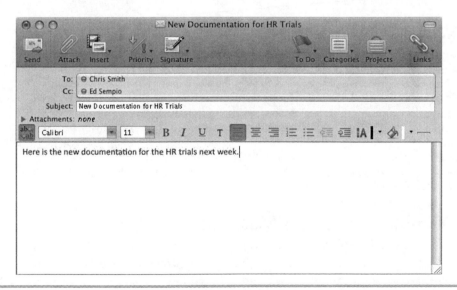

**Figure 16-2** To create a message that the user can finish, use the draft window object.

can also create a signature via AppleScript by using a **make new signature** command and setting three properties:

- **name**   The name you want to give the signature

- **content**   The text to use for the signature

- **include in random**   **true** if you want to include the signature in your random pool; **false** if you don't

When you create a new signature like this, Entourage automatically sets the fourth property of the **signature** object, the read-only **ID** property, to the next unused integer in the signature-numbering sequence.

### Adding a Signature to a Message

To add a signature to a message, set the **signature type** property to **other** and then set the **other signature choice** to the signature you want to apply. Here's an example of using these properties to add the signature named **Business Signature** (referred to as **signature "Business Signature"**) to a message in a draft window:

```
set myDraft to make new draft window with properties ¬
    {content:"New Documentation for HR Trials", ¬
    signature type:other, ¬
    other signature choice:signature "Business Signature"}
```

> **NOTE**
>
> Normally, you'll want to give each message you send a specific signature—preferably one suited to its recipient and contents—or no signature at all. But Entourage also lets you include a signature picked at random from the signatures you've lumped into a random pool. This can be amusing for personal mail or occasionally useful for business purposes (for example, adding a random marketing signature). To add a random signature via AppleScript, set the **signature type** to **random**. To control whether a signature goes swimming in the random pool, set the **include in random** property of the appropriate **signature** object to **true** (to include it) or **false** (to exclude it). When you're working interactively, select or clear the Random check box opposite the signature in the Signatures window.

## Attaching a File to a Message

You can attach a file to either a draft message or to an outgoing message that your script sends without displaying it. To attach a file, set the **attachments** property of the **draft window** object or the **outgoing message** object to refer to the file you want to attach.

For example, the following statement attaches the file named **HR Info.pdf** from the **Server:Information** folder to the draft message referred to by the variable **myMessage**:

```
set myMessage to make new draft window with properties ¬
    {recipient:myRecipients, ¬
    subject:"New Documentation for HR Trials", content: ¬
    "Here is the new documentation for the HR trials next week.", ¬
    attachment:"Server:Information:HR Info.pdf"}
```

# Dealing with Incoming E-mail Messages

Entourage uses the **incoming message** object to represent an incoming message. The **incoming message** object has all the same properties as the basic **message** object (see Table 16-6, earlier in this chapter), plus the three properties explained in Table 16-9.

### TIP

Entourage contains powerful rules for processing incoming messages (and for taking actions with outgoing messages as well, if you like). To work with rules, choose the euphonious Tools | Rules command, and then work from the Rules dialog box.

## Forwarding a Message

To forward a message that you've received, use the **forward** command. This command takes one required parameter and three optional parameters:

- **message** The required parameter—a direct parameter—is a **message** object. For example, you can tell Entourage to **forward the first message in the folder "Inbox"** or **forward myMessage**, where the variable **myMessage** refers to a message.

| incoming message Property | Explanation |
|---|---|
| **SMIME signature** | If the message has an SMIME signature, whether it matches the content (**valid**) or doesn't match (**invalid**). Returns **none** if the message doesn't have an SMIME signature. |
| **SMIME signer** | If the message has an SMIME signature, whether it matches the content (**valid**) or doesn't match (**invalid**). Returns **none** if the message doesn't have an SMIME signature. |
| **SMIME signer info** | Returns an **SMIME signer info** object, which contains details of whether the signer's certificate is trusted, what its e-mail address is and whether it matches that of the sender, and whether the certificate has expired or been revoked |

**Table 16-9** Additional Properties of the incoming message Object

- **to** Use this optional parameter to provide the recipients of the forwarded message. When you're creating a script to forward a message without user intervention, you'll need to use this parameter.

- **html** This optional parameter controls whether Entourage forwards the message as HTML (**with html**) or as plain text (**without html**). Choose the setting you need.

- **opening window** This optional parameter controls whether Entourage opens a window showing the message you're forwarding. When you're scripting the operation, you will probably want to use **without opening window** to prevent Entourage opening a window. If you want to open a window, use **with open window**.

For example, the following snippet forwards the first message in the inbox as HTML, sending the forwarded message without opening a window:

```
set myForward to forward the first message in the folder "inbox" ¬
    to "jramirez@acmevirtualindustries.com" with html ¬
    without opening window
send myForward
```

## Moving a Message to a Folder

To move a message to a folder, use the **move** command. This command takes a direct parameter, which specifies the message you want to move, and a **to** parameter that gives the folder to which you want to move the message.

For example, the following command moves the message identified by the variable **myMessage** to the folder named **Business**:

```
move myMessage to folder "Business"
```

### TIP

If you want to work with a message the user has selected, use the **selection** object. Usually, the best way to use it is to assign it to a variable (for example, **set my_selection to selection**) and then assign the first item from that variable to another variable (for example, **set mess1 to the first item in my_selection**). This gives you a direct handle on the first message in the user's selection (even if there's only one message in the selection).

## Deleting a Message

To delete a message, use the **delete** command and provide your victim's ID as the direct parameter. For example, the following command deletes the message identified by the variable myMessage:

```
delete myMessage
```

## Receiving an Attachment

When you receive a message with one or more files attached, the message has an **attachments** list containing an **attachment** object for each file. Table 16-10 explains the properties of the **attachment** object.

To save an attachment to a folder, you can use the standard **save** command with the **name** property of the appropriate item in the **attachments** object. For example, the following statement saves the first attached file of the selected message (the first message of the selection) to the folder **Server:Process**:

```
set current_selection to selection
set this_mess to item 1 of current_selection
set incoming_files to the attachments of this_mess
set my_file_name to the name of the first item in incoming_files
save the first item of incoming_files in "Server:Process:" ¬
    & my_file_name
```

If the message has multiple attachments, use a **repeat** loop to save each attachment in turn. Here's an example that again uses the **selection** object:

```
set current_selection to selection
set this_mess to item 1 of current_selection
set incoming_files to the attachments of this_mess
repeat with myCounter from 1 to count of items in incoming_files
    set my_file_name to the name of item myCounter in incoming_files
    save item myCounter of incoming_files ¬
    in "Server:Process:" & my_file_name
end repeat
```

| attachment Object Property | Explanation |
|---|---|
| **name** | The attachment's name. This property is read-only. |
| **file type** | The file type of the attachment. This property is read-only. |
| **encoding** | The MIME encoding used for the attachment's data. This can be **no encoding, 7bit encoding, 8bit encoding, binhex, base64, uuencode, AppleSingle, AppleDouble, quoted printable**, or (if you're out of luck) **unknown encoding**. This property is read-only. |
| **file** | The alias to the file |
| **content** | The encoded content of the file (assuming it has been encoded) |
| **properties** | A property that lets you set a list of properties |

**Table 16-10** Properties of the attachment Object

# Working with Contacts

Almost as essential in Entourage as e-mail messages are contacts, which Entourage represents with **contact** objects.

As you'll know from creating contacts manually, Entourage lets you stuff a huge number of different pieces of information into a contact record. Some of these pieces of information are essential, such as the contact's name; most of them are optional; but almost all of them can be useful and so are worth knowing about.

This translates to a fearful list of properties for the **contact** object. Take a deep breath, and then take a look at Table 16-11, which explains the properties of the **contact** object.

| contact Object Property | Explanation |
|---|---|
| id | An integer that contains a unique ID number for the contact within Entourage—for example, **3**. This property is read-only; Entourage assigns the number when you create a new contact. |
| GUID | A text string that contains the item's global unique identifier—for example, **"8280E8CF-44A4-11D9-9080-000A95A27796"** |
| category | The list of categories to which the contact belongs |
| project list | The list of projects to which the contact belongs |
| project sharing list | The list of projects set to share the contact |
| links | The list of items linked to this contact |
| vcard data | The contact's information assembled in vCard (a virtual address card) format |
| first name | The first name of the contact |
| last name | The last name of the contact |
| first name furigana | (Japanese-format contacts only.) The contact's first name in *furigana* (Japanese phonetic characters placed above or alongside ideograms to indicate the pronunciation). |
| last name furigana | (Japanese-format contacts only.) The contact's last name in furigana. |
| title | The title for the contact—for example, **Mr.**, **Mrs.**, **Ms.**, or **Dr.** |
| phone | The default phone number for the contact |
| office | The office for the contact |
| domain alias | The alias for the contact |
| suffix | The name suffix for the contact—for example, **II**, **Jr.** |
| nickname | The nickname for the contact |
| company | The contact's company name |

**Table 16-11** Properties of the contact Object

| contact Object Property | Explanation |
|---|---|
| company furigana | The contact's company name in furigana |
| job title | The job title for the contact |
| department | The department for the contact |
| default email address | Which of the contact's e-mail addresses to use as the default—for example, **email address 1** |
| default instant message address | Which of the contact's IM addresses to use as the default—for example, **instant message address 2** |
| description | A text note added to the contact. (In the Entourage UI, this is the Note field that appears on the Other tab of the Contact window.) |
| default postal address | Which of the contact's postal addresses to use as the default |
| home address | The contact's home address. This is a **postal address** object. |
| business address | The contact's business address. This is a **postal address** object. |
| home web page | The URL for the contact's home web page |
| business web page | The URL for the contact's business web page |
| home phone number | The contact's home phone number |
| other home phone number | The contact's other home phone number—handy for contacts with other homes |
| home fax phone number | The contact's home fax number |
| business phone number | The contact's business phone number |
| other business phone number | The contact's other business phone number |
| business fax phone number | The contact's business fax number |
| pager phone number | The contact's pager number |
| mobile phone number | The contact's mobile phone number |
| main phone number | The contact's main phone number |
| assistant phone number | The phone number for the contact's assistant |
| custom phone number one [through four] | Properties for adding up to four custom phone numbers for the contact |
| custom field one [through eight] | Properties for adding up to eight custom fields of information to the contact |
| age | The contact's age |
| astrology sign | The contact's astrology sign. This is stored as text, so you don't need to confine yourself to the widely recognized signs. |
| spouse | The name of the contact's **husband** object or **wife** object |
| spouse furigana | (Japanese-format contacts only.) The spouse's name in furigana. |
| interests | The contact's interests (leave blank for none) |

**Table 16-11**   Properties of the contact Object *(continued)*

| contact Object Property | Explanation |
|---|---|
| blood type | (Japanese-format contacts only.) The contact's blood type. (This is considered significant for business—it's not a medical courtesy or an indication of imminent danger.) |
| children | A list containing the names of the contact's children |
| custom date field one [through two] | Properties for adding one or two custom dates associated with the contact—for example, a date other than a birthday or anniversary that needs commemoration |
| birthday | The contact's birthday |
| anniversary | The contact's anniversary |
| flagged | **true** if a flag is set for this contact; **false** if no flag is set. This is an old property; use the **flag state** property instead, as it offers three options rather than two. |
| flag state | **flag** if the message has been flagged, **complete** if it has been completed, or **unflag** if it has no flag. (If you have to ask how to "complete" a contact, don't use the **complete** setting.) |
| Japanese format | **true** if the contact uses the Japanese format (which gives you access to the furigana and blood type); **false** if it does not |
| modification date | The date this contact record was last modified. This property is read-only. |
| last sent date | The date you last sent an e-mail to this contact using Entourage. This property is read-only. |
| last received date | The date you last received an e-mail from this contact, again using Entourage |
| properties | A property that enables you to set a list of properties |
| address book | Which address book contains the contact—for example, **address book id 14** |
| has start date | **true** if the incoming message is a To Do item that has a start date; otherwise **false** |
| start date | The start date and time for a To Do item. If you set the **start date** property, Entourage automatically sets the **flag state** property to **flag**. Not usually relevant for a contact. |
| completed date | The completed date and time of a To Do item. Not usually relevant for a contact. |
| has reminder | **true** for a To Do item that contains a reminder; otherwise **false**. Not usually relevant for a contact. |
| has due date | **true** for a To Do item that contains a due date; otherwise **false** |
| remind date and time | The date and time to display a reminder for a To Do item. If you set this property, Entourage automatically sets the **flag state** property to **flag**. Not usually relevant for a contact. |
| image | The image associated with the contact record |

**Table 16-11** Properties of the contact Object *(continued)*

With the possible exception of the Japanese-format properties, most of the properties of the **contact** object are useful in everyday situations.

Now that you've memorized that little list, here are examples of working with contacts.

# Creating a New Contact

To create a new contact, use a **make new contact** command. The easiest way to set most of the properties for the contact is by using the **with properties** parameter and specifying each property for which you want to set a value, like this:

```
make new contact with properties ¬
    {first name:"Estelle", ¬
    last name:"Kalamand", ¬
    nickname:"Stella", ¬
    title:"Dr.", ¬
    business phone number:"510-555-8280"}
```

You can also assign the new contact to a variable and then use that variable to set properties, as in this example:

```
set myContact to make new contact with properties ¬
    {first name:"Estelle", ¬
    last name:"Kalamand", ¬
    nickname:"Stella", ¬
    title:"Dr.", ¬
    business phone number:"510-555-8280"}
tell myContact
    set the business web page to "http://www.acmevirtualindustries.com"
    set the mobile phone number to "707-555-1083"
    set the job title to "Executive Director"
    set the age to 35
    set the children to {"Max (2005)", "Anne (2008)"}
    set the astrology sign to "Sagitto-Gemini Dragon"
end tell
```

## Adding E-mail Addresses to a Contact

These days, most of your contacts will have multiple e-mail addresses, so you'll want to load those addresses into the contact records in Entourage and tell the application which e-mail address to use as the default.

As you may have noticed in Table 16-11, the **contact** object has a property called **default email address**, but it doesn't have different e-mail address properties like it has properties for phone numbers—the **home phone number** property, the **other home phone number** property, the **mobile phone number** property, and so on. This is because Entourage stores the e-mail addresses in **email address** objects and then makes the default one available through the contact's **default email address** property.

If you've added various e-mail addresses manually to a contact record in Entourage, you'll see how this works. On the Name & E-mail tab of the Contact Properties window (see Figure 16-3), you add addresses to the E-mail list box. Entourage gives the first address you add the label Work, but you can change it to Home or Other as needed. Once you've added two or more addresses, you can click one of them and then click the Make Default button to make it the default e-mail address for the contact. The default e-mail address appears in boldface so that you can easily pick it out.

From AppleScript, you add e-mail addresses to Entourage contacts in the same way.

- First, add the e-mail addresses to the contact as **email address** objects, using the **label** property to specify the label (**work**, **home**, or **other**) and the **contents** property to give the e-mail address.

- Then set the **default email address** property to the appropriate **email address** object.

For example, the following snippet sets the variable **myContact** to the long-suffering Estelle Kalamand, adds three e-mail addresses (Work, Home, and Other) for her, and then sets the Work e-mail address as the default:

```
set myContact to contact "Estelle Kalamand"
set WorkEmail to make new email address at myContact ¬
    with properties {label:work, ¬
```

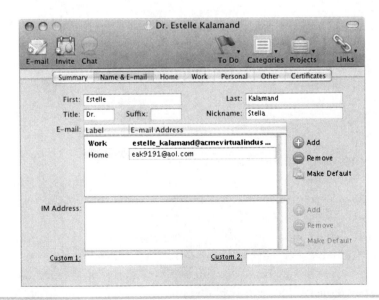

**Figure 16-3** When adding an e-mail address to the list on the Name & E-mail tab of the Contact Properties window, you give the address a label (for example, Work) and decide whether to make it the default e-mail address for the contact.

```
          contents:"e_kalamand@acmevirtualindustries.com"}
set HomeEmail to make new email address at myContact ¬
     with properties {label:home, ¬
     contents:"e_k_dr@aol.com"}
set OtherEmail to make new email address at myContact ¬
     with properties {label:other, ¬
     contents:"personal.medical.guru@gmail.com"}
set default email address of myContact to WorkEmail
```

## Adding Instant Messaging Addresses to a Contact

Entourage treats instant messaging addresses in the same way as e-mail addresses: You can add several IM addresses to a contact, labeling them Work, Home, and Other; and you can then designate one of the addresses as the default IM address.

This means you set up instant messaging addresses for a contact using the same technique as for e-mail addresses.

- First, create an **instant message address** object for each IM address the contact has, setting the **label** property to **home**, **work**, or **other** and the **contents** property to the IM address.

- Then set the **default instant message address** property of the **contact** object to the IM address you want to make the default.

Here's an example of adding two IM addresses to a contact:

```
set myContact to contact "Estelle Kalamand"
set workIM to make new instant message address at myContact ¬
     with properties {label:work, contents:"kalamand@aim.com"}
set HomeIM to make new instant message address at myContact ¬
     with properties {label:home, contents:"ewk_med@hotmail.com"}
set default instant message address of myContact to workIM
```

## Working with a Contact's Postal Addresses

Entourage uses the **postal address** object to represent a complete postal address. The **postal address** object contains five text properties with self-explanatory names: **street address**, **city**, **state**, **zip**, and **country**.

Entourage keeps two different **postal address** objects: a **business** one for the business address and a **home** one for the home address. You can choose which of these objects is the default address for the contact.

To change the business addresses, use the **business address** property of the **contact** object to return the **postal address** object for the business address, and then set the five properties of the address. Similarly, use the **home address** property of the **contact** object to return the **postal address** object for the home address so that you can set its properties.

For example, the following snippet sets the properties of the home address for the contact identified by the variable **myContact** and then sets the home address as the default postal address for the contact:

```
set myContact to contact "Estelle Kalamand"
tell the home address of myContact
    set the street address to "1234 Pacific Ave."
    set the city to "Emeryville"
    set the state to "CA"
    set the zip to "94608"
    set the country to "USA"
end tell
set the default postal address of myContact to home
```

## Getting a vCard of Contact Data

To get a virtual address card containing the contact's data, get the **vcard data** property of the **contact** object. For example, the following statement returns the vCard for the contact named **Wilson Collins**:

```
get vcard data of contact "Wilson Collins"
```

## Deleting a Contact

To delete a contact, use the **delete** method with the appropriate **contact** object. For example, the following statement deletes the contact named **John Sample**:

```
delete contact "John Sample"
```

If you're using an Exchange account, you may find that this method of deleting a contact doesn't work. If so, try telling AppleScript to delete the first contact with that name in the address book—for example:

```
delete (first contact in address book 1 whose name is "John Sample")
```

### NOTE

Ideally, you'll use the **GUID** property to uniquely identify the contact you're planning to nail, as this helps you avoid getting a different contact with a similar name. But unless you can examine the Entourage installation on which your script will run, it's not likely that you'll know the **GUID** for a particular contact. (And if you can examine the Entourage installation, you will probably find it easier to take out the victim manually rather than using AppleScript.)

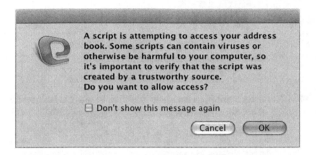

**Figure 16-4** You will probably need to reassure Entourage that your scripts that try to access the address book are genuine, honest, and friendly.

The Number One reason for a script to access your address book is to blitz your contacts with spam offering mail-order brides and pills that will help the recipients retain them, so Entourage displays the alert shown in Figure 16-4. The user must click the OK button to let the script continue.

# Working with Events

Entourage's Calendar feature can be a great help in keeping your schedule organized. To make the most of Calendar, you'll probably want to create and use events.

AppleScript uses the **event** object to represent an event. Table 16-12 explains the properties of the **event** object.

To create a new event, use a **make new event** command. As usual, the easiest way to set the details of the event is to use the **with properties** parameter and then specify each property needed. The following example creates a new event named **Fly to San Jose** and sets essential properties for it. The script assigns the new event to a variable named **new_event**, uses the variable to set the **has reminder** property to **true**, and then sets the **remind time** property to provide two hours of warning:

```
tell the application id "com.microsoft.Entourage"
    set new_event to make new event with properties ¬
        {subject:"Fly to San Jose", location:"LAX", content:"SW 3025", ¬
        start time:date ("20 October 2010 6:45 AM"), ¬
        end time:date ("20 October 2010 8:00 AM")}
    set has reminder of new_event to true
    set remind time of new_event to 120
end tell
```

| event Object Property | Explanation |
|---|---|
| ID | An integer giving the unique ID number of the event within Entourage. This property is read-only. |
| GUID | The global unique identifier for the event |
| iCal data | Text from iCal that you can use to start creating the Entourage event. This property is read-only. |
| subject | The subject (the name) of the event |
| location | The event's location |
| content | The description of the event |
| start time | The date and time at which the event starts |
| end time | The date and time at which the event ends |
| all day event | **true** if the event is all-day; **false** if it is not |
| recurring | **true** if the event recurs; **false** if it does not |
| recurrence | The iCal recurrence rule used for the event's recurrence |
| modification date | The date you last modified the event. This property is read-only. |
| category | The list of categories assigned to this event |
| project list | The list of projects assigned to this event |
| project sharing list | The list of projects that will share this event |
| links | The list of items linked to this event. This property is read-only. |
| properties | A property that enables you to set a list of properties for the event |
| remind time | An integer giving the number of minutes before the start time to sound the reminder |
| has reminder | **true** if the event has a reminder; **false** if it does not |
| to recipient | The recipients for an invitation for the event |
| account | The account associated with the invitation for the event |
| time zone | The ID of the time zone in which the event is set |
| free busy status | The status for the event: **busy**, **free**, **tentative**, or **out of office** |
| calendar | The calendar that contains the event. This property is read-only. |

**Table 16-12**  Properties of the event Object

In most cases, the easiest way to delete an event is to identify it by its **subject** property, as in the following example. The disadvantage to doing so is that Entourage deletes the first event it finds with this subject—so if you have multiple events with the same name, you may get the wrong one.

```
delete event "Fly to San Jose"
```

# Working with Tasks

To keep track of the things you need to get done, you'll probably want to use Entourage's
To Do list—even if you dislike its tyrannical style of micromanagement. Entourage uses
the **task** object to represent a To Do item, and you can use AppleScript to create and
manipulate To Do items automatically.

Table 16-13 explains the properties of the **task** object.

| task Object Property | Explanation |
| --- | --- |
| name | The task's name |
| ID | An integer giving the unique ID number of the task within Entourage. This property is read-only. |
| GUID | The global unique identifier for the task. This property is read-only. |
| iCal data | Text from iCal that you can use to start creating the Entourage task. This property is read-only. |
| completed | **true** if the task is marked as having been completed; **false** if it has not |
| content | The text note in the task |
| recurring | **true** if the task is marked as recurring; **false** if it is not. This property is read-only. |
| has due date | **true** if the task has a due date; **false** if it does not |
| due date | The date and time the task is due |
| remind date and time | The date and time to display a reminder of the due date |
| has reminder | **true** if the task has a reminder set to it; **false** if it does not |
| priority | The priority assigned to the task: **lowest**, **low**, **normal**, **high**, or **highest** |
| modification date | The date and time you last modified the task. This property is read-only. |
| category | The list of categories assigned to this task |
| project list | The list of projects assigned to this task |
| project sharing list | The list of projects that will share this task |
| links | The list of items linked to this task. This property is read-only. |
| has start date | **true** if the task has a start date; **false** if it does not |
| start date | The date and time the task is due to begin |

**Table 16-13**   Properties of the task Object

For example, the following snippet creates a new task named **Clear out the filing cabinet** and gives it a due date. It assigns the new task to a variable named **myTask** and then uses this variable to set the **priority** property and the **category** property of the task.

```
tell the application id "com.microsoft.entourage"
    set myTask to make new task with properties ¬
        {name:"Clear out the filing cabinet", ¬
        has due date:true, due date:date ("20 July 2010")}
    set priority of myTask to high
    set category of myTask to category "work"
end tell
```

To delete a task, identify it by its **name** property—or, if you know the **id** property or the **GUID** property, use one of those for greater certainty. For example, the following statement deletes the task named **Clear out the filing cabinet**, identifying it by the **name** property:

```
delete the task "Clear out the filing cabinet"
```

# Working with Notes

Entourage's notes are handy for keeping your information straight, particularly when you're working in Entourage and need to jot something down.

As you'd expect, Entourage uses a **note** object to represent a note. Table 16-14 explains the properties of the **note** object. Most of these will probably seem familiar by now.

| note Object Property | Explanation |
| --- | --- |
| name | The name of the note |
| ID | An integer giving the unique ID number of the note within Entourage. This property is read-only. |
| GUID | The global unique identifier for the note. This property is read-only. |
| iCal data | Text from iCal that you can use to start creating the Entourage note. This property is read-only. |
| content | The note's text content |
| modification date | The date and time you last modified the note. This property is read-only. |
| category | The list of categories assigned to this note |
| project list | The list of projects assigned to this note |
| project sharing list | The list of projects that will share this note |
| links | The list of items linked to this note. This property is read-only. |
| creation date | The date and time the note was created. This property is read-only. |

**Table 16-14** Properties of the note Object

As you can see from the table, more than half of the properties are read-only—and in fact, for most notes, you'll need to set only two properties: the note's **name** property, which provides its title, and the **content** property, which holds its contents.

The following short script creates a note and then opens it in a window (see Figure 16-5):

```
tell the application id "com.microsoft.entourage"
    set note_content to "Attendees: same as last meeting" & return & ¬
        "add Bill P., M. Sykes, ?director of HR" & return & return & ¬
        "Refreshments: Water, sp. water, fruit" & return & return & ¬
        "Book main conf. room, Pacific Room otherwise" & return & ¬
        return & "Run agenda past Bill P."
    set new_note to make new note with properties ¬
        {name:"Planning Meeting Notes", content:note_content}
    open new_note
end tell
```

To delete a note, identify it by its **name** property—or, if you know the **id** property or the **GUID** property, use one of those for laser-guided targeting. For example, the following statement deletes the note named **Planning Meeting Notes**:

```
delete the note "Planning Meeting Notes"
```

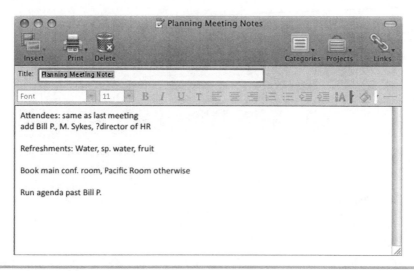

**Figure 16-5**  The new note created by the sample script

# Index

## A

a reference to operator, 66
access mode property, 345–346
account directory property
    explained, 274
    for locating stored mail, 276
account mailbox property, 278
account object properties, 274
account type property
    explained, 274
    for smtp server object, 275
accounts. *See* Mail accounts
activate command
    to Excel, 339, 348, 355
    explained, 8
    on window object, 371–372
    to Word, 293, 300
activate object command
    with document keyword,
        300–301
    with workbooks, 348
    with worksheets, 355, 358
activateWord variable, 228–229
active cell class, 358
active end page/section number
    information, 315
active printer property, 304

active sheet object, 339
active window class, 306, 371
active workbook parameter, 373
active worksheet class, 355
add title parameter, 140–141
add to most recently used list parameter,
    341–342
adding folder items event handler
    creating folder action
        scripts, 240
    writing folder action scripts,
        227–229
additional headers account object
    property, 379
address property
    for mail recipients, 282
    for outgoing messages, 389–390
after losing parameter, 230
after parameter
    for copying worksheets, 352–353
    for inserting worksheets, 350
    to search for data, 375
after receiving parameter, 228–229
album object properties, 263
album(s)
    artist, rating, and track
        properties, 251
    creating new, 264

locate existing and deleting, 265
types, 264
alerts
    choosing icons for, 152
    creating, 153–154
    for custom error messages,
        208–209
    differing from dialog boxes,
        151–152
    suppressing, 352
alias class, 77, 79
alias file, 122
alias references
    reaching objects with, 108–109
    using, 110–111
alignment property constants, 321
all headers message property, 284
altitude photo object property, 266
AppleScript
    attaching folder action scripts,
        238–239
    cell type constants, 360
    chart type constants, 365
    constants for white space
        characters, 85
    creating charts from, 363
    defined, 4
    dialog type constants, 330
    learning, 5